Transatlantic Connections

Transatlantic Connections

THE MOVEMENT AND NEW FORMALISM

Theresa Malphrus Welford

Story Line Press | *Pasadena, CA*

Transantlantic Connections: The Movement and New Formalism

Book design by Mark E. Cull

Library of Congress Cataloging-in-Publication Data

Names: Welford, Theresa M., author.
Title: Transatlantic connections : the Movement and New Formalism / Theresa Malphrus Welford.
Description: First edition. | Pasadena : Story Line Press, 2019. | Includes bibliographical references and index.
Identifiers: LCCN 2019019298 (print) | LCCN 2019019561 (ebook) | ISBN 9781586540548 (print) | ISBN 9781586540555 (ebook)
Subjects: LCSH: Movement, The (English poetry) | English poetry—20th century—History and criticism. | New Formalism (American poetry)—History and criticism. | Narrative poetry, American—History and criticism.
Classification: LCC PR605.M68 (ebook) | LCC PR605.M68 W35 2019 (print) | DDC 821/.91409—dc23
LC record available at https://lccn.loc.gov/2019019298

The National Endowment for the Arts, the Los Angeles County Arts Commission, the Ahmanson Foundation, the Dwight Stuart Youth Fund, the Max Factor Family Foundation, the Pasadena Tournament of Roses Foundation, the Pasadena Arts & Culture Commission and the City of Pasadena Cultural Affairs Division, the City of Los Angeles Department of Cultural Affairs, the Audrey & Sydney Irmas Charitable Foundation, the Kinder Morgan Foundation, the Meta & George Rosenberg Foundation, the Allergan Foundation, and the Riordan Foundation partially support Red Hen Press.

First Edition
Published by Story Line Press
an imprint of Red Hen Press
www.redhen.org

Contents

CHAPTER 1

Bridging the Atlantic

THE MOVEMENT AND NEW FORMALISM

We owe a great debt to poets like Richard Wilbur, Anthony Hecht, X. J. Kennedy, Thom Gunn (to name a few—add J. V. Cunningham and Philip Larkin to the list . . .), who held the fort, so to speak, during the siege.[1]

—*Leslie Monsour*

Many American poets have probably never heard of a short-lived literary group of the 1950s called, simply, the Movement, though they may be familiar with individual members of the group: Kingsley Amis, Robert Conquest, Donald Davie, D. J. Enright, Thom Gunn, Elizabeth Jennings, Philip Larkin, and John Wain. The New Formalists, often at variance with their American peers, gravitated to several of these English elders during their own poetic development twenty years later.

As I shall outline in this study, the New Formalists—including Dick Allen, Dick Davis, Annie Finch, John Gery, Dana Gioia, R. S. Gwynn, Marilyn Hacker, Mark Jarman, Paul Lake, Charles Martin, David Mason, Robert McDowell, Leslie Monsour, Marilyn Nelson, Molly Peacock, Katha Pollitt, Vikram Seth, Robert B. Shaw, Maura Stanton, Timothy Steele, Diane Thiel, and Rachel Wetzsteon—have been inspired by Movement poets, have learned from their craft, and have responded to their poems and philosophy in a variety of ways.

If critic Blake Morrison's assessment is correct that the Movement poets were "probably the most influential in England since the

Imagists," it is not surprising that they have had an impact extending over the decades and even across the Atlantic.[2] As recently as a 2004 interview with Robert Conquest, in fact, American poet and critic William Baer notes that *New Lines*—the anthology that introduced the Movement to the literary world—is "still generally considered to be the most important British anthology in the second half of the twentieth century."[3] For the New Formalists, their admiration for the Movement writers was more than a passing fancy; indeed, it grounded much of their early and their mature poetry.

After describing the formation of the two groups, I shall examine the personal and textual connections between the New Formalists and Movement writers. In some instances, the American poets freely acknowledge this influence in their correspondence, criticism, interviews, and poems. In other cases, the connecting link is unacknowledged or even denied.

Beginning in the late 1970s, a handful of critics have hinted at the possible influence of the Movement writers on the New Formalists. Keith Tuma, author of *Fishing by Obstinate Isles: Modern and Postmodern British Poetry and American Readers*, noted in a 2003 email that the "main connections between the so-called New Formalists and the Movement . . . would come via Donald Davie and, behind Davie, Yvor Winters."[4] Tuma also pointed out the connection between Gunn and "the Wintersian legacy." He went on to say, "So from my perspective, the link between the Movement and New Formalism is strong and, like much else in Anglo-American relations in poetry, has Davie as its center, less as poet than as critic and teacher." H. T. Kirby-Smith includes both Larkin and Winters in his list of "anti-experimental" poets who have influenced the New Formalists.[5] In addition to stating that Larkin has been a model for Steele, Gordon Harvey specifically compares Steele's "Old Letters" and Larkin's "Love Songs in Age" (both of which I shall discuss in Chapter Five).[6] Joe Francis Doerr, in *The Encyclopedia of American*

Poetry: The Twentieth Century, mentions Davie as an influence on New Formalism.[7]

Other than these few examples, the Movement writers are rarely credited with having caused much of a ripple in the United States. Yet, as I shall demonstrate, the poetics and poetry of this group have had a major impact on many American writers associated with New Formalism.

After interviewing more than a dozen New Formalists about their reactions to the Movement writers, I noticed a clear pattern: they first encountered the work of the elder English writers at important moments in their own literary development, usually as undergraduates or young graduate students.

As an undergraduate at Brown University in the late 1950s, Dick Allen encountered the work of Thom Gunn in *New Poets of England and America*.[8] When he read Gunn's "On the Move," his first thoughts were of pop culture icons such as James Dean and Marlon Brando. Allen was also drawn to the daring combination of "contemporary subject matter and rhyme and meter and power."[9] He says that Gunn has been a long-term influence on his own work, from formal poetry to free verse. From his very first reading of Gunn's poems about motorcyclists, he found them inspiring because of "how wonderfully they combined the contemporary with narrative and rhyming form." Larkin's "Church Going," in the same anthology, struck him as a "major poem" and Larkin himself as an "obvious master" because of his "combination of form and important subject matter."

In 1964, Charles Martin first read poetry by Gunn, Larkin, and Davie, also in *New Poets of England and America*.[10] Martin says, "Larkin made an immediate impression on me, and I shortly thereafter read his *Whitsun Weddings*, which was the only book of his that I could find back then." Martin goes on to say, "Davie and Gunn did not make as much of an impression on me at the time," but he later read Gunn's book *Moly* and saw the poems in that book (along with those in Anthony Hecht's *The Hard Hours*) as "perfectly contemporary in language and subjects." He read Davie's early poetry around the same time. Although he found Davie's poetic development "odd and finally rather disappointing," he continues to respect Davie's criticism. For Martin, Larkin is "the best of them, an indisputably great poet in an indisputably minor way." At the same time, he says, Gunn "is my favorite of the three, and his elegy for Robert Duncan seems to me as great a poem in its way as Auden's elegy for Yeats." He points out that he didn't read *New Lines* until "a few years ago" but when he did, he "recognized that the Movement's principles were similar to those of the New Formalists." He suspects that some New Formalist critics "had read the Movement anthology and were influenced by it."

Timothy Steele was studying in London in 1969 when he read the Faber paperback *Selected Poems* by Thom Gunn and Ted Hughes. He was immediately taken with Gunn's poems: "They had an intellectual energy, and a gift for extended metaphor, that called to mind the work of my favourite poets at that time, Shakespeare and Donne. Yet Thom's verse was contemporary in matter and diction. It was alert to the living moment."[11] That same year, Steele discovered Larkin's poetry and was similarly impressed. Moved by its "unassuming freshness and authenticity," he purchased Larkin's *The Less Deceived* and, a year later, *The Whitsun Weddings*. Interviewed by William Baer in 2002, Steele included Gunn and Larkin among a group of elder poets to whom he feels "indebted."[12]

As an undergraduate in the 1970s, Mark Jarman had encounters with the work of Gunn and Larkin that were much like Steele's. Of Gunn, Jarman recalls, "Partly he fascinated me because he wrote about California, where I was from, and he did it in ingenious verse forms, like rhyming syllabic verse. . . . When I was learning to write, I imitated him a lot."[13] Later, Jarman's graduate school advisor and thesis director Donald Justice introduced him to the poetry of Larkin and discussed poems in *High Windows* in which Justice "thought the meter was just off."[14] Although Jarman says he didn't know enough about the technical aspects of poetry to understand how the meter was "off," these sessions led to "a deepening appreciation" of Larkin. Jarman came to believe that Larkin is "actually very innovative in his verse" but that he "disguises his innovations, rather the way Frost did," and that Larkin's poetry encompasses an impressive "range of diction within a strict space," with imagery that is phrased in "original yet totally accurate" ways.[15] Jarman also admires Davie, but says that Larkin is his favorite Movement poet and that he knows many Larkin poems "by heart."[16]

As a graduate student at Harvard University in the 1970s, Dana Gioia had his own eye-opening encounter with Larkin's poem "Poetry of Departures": "I had no idea who Larkin was then, but I knew immediately that he was the writer I had been looking for—not merely a master but a confidant."[17] In December 2001, Gioia recalled the first time he heard Larkin's poetry, when a classmate read aloud two poems, one by Gary Snyder and the other by Larkin, then praised Snyder's poem for such ostensibly American qualities as openness and inclusivity and criticized Larkin's poem for its ostensibly British qualities, which were the exact opposite.[18] On hearing the Larkin poem, Gioia did not react as he was evidently expected to. Instead, he said, "Wow." Immediately after class, he went to a bookstore and ordered a Larkin collection. "What I was trying to do," he recalls, "was write poems that were formal yet conversational." When he read Larkin, he "suddenly . . . realized that this was the guide who was doing what [he] was trying to do."

While some New Formalists discovered the Movement writers by chance, others sought them out. John Gery applied to Stanford University in the 1970s precisely because Donald Davie taught there: "When I learned that Davie taught at Stanford, where I knew [Yvor] Winters had found a sanctuary for his unorthodox ideas for years, I decided that Stanford was where I would need to go to study the writing of poetry; I was afraid that otherwise my own compulsion to write in meter and rhyme would be ridiculed as old-fashioned or squelched under the influence of the 'free verse' poets teaching at such places as the Iowa Writers' Workshop."[19] As a teacher, Davie turned out to be "as complex and challenging" as Gery had hoped. He was further pleased to find classmates who were committed to using traditional forms, including several subsequent New Formalist poets—Dana Gioia, Vikram Seth, and, later, Paul Lake.

THE MOVEMENT: BIOGRAPHY, HISTORY, AND IDEOLOGY

Although Larkin and Gunn are generally well regarded as poets, and Davie as both a poet and a critic, the 1950s poetic movement known as the Movement, which first brought them to attention, is only occasionally described as having had a long-lasting impact.[20] In addition to Davie, Gunn, and Larkin, the other members of this group were Kingsley Amis, Robert Conquest, D. J. Enright, John Holloway, Elizabeth Jennings, and John Wain. In 1955, Enright edited one of the formative anthologies of the Movement, *Poets of the 1950s* (living in Japan at the time, he intended his collection for a Japanese audience). It includes eight of the nine principal Movement writers, leaving out only Gunn. In 1956, Conquest published *New Lines*, which included all nine. The history of the Movement has been delineated by John Press, in *Rule and Energy* (1963); by Jerry Bradley, in *The Movement: British Poets of the 1950s* (1993); and, most extensively, by Blake Morrison, in *The Movement: English Poetry and Fiction of the 1950s* (1980). All nine poets have also spoken or written about their involvement in the Movement (to whatever extent they see themselves as having been involved). Even though one tendency of Movement writers is to deny the reality of the Movement in the first place, its existence has by now been sufficiently established.

Blake Morrison, although not an uncritical admirer of the Movement, set out to prove "that it was a literary group of considerable importance."[21] Most contemporary critical reactions, writes Morrison, involved "dismiss[ing] it as being of small consequence" or otherwise "downgrading" it, but he contends that "the Movement is as central to [the 1950s] as was 'the Auden generation' to the 1930s."[22] He argues that "it is remarkable how many key texts of the post-1945 period . . . should have sprung directly from the collaboration and interaction which the Movement represented."[23] Since their collaboration lasted no more than a decade, it is indeed remarkable how many important works the Movement writers produced, though some of these came shortly before the nebulous period when the group "officially" formed and some shortly after the equally nebulous period when it "officially" dissolved. As Morrison rightly points out, however, the "criterion for judging certain texts to be Movement texts cannot be purely chronological: the crucial consideration is whether the particular text embodies a sensibility (and this includes questions about subject matter, form, tone and attitude) which is characteristic of the Movement."[24] He noted that critics still (in 1980) sometimes "identify a 'Movement tone' or 'Movement manner' in texts not necessarily produced from within the group and not necessarily written in the 1950s. . . . The identity of the Movement has, it seems, transcended both the group and the decade, coming to stand for certain characteristics in English writing—rationalism, realism, empiricism—which continue to exert their influence today."[25] These characteristics even include "an identifiable 'line' on sex, religion, politics and other non-literary matters."[26]

In a 1949 poem called "Modesties," Larkin advocates "modesty and simplicity" and even "shyness" in poetry:

> Words as plain as hen-birds' wings
> Do not lie,
> Do not over-broider things—
> Are too shy.[27]

The Movement poets were reacting against the supposed excesses of poets such as Yeats, Pound, and Thomas. In *Purity of Diction in English Verse* (1952), Davie expresses a preference for poetry that is "chaste" and thereby "central" while Matthew Arnold thought of it as "express[ing] the feeling of the capital, not the provinces" and "central to the language, conversational not colloquial, poetic not poetical."[28] The effect, says Davie, is a "valuable urbanity, a civilized moderation and elegance." Twenty-five years later—in an interview conducted by Gioia—Davie would describe *Purity of Diction* as "a sort of concealed manifesto" for the Movement.[29]

The group also demonstrated a desire for "the return of clarity," a contention that "to follow the Modernist tradition was . . . a retrogressive act," an insistence that poetry should be characterized by "toughness and modernity" (with "modernity" obviously meaning something different from "Modernism"), and an "approval of a modest and oblique approach to 'big subjects.'"[30] *Mandrake*, a literary journal with which several Movement poets were associated, echoed their determination "to oppose sham and cant (not by irritable polemic but by quietly fostering honest workmanship)."[31] Elizabeth Jennings's early poem "Modern Poet," a manifesto for a movement that did not yet exist, lists poetic ills that the Movement poets would repudiate: "fine phrases," "inflated sentence[s]," "words cunningly spun," "floreate image[s]," "relaxing pun[s]," "sentimental answer[s]."[32] Her manifesto echoes statements made by predecessors such as Wordsworth and Pound.

Critic Richard J. Gray states that, although there were "different consequences" to the efforts of the Movement writers, they were "reacting in terms similar to those of many of the Imagists" and "some of the Romantics," as well as others who wished to "strip away the layers of habit and artifice from the inherited poetic language."[33] In "Modern Poet," Jennings also describes "the poet's art," which, she says, "is to speak and not to be sung." Furthermore, "sympathy must turn away to anger."[34] Here, whether intentionally or not, Jennings yields to gender-based stereotypes: poetry must reject sympathy, often regarded as a "feminine" feeling, and must instead express anger, often regarded as a "masculine" feeling. In her implication that sympathy is powerless and hence useless, while anger is powerful and useful, she is also voicing a notion based on pragmatism, another plank in the Movement platform. (This preference, incidentally, foreshadows the development of a related group, the so-called Angry Young Men, with which Amis and Wain were associated.)

Clearly, the Movement writers were dissatisfied with much of the poetry around them, whether written by their contemporaries or their predecessors. Such dissatisfaction is, of course, among the motivating factors behind the formation of literary movements. According to Morrison, those poets who would become the Movement (along with many others in the 1950s) admired "anti-Romantic" writers such as William Empson and W. H. Auden and abhorred "neo-Apocalyptic" writers such as Dylan Thomas, David Gascoyne, Edith Sitwell, and W. R. Rodgers.[35] In an essay originally published in the 1950s and reprinted in *Memoirs,* Amis states that Thomas "strikes me as a very bad poet indeed."[36] Amis also attacks Thomas personally as "an outstandingly unpleasant man, one who cheated and stole from his friends and peed on their carpets." He then goes on to say, "at the start [Thomas] boozed a lot because it fitted his image of a poet, rather than out of any thirst or need... But for the last eight years or more of his short life he had something to drink about."[37]

The ad hominem nature of Amis's remarks may still seem shocking. However, the Movement writers often engaged in such personal criticism, for they believed that literature is directly and unavoidably affected by the character of the writer. (As I shall discuss elsewhere, some New Formalists—and their opponents—evidently share this belief.) With "anti-Romanticism" becoming "an increasingly important part" of their ideology, the Movement writers rather misleadingly labeled the "neo-Romantic" as "the poets of the 1940s," while characterizing their own work as "a radical departure, the 'new poetry.'"[38] Although the Movement's dislike of Thomas (and writers they considered similar to him) is only one of the many traits unifying them as a group, it is among the most prominent. Still, as Morrison notes, "One must be careful to distinguish hostility to Thomas's work from hostility to the 'Thomas legend': it was the legend—Thomas as drunk, fornicator, rebel, etc—which most annoyed them."[39] In fact, he says, Movement references to Thomas often reveal a respect for much of his poetry but a "Leavis-like contempt for those in the literary world who contributed to, and cashed in on, his early death."

In "My Life Up to Now," Gunn—who argued, quite exasperatedly, that he was *not* a member of the Movement—says that around 1954, when his first book, *Fighting Terms*, was published, he "first heard of something called the Movement. . . . To my surprise, I learned that I was a member of it."[40] In a 2001 letter to me, Gunn is even more emphatic:

> I was never a *member* of the Movement, in fact my contention is that it never really existed, the poets "in" it having in common . . . merely a period style. I never met some of the other poets in it (e.g. Larkin or Holloway) and admired only two of them—Larkin and Davie. . . . I think I was pretty different in intention and outlook from the others, and was associated with them because of the time I started publishing.

Throughout his career, Gunn says, he has been influenced far less by Movement writers than by Charles Baudelaire, who "has been from the start one of the poets I have most emulated" because "I like the way he writes about extreme subjects by means of understatement."[41] He goes on to suggest that the Movement writers themselves rarely dared to write about "extreme subjects" but that when they did they, too, used "understatement." Gunn closes his letter by saying, "This must all seem very sour, but I think if you read the essays in *Shelf Life*, you will understand a bit better what I have been up to." Although Gunn's involvement with the Movement was undoubtedly as tenuous as he always said it was—since he was several years younger than the other Movement poets, since he didn't know the other members of the group at the time (except for Jennings, whom he traveled to Oxford to meet in 1953), and since he was no longer living in England when the Movement began to attract notice—his reluctance to admit his membership in the group adheres to the Movement pattern.[42] In his 1959 essay "Remembering the Movement," which appeared several years *before* the Movement officially ceased to exist, Davie admits that he and the others "ridiculed and deprecated 'the Movement' even as we kept it going."[43] He defies the typical Movement impulse, however, and insists that he and the others were genuinely like-minded poets and critics and that it was "craven defensiveness," "pusillanimity," and "the unforgivable literary sin of going much further than halfway to meet [their] readers" that led them to "pretend that the Movement didn't exist, that it was an invention of journalists, that we had never noticed how Larkin and Gunn and Amis had something in common, or that, if we had noticed, it didn't interest or excite us."

Each time the Movement writers engaged in their habitual pattern of denial, they relied on certain stock phrases. Decades later, as Timothy Steele describes the origins of his own group, he uses remarkably similar terms: "New Formalism was never organized or announced in the way that, for instance, F. S. Flint and Ezra Pound organized and announced Imagism. This distinction is worth making because many people today are understandably suspicious of movement-mongering."[44] Steele says that he and other young poets were writing poetry that gradually began to be noticed, "and to my surprise and probably to others' as well, critics informed us that we were a movement."[45] Such denials are not unusual, since many poets wish to be seen as independent creators or free spirits with no interest in non-artistic matters, including organizations or movements. It is striking that Steele's denials and those of the Movement are expressed in virtually identical language.

THE DEATH OF THE MOVEMENT

In his article "Davie, Larkin, and the State of England," Bernard Bergonzi describes the "necessary, emblematic relationship" between Larkin and Davie.[46] As he does, he summarizes what he views as the most serious causes for the death of the Movement: "Larkin stays still, does not travel, rereads Hardy; and writes about what he sees. Davie, on the other hand, moves on, reads many literatures—though returning constantly to Pound, the master voyager of modernism—and longs for the heroic and the imaginatively possible, as well as what is actually and inescapably there."[47] For Bergonzi, Larkin represents the Movement poets' tendency to look to poetic models from the past rather than modernist or contemporary ones, to be provincial, even to be stubbornly "English." As he blatantly revealed in a 1982 interview conducted by American poet and critic Robert Phillips, Larkin never outgrew his opposition to anything that was not English: "deep down I think foreign languages [are] irrelevant. If that glass thing over there is a window, then it isn't a Fenster or a fenêtre or whatever. Hautes Fenêtres, my God! A writer can have only one language, if language is going to mean anything to him."[48] Davie, Enright, Gunn, Jennings, and others chafed against such narrow thinking. Both Davie and Jennings translated poetry, Davie from Russian and Jennings from Italian. Conquest obviously rejected Larkin's view, for he became a fluent speaker of Bulgarian and Russian, as well as a renowned expert in Soviet history, politics, and literature. According to Bergonzi, Davie and other Movement writers who "long[ed] for the heroic and the imaginatively possible," although still wishing to pay proper heed to "what [was] actually and inescapably there," found it necessary to break free, to read "many literatures," even to join modernist "master voyager[s]" as they embarked on journeys both imaginary and literal.[49]

In his book about Philip Larkin (which is called, simply, *Philip Larkin*), Bruce Martin describes the relationships among the Movement writers—and, implicitly, the problems leading to the group's demise—in an entirely different way.[50] Larkin's poetry, he says, shows too much emotion, as well as too much "understanding and compassion," to meet the "standard" of "emotional detachment" characterizing Movement poetry. Martin also implies that Larkin was too good a poet to have remained within such a group: "Beside Larkin's writing, most of Davie's seems stiff and hopelessly academic, while that of Amis seems flippant. . . . Comparing Larkin with Davie or with Amis suggests how much wider was the range of his talents even when there seemed to be a Movement to which they all belonged."

Whether Bergonzi or Martin is correct is not a matter that can be settled here. What is clear is that the Movement's lifespan was brief yet productive, and that the influence of the Movement reached much further than any member of the group had anticipated.

Although Larkin, Amis, and Conquest continued to criticize modernism even after the "death" of the Movement, Davie and Gunn embraced it. Samuel Maio attributes Gunn's and Davie's advocacy of modernism to their "Americanization," because of which they "fashionably abandoned most of the poetic principles of the Movement."[51] In a 1979 review of Davie's *The Poet in the Imaginary Museum*, Dana Gioia also describes Davie's "conversion" to modernism. Gioia, however, does not imply that it was a "fashionable" or frivolous move:

> Pushed into the public limelight as a member of "The Movement," a group of British poets who insisted on the continuing vitality of native literary traditions and on the incompatibility of modern experimentalism with English genius, the personally conservative Davie emerged as an apologist both for foreign poetry and for experimental writing.

Gioia maintains that Davie's "sense of himself as an Englishman was always strong enough not to be threatened by foreign cultures" and that Davie made important contributions to international poetry, translating Mickiewicz, Pasternak, Bassani, and Mandelstam and "carefully demonstrat[ing] the relevance of the modern masters like Pound and Valéry to his contemporaries." What's more, in addition to "proving the centrality of Hardy and Graves to the modern English tradition, he also secured Olson, Bunting, and Winters a place on the required reading list."[52]

YEARNING FOR ANOTHER MOVEMENT

In a 1977 interview with Gioia, Davie looks back rather fondly on his involvement with the Movement:

> I discovered, and half a dozen other poets subsequently my friends discovered, that though we were starting from very different points we were mov-

> ing upon a common area, a point at which our different careers, and the styles we were working out for ourselves, intersected in an important way. And that moment in history is marked by what was the fighting anthology of the Movement, *New Lines*, edited by Robert Conquest.[53]

Although Davie claims that the Movement had casual, unpremeditated origins, without a "manifesto all afloat around a café," he agrees that his early critical study *Purity of Diction in English Verse* (1952) was a "sort of concealed manifesto" for the Movement.[54] Describing the founding and the relatively rapid dissolution of the group, he says, "It wasn't like a Parisian French movement . . . so it didn't break up in vituperations on matters of abstract principle. Simply, it happened, then it dissolved itself."[55]

In addition to his denial that there was a manifesto for the Movement, followed one page later by his admission that he had indeed penned such a document, Davie's remarks are telling. He implicitly pokes fun at the cerebral and deliberate poets who would pen such a manifesto, along with those poets whose pretensions include gathering at artsy places like cafés; suggests an impatience with the kind of unpragmatic intellectualism that might lead to "vituperations"; implies that the English are more levelheaded than the French; and, in his description of the group's lifespan, hints at a worldview predicated on a resigned acceptance of the way things are. In short, as he describes the origins and the demise of the Movement, Davie reveals that he hasn't surrendered Movement ideas. Indeed, Richard J. Gray states that Davie's description is "symptomatic of a particular—perhaps *the* particular—tradition of English thought, a tradition epitomized by the Movement."[56]

In his interview with Gioia, Davie describes his longing for a new movement similar to the one in which he had been involved. Since he was speaking to a founding member of New Formalism shortly before the younger group began to coalesce as a movement, his words seem prescient. Indeed, it is tempting to see them as a direct inspiration: "One wishes that that sort of thing happened more often. Others have said this. People who weren't in the Movement, younger people who were hardly even born then, have said that they wished something like that would happen to us now." Even as he briefly describes the potential value of such a movement, it is clear that Davie continues to adhere to Movement beliefs. Poets should have "something to focus on," whether they agree or disagree with it. The entire "poetic landscape," in his view, should "make sense," and it should be unified rather than "totally eclectic." He goes on to say, "If there did emerge such a movement in which variously talented but serious writers clung to their little things in common for a while, this would be a very good thing. I suppose it would be a very good thing in American poetry too."[57] Even here, his language hints at a Movement-like modesty, or perhaps a Movement-like belief that excessive literary ambition is unwise.

This interview with Davie is equally significant for what it reveals about Gioia:

> Americans, even cosmopolitan ones like Lowell, often criticize British poets, especially ones like Larkin, or the current poet laureate, John Betjeman, or even you, as having retreated from the world at large. Whereas earlier British poets spoke for England as one of the centers of the world, now they have shrunken to the stature of local poets. . . . How would you answer this criticism?[58]

Clearly, as far back as 1977, Gioia was well acquainted with the Movement and its view of the diminished British Empire. In reply to Gioia's question, Davie said, "I would answer that [the criticism is] very ungracious indeed because I believe it is true of Larkin and Betjeman and not of me."[59] Although Davie was joking, he makes a valid point about himself and the others who left the Movement behind. Nevertheless, given the connections between New Formalism and the Movement, it is equally significant that he continued to embrace many ideas that characterized the Movement.

A new poetic movement similar to the one described by Davie was not long in coming. In the 1970s, certain poets and critics in the

United States were becoming disenchanted with contemporary American poetry. In addition to an interest in traditional poetic resources such as rhyme, meter, narrative, and form, they shared a surprising number of ideas with the poetic and critical movement to which Davie had belonged.

In the late 1970s and early 1980s, young American writers who wished to engage in the paradoxical endeavor of *experimenting* with poetic *traditions* found themselves "very uncomfortably isolated, even scorned," because the majority of other poets viewed "artistic form itself not as liberating but as confining."[60] After years of isolation, relieved only by the support of a few members of the "older generation who were misunderstood by their followers or who resisted the drift of the times and were isolated themselves," the young and tenacious poets finally discovered each other and became an "odd underground." Then, one evening, a meeting signaled the beginnings of what would become New Formalism: "The first time we really felt that a genuine movement was afoot was in early 1981, when Dick Allen, Frederick Feirstein, and Frederick Turner met for the first time at the Minetta Tavern in Greenwich Village."

The above account appears in the 1989 edition of *Expansive Poetry*, edited by Feirstein and Turner. David Mason pungently calls it "bullshit."[61] In a review of *Expansive Poetry*, he uses more diplomatic language but maintains his skepticism: "Indeed, the biased introduction (which seems calculated to place Feirstein, Turner, and a few others in the position of revolutionary leadership) goes so far as to imply that the movement began with a single meeting in a Greenwich Village pub, as if postwar formalism had disappeared except in the work of a few heroic survivors recently emerged from their caves."[62] Mason makes an important point. For one thing, Feirstein and Turner's history implies a far greater level of organization than would likely have been the case. It also implicitly locates the founding of New Formalism on the East Coast, whereas similar shifts in poetic sensibilities were occurring across the United States. In reality, argues Mason, there was no "founding."

Whatever the actual details may be, the poets who met at the Minetta Tavern that evening in 1981—along with dozens of others—were united in several ways, including an interest in employing traditional poetic resources, a feeling that the quality of criticism needed to be improved, and, as Feirstein and Turner put it in their introduction to *Expansive Poetry*, a "distaste for the scribbling going on in the Establishment's workshops."[63] As it turns out, many of them were also united in their attraction to a group of English writers known simply as the Movement.

Even a partial list is surprisingly long: Dick Allen, Bruce Bawer, Rafael Campo, Dick Davis, Thomas M. Disch, Michael Donaghy, Frederick Feirstein, Annie Finch, John Gery, Dana Gioia, Emily Grosholz, R. S. Gwynn, Marilyn Hacker, Rachel Hadas, Andrew Hudgins, Mark Jarman, Paul Lake, Sydney Lea, Brad Leithauser, Charles Martin, David Mason, Robert McDowell, Marilyn Nelson, Molly Peacock, Frederick Pollack, Katha Pollitt, Wyatt Prunty, Mary Jo Salter, Gjertrud Schnackenberg, Vikram Seth, Robert B. Shaw, Timothy Steele, and Frederick Turner. Many of these poets and critics came together in a movement that, by the mid-1980s, would be labeled New Formalism. Quite a hardy movement, it has endured long enough to engender second-generation or even third-generation poets, such as Diane Thiel, Rachel Wetzsteon, and recent MacArthur "genius grant" winner A. E. Stallings, who share New Formalist ideas. It has also become solidly established, as witnessed by the articles, books, journals, websites, publishing houses, and poetry conferences associated with it. Like other movements before it, New Formalism has, as a result of its success and longevity, moved from counterculture status into a more or less mainstream position. Mark Jarman states that it was dead as a movement by 1996, when he and coeditor David Mason "identified it" in *Rebel Angels*.[64] Others, though granting that it has outgrown the rebelliousness and abrasiveness that characterized its youth, insist that New Formalism is far from dead, in the sense that its poetry and its ideology continue to inspire writers.

In a 1987 review of Morrison's groundbreaking book *The Movement*, Pulitzer Prize-winning critic Michael Dirda makes several relevant points about the poetic climate in the United States at that time, including the rise of formal poetry. While acknowledging the difficulty of making generalizations about American poetry, since "there are no doubt young people who still emulate Sylvia Plath or chant along with Allen Ginsberg," Dirda says that "a spirit very like that of the Movement's does seem abroad in the land."[65] Although he never names the group specifically, Dirda is clearly referring to New Formalism. Of the three emerging poets that he considers "gifted," two—Vikram Seth and Brad Leithauser—are among the earliest New Formalists. Dirda also notes that "fixed forms have returned with the vengeance of the repressed." Indeed, although some American poets, such as Richard Wilbur, continued writing in forms throughout the 1960s, 1970s, and 1980s, most poets—particularly those publishing in prominent venues—wrote free verse. In "Notes on the New Formalism," which appeared around the same time as Dirda's review, Gioia suggests that many young American poets believed free verse had become as established and orthodox as the traditional forms it had originally been intended to supplant: "The new formalists put free verse poets in the ironic and unprepared position of being the status quo."[66] Further, as Dirda observes, "the once underrated Richard Wilbur and Anthony Hecht—masters of a poetry of statement and wit—now earn the accolades of gifted newcomers like Brad Leithauser." Dirda's description is apt, for the New Formalists were largely responsible for the increased recognition that Wilbur and Hecht began to receive at that time.[67] Most important, the Movement-like "spirit" that Dirda sensed actually did emanate, in part, from the Movement writers themselves, especially Davie, Gunn, and Larkin.

FAMILY RESEMBLANCE: THE MOVEMENT WRITERS AND THE NEW FORMALISTS

In the introduction to *Contemporary British Poetry*, coeditor Romana Huk recalls Morrison's depiction of the typical young English poet of the 1970s as a male with a background in the professional or middle class (or, if a member of the working class, less assertively so than in the 1960s) and an education in English literature, probably from Oxford or Cambridge. "His politics," Morrison says, "are on the whole quietly conservative, and where they intrude into the poetry at all, it is as a kind of nostalgic liberal humanism."[68] This poet also "has a surprisingly strong respect for 'traditional' forms, even strict meter and rhyme."[69] Perhaps even more surprisingly, this young poet rejects the Romantic motif of the poet as "risk-taker, 'mad genius' or bard" and chooses instead to affiliate himself with "the tradition of the poet as *clericus*."[70] Morrison states that the Romantics and the modernists have not influenced this poet; instead, dominant British poets, especially Hughes and Larkin, have been his models.[71] Morrison is clearly dismayed by the influence of Larkin. Even those who have "managed to escape the suburbs of Larkinland," he says, "have tended to come back with the same message: that what counts in poetry is 'craft' and 'rational intelligence.'"[72] Morrison feels that an overzealous concentration on these attributes has led to the development of "young poets who are competent, restrained, craftsmanlike—and dull."[73]

Huk speculates that the "nonpolemical writer nostalgic for premodernist paradigms for poetry" described by Morrison may indeed be a remnant of the Movement, which "took good enough hold of the poetry scene to weather the cultural revolution of the 1960s . . . and come out ostensibly on top again in the1970s."[74] In the introduction to *British Poetry Since 1970* (which features Morrison's depiction of the "1970s poet"), coeditors Peter Jones and Michael Schmidt allege that the 1960s "were spoiled by excess of opportunities and choices and by the paucity of generously stringent critics."[75] According to Huk, the Movement poets would agree.

Many New Formalists, who began to emerge in this same era, would agree as well. Both groups have, in fact, lamented an "excess of opportunities and choices" when those have led to vast quantities of what the two groups view as mediocre poetry, and both groups have formed their own poetic criteria and movements in reaction to such poetry. Both lament the "paucity" of "generously stringent" criticism, stating that it contributes to an atmosphere in which mediocre poetry predominates. Both argue that good poetry balances emotion and intellect, freedom and control. To varying degrees, both emphasize the importance of writing poetry (and criticism) capable of interesting a fairly broad audience.[76] Both maintain that poets should write about subjects other than themselves and that notions of culture, including suitable topics for poetry, should be enlarged to include not only "highbrow" subjects but also "popular" ones. Taking issue with those who see poetic resources such as rhyme, meter, and form as outdated, both groups believe these resources are, as Mark Jarman puts it, "evergreen."[77]

These ideas are far from unique to these two groups. However, other characteristics and concerns shared by the Movement writers and the New Formalists set them decidedly apart from the majority.[78] Notably, the two groups share an affection for popular poetic forms, from light verse to limericks, that are often belittled by academics and mainstream poets and critics. In the United States, while free verse still enjoys wide popularity in university programs and leading publications, the New Formalists and their advocates deserve much of the credit for the increased interest in traditional forms such as sonnets, villanelles, sestinas, ghazals, rondeaux, pantoums, and ballads. People on all sides of the controversy have been guilty of extremism, exaggeration, and outright silliness, but what matters most is that formal poetry is no longer dismissed or ridiculed as it often was in the 1960s, 1970s, and 1980s.

The two groups also share a dedication to championing or at least reappraising writers who are little known or who have become unfashionable, *especially* ones who have been shunned by academics. Both groups present themselves as oppositional "outsiders." The title of the "manifesto anthology" of the Movement—*New Lines*—hints at such a self-depiction. The title of the manifesto anthology of the New Formalists—*Rebel Angels*—could hardly be more blatant.[79]

Since at least the Romantic Era, poets have often depicted themselves as free spirits and nonconformists. Although the Movement writers and the New Formalists embrace the outsider pose of most of their peers and predecessors—a pose that is itself paradoxical, since it is virtually the norm—these two groups also go against the grain in their own distinctive and self-contradictory ways, viewing it as less important to distance themselves from society at large than from what they view as the stiflingly bureaucratic rules and confines of the poetic establishment. Ironically, as the members of both groups position themselves as societal insiders, they position themselves as outsiders to all those poets who view themselves as outsiders.

Donning the emphatically un-Romantic gray flannel suit of "the poet as *clericus*" and "a responsible citizen responsibly employed," the Movement writers and the New Formalists often characterize themselves as commonsensical and pragmatic members of society, not eccentric *artistes* prone to fits of brooding melancholy or flights of wild inspiration.[80] Gunn cultivated the image of a leather-clad Bohemian, but otherwise both groups have repudiated what Morrison calls "traditional Romantic or Bohemian interpretations of the poet as a man apart."[81] The Movement writers, says Morrison, "tended to understate rather than advertise their poetic activities, as if anxious not to look like poets."[82] When asked what sort of poetic persona, if any, Jarman presents in his poetry, his answer echoed the Movement: "I do try to avoid the appearance that I am in any way special or heroic or exciting because I write poetry."[83] The Movement writers would likely have agreed with David Mason's contention that we must have "more than one image of the living poet—the responsible citizen as well as the romantic rebel or the hysterical suicide."[84] As Jarman points out, it was Keats who said that "a poet is the most unpoetical of people."[85] Gunn summed it up neatly in a 1986 review: "To be a poet you have to be both ordinary *and* extraordinary."[86]

As the Movement writers and the New Formalists describe what sort of person a poet should be, they reveal shared ideas about the nature and purpose of poetry itself. Poetry should be quiet and "modest," as suggested in Larkin's poem "Modesties." It should not prophesy, preach, or deliver political speeches. It should not be highly autobiographical or confessional, nor should it "celebrate the self" in a Whitmanian sense. It should not perpetuate outdated images of the poet as courageous rebel, irresponsible Bohemian, or potential suicide. It need not comply with the early twentieth-century notion that the difficulties and complexities of the modern world demand difficult and complex poetry. It should not exclude "ordinary readers" or pander to those with elitist views of literature. Both groups break their own rules at times, but such shared ideas underlie the close connections that the younger poets feel with the older ones.

Morrison's contention that young poets of the 1970s have a "less partisan" attitude toward modernism than "most of [their] twentieth-century predecessors" may be true of the poets he has in mind, but it tends not to be true of the New Formalists, just as it was not true of the Movement writers.[87] Both groups have set themselves apart from most twentieth-century (and twenty-first-century) poets by criticizing modernism and actively defying its mandates. As Eliot put it, poets "in our civilization, as it exists at present, must be *difficult*," and as Pound asserted, poets must "make it new!" But both the Movement writers and the New Formalists insist that writing poetry of the type recommended by Pound and Eliot—non-formal, fragmented, heavily allusive, often alienatingly difficult—is not necessarily a valid response to the chaos of the modern world and that it is certainly not the *only* response.[88] Some have gone further, saying that those who write such poetry are surrendering to the chaos and even *contributing* to it. As Christian Wiman points out, Wallace Stevens made exactly the same point:

> This structure of ideas, these ghostly sequences
> Of the mind, result only in disaster. It follows,
> Casual poet, that to add your own disorder to disaster
>
> Makes more of it.[89]

Robert Frost, Richard Wilbur, and others have made very similar statements. Nevertheless, in holding such a view in a modernist and postmodernist environment, the Movement writers and New Formalists have joined the ranks of a fairly small and unfashionable minority. Taking the opposite approach to that implicitly urged by Eliot's *The Waste Land*, both groups believe that, as John Wain said in 1950, shoring "regular and disciplined verse forms" against the "ruins" is more *constructive* than shoring "fragments" against them.[90] Wain emphasizes discipline, regularity, and rebuilding in the midst of destruction, citing "two decades of meaningless peace" followed by "a global war" that "ended with the fearful savagery of Hiroshima and Nagasaki. . . . At such a time, . . . it is natural that a poet should feel the impulse to *build*. Writing regular and disciplined verse forms is building in a simple and obvious sense, like bricklaying. Too simple, too obvious? Perhaps. But we were all very young and were doing the best we could to make something amid the ruins."[91] New Formalists Steele, Gioia, and Annie Finch have made similar comments about their own desire to "make something amid the ruins."[92] The Movement writers and the New Formalists both condemn the prevailing poetry written by their contemporaries, calling it flat, "prosy," unnecessarily baffling, excessively figurative, unrelentingly self-indulgent, and pointlessly obsessed with novelty and experimentation. Such criticisms are not unique to these two groups, but the Movement writers and the New Formalists put much of the blame on the same culprit. Much contemporary poetry, they argue, is flawed largely because it is chained to a century-old modernist program involving a "Permanent Revolution," in Robert Conquest's words, or the "eternal avant-garde," in Gioia's.[93]

By using "plain" language, maintaining a relaxed, often humorous or ironic tone, and avoiding dense, showy metaphors, the Movement poets were, in general, attempting to appeal to a broad audience. In addition, as critic Paul Giles says, they were deliberately striving to serve as an "antidote to the obscure, overwrought symbolism of a decadent modernism."[94] Morrison points out that "the Movement writers' chatty familiarity with readers was also intended as an implicit rebuke to the Modernist writers against whom they were reacting"—especially Pound, whom Davie "accused . . . of 'scrapping the contracts traditionally observed between poet and reader' by failing to provide 'metrical landmarks to assist us.'"[95] Although they *were* intellectuals pretending to be "just folks," and although they often made statements seemingly calculated to offend, the Movement poets were motivated, at least in part, by admirable goals. They deliberately set forth to create "an artistic programme in which 'ordinariness' is to be dignified," and underlying much of what they did was their desire to "demystify and democratize" literature and literary criticism.[96] Of course, there were differences among the members of the group, with some believing that a small, "elite" audience was most desirable, others preferring a broad readership, and still others falling somewhere in the middle. Larkin was perhaps the most adamant about the need to appeal to "ordinary" people. Bruce Martin says, in fact, that Larkin was popular largely because he "manage[d] to project a very personal concern for the things which personally concern most people living in the modern world."[97] Along these lines, the Movement writers wanted to "enlarge the notion of culture."[98] Amis, for instance, attempted to demonstrate "that film, science fiction, jazz, Ian Fleming and the detective novel" merit serious attention.[99] Larkin and Conquest championed some of the same popular genres. As I have suggested, these are among the ideas and characteristics that the New Formalists share with the Movement.

CHAPTER 2

Choosing Sides

THE POETRY WARS IN THE UNITED STATES

Philip Larkin's poetry has been a constant inspiration over the years. . . . And Thom Gunn's motorcycle poems from as soon as I read them, how wonderfully they combined the contemporary with narrative and rhyming form.[100]

—*Dick Allen*

In the introduction to *Expansive Poetry: Essays on the New Narrative and the New Formalism* (1989), Frederick Feirstein and Frederick Turner describe what they saw as the "narrow and doctrinaire . . . world of poetry in the seventies" in the United States: "Both narrative and meter were considered at best out of date, and at worst the instruments of bourgeois capitalism." Despite the fact that popular music was (and is) invariably governed by "strict meter and narrative impulses . . . the high priests of the ruling ideology proclaimed that narrative and meter were elitist European importations and that the true American voice could only be heard in 'free verse.'" Often "gleefully pessimistic about the future," most poets wrote "solipsistic confessions about their darkly perceived past." And they shared with their publishers the "cynical opinion that good writing was automatically unpopular, and popular writing was automatically bad."

Tracing the history of American poetry in the second half of the twentieth century, Feirstein and Turner describe the free verse movement's "revolt against the social conventions of Puritan America that permeated all levels of society, epitomized in the fifties."

Rather strangely, they compare the efforts of "the underground culture" within poetry to those of "Chuck Berry, Little Richard, Bill Haley, and perhaps most importantly Elvis Presley." The "sexuality and passionate optimism" of John F. Kennedy, they say, also inspired those poets who wanted to "throw off the stifling boring age of Eisenhower." Unfortunately, the free verse movement, which "had begun as experimentation," became as "bureaucratic" and dictatorial as the orthodoxy it was originally intended to overthrow, and in the process "the freedom to truly experiment" was lost: "such spokespeople as Diane Wakoski began to declaim that anything but the kind of poem she and others like her were writing [was] un-American. . . . Poets became afraid of writing what was not au courant . . . . And the magazines and presses were taking almost uniformly only short free verse autobiographical imagist lyrics." In addition to inflating the centrality of their own role and that of the East Coast in their history of New Formalism, Feirstein and Turner indulge in personal attacks on their contemporaries as well as their Modernist predecessors and make sweepingly broad generalizations about the political and literary climate of the United States. What's more, their self-descriptions become almost comically hyperbolic: "young and tenacious" hero-poets, scattered "voices crying in the wilderness," surrounded by bureaucratic "poseurs."

Such hyperbole is not unusual in the rhetoric of those attempting to shake up the "Establishment," but it weakens Feirstein and Turner's argument. Nevertheless, some of their statements are valid. Feirstein and Turner are probably correct that many poems published in journals over the last few decades *have* been "prosy little poems propped up by corny rhetorical devices." Similarly, a survey of journals would likely validate the accuracy of their claim about the dominance of "short free verse autobiographical imagist lyrics." They are also right that poets who wished to use meter, rhyme, or narrative, and who dared to criticize the poetry of their contemporaries, often were—and sometimes still are—condemned on political bases and subjected to ad feminam or ad hominem attacks far more vicious than those perpetrated by Feirstein and Turner themselves. As an aside, it is interesting to note that the personal attacks engaged in by the New Formalists and their opponents closely resemble those made by the Movement writers and *their* opponents. Since some New Formalists have gone out of their way to offend and provoke members of the "Establishment," and since some have been guilty of offenses including stereotyping, polemicism, and self-aggrandizement, it is not surprising that the reactions have tended to be heated and personal. All involved, evidently, believe that poetry is worth such fiery passion, even when that passion is expressed in ways that are generally considered inappropriate.[101]

Ironically, a few years after the earliest shots in these American "poetry wars" were fired, a member of the "enemy camp" provided the movement with its name. In a 1985 *AWP Newsletter* editorial, poet and creative writing teacher Ariel Dawson condemns poets who are interested in form—whom she likens to "yuppies"—saying that she suspects they "longed after form because they had few natural means of acquiring it, no strong view of the world, no personal vision."[102] She believes these poets are turning to "reactionary conservatism" in place of a "journey of the self," embracing New Formalism while remaining ignorant of the "old" formalism and reminding her of "the average Christian fundamentalist's knowledge of the Bible and the evolution of his own religion." According to Dawson, "the reemergence of formalism is perfectly harmonious with the yuppie knack for resurrecting elitist traditions." Dawson was not the first "enemy" to attack, nor was she the most vitriolic. In a 1977 article, "Trivial or Mechanistic Sound Versus Cosmic or Superior Sound," Duane Locke bombards those he calls "dehumanized writers of preconceived forms" with an astonishing fusillade: they are "enemies of poetry," "barbarians" (backed up by their "stooges," college professors, who are themselves "fortified and well equipped by a misdirected and deadening education"), "weaklings who have no interiority or mystic openness," "victims and slaves of the illusions self-manufactured by their conscious minds," and "verbal mechanists."[103] Poets who wield "sestinas and other weapons to destroy the recent and rare return to true poetic expression" represent "a society of diseased split brains and abject ego imprisonment." In relying on a "degenerate and debased handbook technological approach to poetry," they have "committed aural suicide, thus deafening themselves and destroying their capacity to hear cosmic sounds." Surprisingly, Locke's hostility toward formal poetry predates any provocation coming from the New Formalists.[104]

When the revised edition of *Expansive Poetry* was published in 1999, under the name *New Expansive Poetry*, Feirstein and Turner's introduction was replaced with one by the new editor, R. S. Gwynn, who approves of the "lively adversarial spirit" of the earlier introduction but offers a slightly less partisan view of New Formalism's origins.[105] Gwynn is reluctant to use any of the labels attached to this particular movement, though he finally chooses "expansive poetry" without capitalization.[106] Any hesitancy in settling on a name for the group from the given possibilities is understandable. Some are overly narrow or carry undesirable political connotations, such as "New Formalists," "New Narrative Poets," or "Neo-Formalists," while others, such as "Expansive Poets" and "Natural Classicists," are vague.[107] Their more vehement detractors have offered amusingly negative alternatives: "commuter poets," "wimps," "café Republicans," "the radical right of poetry," "cultural neoconservatives," "yuppie poets," "piddling Pounds," "prince[s] of the Blanc Mange Mode," "Rebels Without a Case," "il-literati," "low proppers-up of state ideology," "the Reaganites of poetry," and "anti-Americans."[108]

When John Hollander, an American forerunner of New Formalism, spoke at the 1985 Modern Language Association Conference, poet Diane Wakoski compared Hollander to "Milton's Satan" and stated that he was "denouncing, basically, the free verse revolution, denouncing the poetry which is the fulfillment of the Whitman heritage, [and] making defensive jokes about the ill-educated, slovenly writers of poetry who have been teaching college poetry classes for the past decade."[109] As Kathrine Varnes, a second-generation New

Formalist, describes the conflict between twentieth-century formalists and free-verse writers, she could also be describing the conflict between the New Formalists and many of their contemporaries and elders: "The free verse writers had the rhetorical and associational advantage of being considered more innovative, more rebellious, more American. Those who wrote in predetermined verse forms, or with accentual-syllabic meters and rhyme, were often associated with political conservatism, Britophilia, and the status quo."[110]

Varnes's description is relevant in another way as well. Since many twentieth-century poets—perhaps especially Americans—are apparently eager to be seen as "innovative" and "rebellious," and since many Americans are apparently reluctant to be seen as "Britophilic," it would be unsurprising if the New Formalists rejected efforts to link them with the Movement writers. Indeed, some New Formalists have come close to doing exactly that. Dick Allen says, for instance, that the "emphasis on traditional form, rhyme, meter, [and] audience in the Movement is somewhat stricter and more expected, perhaps even old hat" compared to that of the New Formalists.[111] Movement poetry is also, in his view, "apt to be more 'upper class' than American New Formalists and Expansive poetry, which is mainly middle class"—an ironic perception, for the Movement writers were condemned in England for being overly middle class and even middlebrow. Regardless of these minor quibbles, Allen says that Movement poetry has been important to him.[112]

As suggested earlier, both the Movement poets and the New Formalists have been called anti-academic and anti-intellectual. Both groups have been accused of idealizing the "good old days" before modernism, and, in the case of the New Formalists, the "good old days" before postmodernism. Both have been called old-fashioned, narrow-minded, and reactionary. Both have been condemned for their political beliefs (or perceived political beliefs). Davie said, for instance, that he and other writers of the 1950s were aiming toward a "rational conservatism" in their "poetic technique."[113] In contrast, as seen above, those who oppose the New Formalists have used the term "conservative" as a dire insult. Even "rational" has been used as an insult. The two groups also share the dubious distinction of being subjected to class-based attacks, with another interesting twist: the attacks in England seem to have been motivated by *snobbery*, while those in the United States seem to have been motivated by *reverse snobbery*. Critics of the Movement allege that these poets' impoverished backgrounds have made them stunted, limited, and "mean," whereas critics of New Formalism allege that these poets' affluent backgrounds have made them elitist and anti-democratic. Epithets such as "yuppie" and "café Republican," as well as claims that an attraction to poetic form is equivalent to an attraction to country clubs, vividly illustrate this perception. In the tellingly titled "Dana Gioia and the Poetry of Money" (1988), Greg Kuzma engages in a blatant class-based attack.[114] That his comments still seem shocking decades later attests to the rarity of such attacks in the United States, where the pretense that class distinctions do not exist is a major component of the national identity. In contrast, Somerset Maugham, responding to the characters in Kingsley Amis's *Lucky Jim*, unhesitatingly engages in class-based stereotyping, insisting that the young people supposedly represented by that novel are "mean, malicious, and envious."[115] Similarly, although Stephen Spender invited Elizabeth Jennings to contribute poems to *Encounter* in the early 1950s, he soon denounced the Movement poets, calling them "Lower Middle Brows."[116] Edith Sitwell speculated that perhaps the Movement poets wrote "lifeless quatrains" because they spent their childhoods in "the cramped dimensions of prefabricated houses."[117] Evelyn Waugh saw them as "grim young people coming off the assembly lines," representing a "new wave of philistinism."[118]

While only Sitwell refers to the Movement writers' use of traditional poetic forms, critics of the New Formalists often condemn them for this very reason.[119] In *The Oxford Encyclopedia of American Literature*, Gerry Cambridge states that Britain has a long-standing "poetic tradition in which there is no necessary association between formal poetry and social status."[120] America also has such a tradition, he says, but many poets and critics in the twentieth century have apparently forgotten about its existence.[121] Thanks to the efforts of William Carlos Williams and others—and to gross oversimplifications of their views—formal poetry developed a bad reputation in the United States in the twentieth century. Thom Gunn, an Englishman who lived in the United States for fifty years, comments on "Englishness" and "Americanness" in poetry:

> What people say about me, and it's probably true, is that in many of my poems I write about an American subject matter in an English way, by which they mean metrical and in rhyme—which may be an English way, though it's been used by some Americans. Of course free verse is not particularly English; very few English people have written decent free verse.[122]

In this case, Gunn is not being especially political, nor is he speaking of the New Formalists, but his remarks call to mind a question that sometimes arises. If writing in form is "English," or, more broadly, "European," are the New Formalists therefore "un-American"? Many American poets and critics think so, or at least they did when New Formalism first emerged. Dana Gioia describes "threadbare clichés" about poetic form "which somehow still survive from the Sixties": "Form, we are told authoritatively, is artificial, elitist, retrogressive, right-wing, and (my favorite) un-American."[123] Timothy Steele once received a "threatening anonymous phone call" from someone who said, "American poetry comes from Walt Whitman, you S.O.B.—and you better wise up!"[124] Writing in 1986, poet-critic Lewis Turco, who sympathizes with many New Formalist aims, sensibly counters such comments by pointing out that "the work of Robert Frost is as American and as American-sounding as anything William Carlos Williams ever wrote. As though any of this had any importance at all. What is the difference whether a poem is American or English or Canadian or Australian if it is a good poem?"[125] Gioia proposes "the radical notion that American poetry is whatever poetry happens to be written by Americans."[126]

In his 1999 introduction to *New Expansive Poetry*, R. S. Gwynn describes New Formalism's history in a less "adversarial" way than Frederick Feirstein and Frederick Turner did in 1989. However, Gwynn does cast that history in terms of generational conflict—as those attempting to shake up the "Establishment" frequently do—pointing out that many poets associated with New Formalism "came of age in the 1960s, when Beat, Confessional, and Deep Image poetry, in their respective turns, dominated the poetic *table d'hôte*." These younger poets, he says,

> watched bemused while their mentors, the poets of their parents' generation, emerged from mid-life with a vengeance, turning away from tradition toward open form and increasingly subjective approaches to autobiographical material. . . . These younger poets, unlike many of their contemporaries, turned back to earlier models—Frost, Hardy, Jeffers, Millay—and in some cases attempted to counter Modernism by recovering and reconstituting the forms and genres of earlier literary periods.

"This strategy," he says, far from being an uninformed step backward, "could thus be compared to the way in which post-modern architecture successfully imports the flying buttress and arched nave into a world of concrete and steel or how a return to traditional musical forms can rightly be celebrated as 'new.'" Rather than being "nostalgic for pre-modernist paradigms for poetry," the New Formalists might say—and some of them have said—that they are in fact making a *post*modernist move, melding the old and the new, the traditional and the innovative, the "elite" and the "vulgar," the artifacts of "high" culture and those of "popular" culture.[127]

Gwynn points out that, although the New Formalists have certainly rebelled in an unorthodox manner—by declining to take part in what Conquest has called the "Permanent Revolution" of modernism and, instead, looking back to traditions that originated *before* modernism—their rebellion fits into the "curious manner of literary dialectic" and can be viewed as "yet another manifestation of a generation's revolt against the authority of its elders—not this time as wild-eyed revolutionaries urging even further extremes but as counter-insurgents in the Culture Wars—hence [Mark] Jarman and [David] Mason's designation of them as 'rebel angels.'"[128] Gioia also touches on the generational conflicts, speculating that those older poets who were "antagonistic" toward New Formalism "wanted to be rebels, wanted to be avant-garde, [but] when you are fifty, you no longer feel so avant-garde as you were, and so you don't want younger people doing something different from you."[129] As Larkin put it in 1970, referring to modernism in general and modern jazz in particular, "Nothing is funnier than an upstaged revolutionary."[130] Morrison's description of a similar generational conflict, this one between the Movement and the 1930s generation, highlights an important and paradoxical parallel between the Movement and New Formalism: "common to these various caricatures" within Movement manifestos and poetry "is the assumption that although the Movement writers are 'sons' reacting against 'fathers', it is they, not their predecessors, who are politically mature: responsible youth reprimands reckless middle age."[131]

As he describes *The Reaper Essays*, which its editors, Mark Jarman and Robert McDowell, characterized as "adversarial—aimed to explode the complacency of contemporary letters," Gwynn paints the poetic scene of the 1970s in boldly unflattering colors:

> The tribal music of Poetryland—the murky manifestos of Projective Verse and breath-units, the proliferation of cut-rate knock-offs of 'Howl' and 'Daddy,' the shamanism of the deep image and the multiform brain—had begun to resemble ritualized incantations, mumbled by the multitudes but comprehended by few, and a sense emerged that certain types of poetry had overstayed their welcome.

In the midst of such "murky manifestos," "cut-rate knock-offs," and pretentiously arcane "shamanism," what were young poets to do? Some, says Gwynn, turned to "Language" poetry, "go[ing] further into disorder and subjectivity" and "dispensing with an audience entirely." But, says Gwynn, this choice did not appeal to the New

Formalists or the New Narrative poets, who chose instead to return to a "more accessible vision" and who, furthermore, believe that an audience is "entirely indispensable." It is worth reiterating that, in addition to the inverted generational divide mentioned above, these emphases on clarity and accessibility, along with scoffing attitudes toward "shamanism," are among the many characteristics shared by the Movement poets and the New Formalists.

By the early 1980s, the New Formalist movement was well underway, though, as noted earlier, it did not have a name until 1985.[132] In "The Poet in an Age of Prose," which first appeared in 1990, Gioia describes New Formalism in these terms:

> The use of rhyme and meter is only one aspect of a deeper aesthetic shift away from the coterie culture of the universities. The new sensibility also has led to the return of verse narrative, the exploration of popular culture for both forms and subjects, the rejection of avant-garde posturing, the distrust of narrowly autobiographical thematics, the unembarrassed employment of heightened popular speech, and the restoration of deep, unironic emotion.[133]

As Gioia's description suggests, there were loose associations of poets, scattered across the United States, who valued rhyme, meter, and poetic form, and others who argued that narrative needed to be brought back into contemporary poetry. Some emphasized a conservative Western tradition, while others, including Annie Finch and Kathrine Varnes, encouraged a global "multiformalism" or "omniformalism."[134] Many wanted their poetry to be different from the "bodiless unfocused meditative verse of John Ashbery and those he appeared to be influencing."[135] They were also dissatisfied with most contemporary criticism, suggesting that it trivialized poetry by not taking it seriously enough; that it focused more on promotion than on criticism and evaluation; and that it was often so difficult and jargon-laden that it drove away potential readers. They considered it important to reappraise poets whom they viewed as underappreciated, especially those who were shunned by the "coterie culture of the universities."[136] Since audience was important, even indispensable, to many of these poets, they wanted to win back the intelligent "common" readers of poetry that they felt had been lost since the modernist dicta issued by Pound and Eliot. Many felt that re-energizing and democratizing poetry by expanding the range of possible subjects would be one way to win back those readers. Although their own poetry demonstrates that they didn't reject autobiographical subjects, most also believed that poets should be encouraged to write about topics other than themselves. Whereas some seemed to wish that modernism (and postmodernism) had never happened, most simply wanted to revitalize poetic traditions and take advantage of resources that had been in disfavor since the advent of Modernism.[137]

In a 1983 overview of "The Year in Poetry," Lewis Turco hints at exactly this kind of revitalization in his reference to the "rumors and siftings of a return to formalism in American poetry."[138] In fact, a "return to formalism," as well as the corollary "return to narrative," can be traced to at least the early 1970s. For instance, in a 1971 review of *The Contemporary American Poets: American Poetry Since 1940* (edited by Mark Strand), Dick Allen expresses ideas that would later become central to New Formalism. While granting that the anthology under review is "good" and that it includes "a lot of beautiful poems," he says that the focus on one "*kind* of poetry," with almost all of the featured poems stemming from the "*lyric* tradition," is a serious limitation.[139] This collection may feature "all the 'right' poets," but it leaves out far too many, featuring "almost no black poets," "no folk rock poetry," and "no concrete poetry." By featuring the poems that it *does* feature, says Allen, the anthology "demonstrates the terrible sameness of American poetry since 1940."[140] Furthermore, although it aspires to show the development of the featured poets, the anthology "demonstrates how little most of these poets have developed." Allen's call for a poetic rebellion foreshadows the New Formalist movement:

> So many of our poets have become so finely tuned, so unique, so heightened, so intellectual, so precious, so observant, they no longer speak out of the voice of the ground, out of the voice of the people, but only out of the voice of *their* crowd....
>
> The style of the whining self cannot much longer be the main concept of modern poetry. It is time to return to storytelling; it is time for the poets ... to take on a sense of duty. Poetry may (as it did in the past) help to once again teach the people how to speak profoundly among themselves, instead of assuming that "ordinary" people are such dolts.

Ironically, the New Formalists have been criticized for their elitism, for their exclusion of outsiders, and for the "sameness" of their poetry.

Marilyn Hacker, who would eventually (albeit reluctantly) find herself classed among the New Formalists, published *Presentation Piece*, a collection of formal poetry, in 1974. Other collections soon began to appear, including Charles Martin's *Room for Error* (1978); Timothy Steele's *Uncertainties and Rest* (1979); Frederick Feirstein's *Manhattan Carnival*, Frederick Turner's *The Return*, and Richard Moore's *Empires* (all in 1981); Gjertrud Schnackenberg's *Portraits and Elegies* (1982) and *The Lamplit Answer* (1985); and Brad Leithauser's *Hundreds of Fireflies* (1982).[141] Vikram Seth's *The Golden Gate*, a book-length narrative poem in an elaborate rhyming form, appeared in 1986. In 1988 Robert Richman published *The Direction of Poetry: An Anthology of Rhymed and Metered Verse Written in the English Language Since 1975*. Davie is included, as are several writers associated with New Formalism.[142] In the introduction, Richman praises Larkin's skill with blank verse, and in a footnote, he states that he wanted to give "Larkin's last poems ... a central place in both the introduction and [the] text" of this collection but that he was unable to attain permission to use them.[143] In 1996, New Formalist poets appeared together for the first time in *Rebel Angels* with the exception of its editors, Jarman and Mason, as well as any poets born before 1940.[144] It is telling that, when Jarman and Mason were writing the introduction to *Rebel Angels*, Gioia recommended "Robert

Conquest's preface to *New Lines*, the Movement manifesto anthology," as a model.[145]

In the introduction to *New Expansive Poetry*, Gwynn states that a special 1977 issue of *Mississippi Review* entitled "Freedom and Form: American Poets Respond"—which contains the attack by Duane Locke described earlier, as well as poems and essays by many others—was an early indicator of the emergence of New Formalism. Another early salvo in the "poetry wars" was Frederick Turner's "'Mighty Poets in Their Misery Dead': a Polemic on the Contemporary Poetic Scene," which appeared in the Fall 1980 *Missouri Review*.[146] Brad Leithauser's "Metrical Illiteracy," an article that Keith Maillard (inaccurately) describes as "the first shot in what might be called 'the form war,'" appeared in 1983.[147] Gioia's "The Dilemma of the Long Poem," also appearing in 1983, was a survey of current American poetry, which Gioia called a "very limited enterprise" focused almost entirely on short lyrics.[148] Gioia's "Notes on the New Formalism" and Leithauser's "The Confinement of Free Verse" appeared in 1987. In 1989 Dick Allen guest-edited an "Expansive Poetry" issue of the American journal *Crosscurrents*, and in 1992 Robert McPhillips guest-edited a "New Formalist" issue of the English journal *Verse*.[149] Book-length critical works or anthologies that attracted widespread—and often heated—attention to the New Formalists include the aforementioned *Expansive Poetry* (1989), edited by Feirstein and Turner; *Missing Measures*, by Steele (1990); *Poetry After Modernism*, edited by Robert McDowell (1991); *Can Poetry Matter?* by Gioia (1992); *The Ghost of Meter*, by Finch (1993); and *A Formal Feeling Comes*, edited by Finch (1994). From 1980 to 1990, Jarman and McDowell edited *The Reaper*, and their polemical "Reaper Essays" appeared in book form in 1996.

NEW FORMALISM: ALIVE AND WELL?

New Formalism is no longer a movement in the sense of a group of activists fighting for a particular literary and critical agenda; instead, it appears to have moved from outlaw status to a canonical position.[150]

David Mason speculates that New Formalism may have endured for quite some time because it "arose at a point when some . . . revolutionary movements of the post-war era"—he specifies the Beats, the Black Mountain poets, and the Confessionals—"had become enervated, an establishment unto themselves."[151] In addition, Mason says, "I suspect our longevity is due to the fact that we're part of a larger trend, and lots of people not associated with our movement have been drifting back to form again anyway."[152] While he is undoubtedly correct, it is also true that the ongoing and well-publicized efforts of the New Formalists have contributed to a reawakened interest in rhyme, meter, narrative, and poetic form in the United States. According to Annie Finch, one key factor in the group's lengthy lifespan is the inherent versatility of form itself, which allows New Formalism to "link into" various "grass-roots" or "people's poetry" movements.[153] Finch believes, too, that the "extreme dedication and organizational drive of one or two core people" has been a factor in the longevity of New Formalism. She gives Gioia, McDowell, and Jarman credit for laying a "very strong foundation."[154] In addition, New Formalism's energetic and unabashed self-promotion through reviews, articles, books, conferences, and websites has undoubtedly contributed to the group's long-term survival.[155] In contrast, although the Movement writers and their allies vigorously promoted that group and its ideas, they were apparently unwilling to go nearly as far as the New Formalists.[156]

Another likely reason for New Formalism's longevity is that some of its ideas, including the insistence by most members of the group that poets should be encouraged to write free verse *and* formal verse if they wish, are simply sensible and widely acceptable. A similarly sensible—if not obvious—idea of many New Formalists is that poets benefit from training in prosody even if they do not plan to write formal verse. Annie Finch has suggested that if poetic movements wish to survive, they must be willing to embrace change—and even to embrace conflict. Thus far, New Formalism appears to have done exactly that, allowing it to live, albeit quietly, into its fourth decade.

Perhaps the most important reason for New Formalism's longevity—and another major difference between this group and the Movement—has been this willingness to evolve. Much of the impetus has come from women. Annie Finch and Kathrine Varnes have spoken to me about their struggles to make themselves heard at New Formalist gatherings and to introduce "new" ideas, such as feminist and postmodernist theory.[157] The situation has, however, improved. Finch, Varnes, Kim Addonizio, Marilyn Hacker, Allison Joseph, Marilyn Nelson, Molly Peacock, Dana Gioia, H. L. Hix, Dick Allen, David Mason, and Mark Jarman are among the provocateurs who have actively urged the group to evolve—or who have quietly but insistently served as models of poetic and critical openmindedness.[158] In her essay "Feminist Formalist: A Critical Oxymoron?" Varnes suggests that feminism and formalism *can* coexist.[159] In an article called "New Formalism Among the Postmoderns," Hix argues that some postmodernist ideas could benefit the New Formalists.[160] Those New Formalists who prefer not to be dismissed as hopelessly sexist, reactionary, retrograde, or worse have heeded such criticisms and suggestions. Much-needed changes have taken place within the group: a decrease in the number and vehemence of attacks on "the academy"; an increased openness to a variety of poetic approaches; an increased interest in feminism, poststructuralism, and postmodernism; a broadening of geographic boundaries; and an increase in the presence of women and people of color.

Of course, there has been resistance. I have heard Finch described as the "political correctness police," and I have read attacks on the New Formalists coming from conservative sources such as *Edge City Review* and *Expansive Poetry & Music Online*. Some have argued that the concept of "form" can become meaningless when used as broadly as it is in Finch's *A Formal Feeling Comes* (1994) or in Finch and Varnes's *An Exaltation of Forms* (2002).[161] Some have asked why anyone who wishes to write both free verse and formal verse or to explore feminism or postmodernism would even *want* to be counted as a New Formalist. Kim Addonizio, who has her own "reservations about the 'formalist' label," offers one pragmatic answer: "I guess I'm happy to be considered one if it gets my work out there to people."[162]

CHAPTER 3

Personal and Textual Connections

Thom Gunn will no doubt prove to be a pivotal figure. For one thing, many of us looked up to him when we were young as a model of what the poet could be, and what we were so often told we could not be—that is, he felt free to write in any verse form he chose and never restricted himself in terms of subject matter. . . . Gunn, as an Englishman living in America, seemed a bridge to multiple possibilities for the art.[163]

—David Mason

In any examination involving influence or related phenomena, several cautions are crucial. For one thing, as Claude Lévi-Strauss points out, "Similarity does not denote influence." In addition, as every student of logic learns, *post hoc* does not necessarily mean *propter hoc.*[164] An old proverb, recast to fit the situation, makes another important point: Familiarity may breed *contempt* rather than *influence.* Also, since writers themselves are not always aware of their influences, tracking down the connections can be difficult or even impossible. Even when evidence of possible influence can be found, it proves no more than that—*possibility.* Indeed, many factors that appear to suggest that one writer has influenced another may be merely coincidental, since writers, even those living in different eras and different countries, often live through analogous personal, societal, historical, cultural, and literary experiences. Furthermore, writers may *state* that someone has influenced their work, but evidence of such influence may be sparse or even nonexistent—and the work itself may, in fact, call the writers' claims into question. While keeping these cautions in mind, we can add to our understanding of poets and their work by tracing influences and related phenomena.

Dialogism, as defined by Mikhail Bakhtin, is a productive way of looking at relationships between writers—and relationships between texts. Richard J. Gray describes his own adaptation of Bakhtin's notion thus:

> Texts 'talk' to each other. They, and their authors, are engaged in a constant debate with each other, a debate that allows for difference as well as 'influence.' And the debate is, of course, more intense between those of 'like mind': e.g. Southern writers and Faulkner, the New Formalists and the Movement poets.[165]

In this version of a dialogic relationship—which, admittedly, takes liberties with the original Bakhtinian notion—a poet may consciously or unconsciously engage in such acts as replying to, arguing with, expanding on, toying with, or parodying the ideas, themes, images, language, style, formal aspects, and so on, of the poetry and criticism of a predecessor or a peer. To borrow Bakhtin's terminology, the *texts* engage each other in these ways.

Signifying, as defined by Henry Louis Gates in *The Signifying Monkey* (1988), is similar in some ways to *dialogism*. As Gates uses the term, *signifying* generally describes literary relationships between African American writers and their Anglo-European forebears, but the concept is potentially useful even in a discussion of the Movement writers and the New Formalists—where most of the poets have Anglo-European backgrounds—because of its combination of parody, irreverence, and downright subversiveness, as well as its emphasis on the possibility and the value of learning from a wide variety of authors.

While modernist and postmodernist theorists have demonstrated that influence can be problematic, many writers still use this term to describe their relationships with their predecessors and contemporaries. Molly Peacock's ideas about influence stem from the ancient meaning of *inspiration*:

> By "influence" I mean something in the voice and music of the writer that goes straight into my physical body and literally inspires me, changing something about the way my diaphragm breathes, and making me say, "I want to do THAT!" And, miraculously, the influence allows me to do what that other poet is doing, it permits me, encourages me, even, if you will, acts as a benign parent, urging me along to do what it is doing, then take off on my own.[166]

Marilyn Hacker's ideas are similar to Peacock's. Hacker says, simply, that poets who have influenced her have "made [her] want to write poems!" and have "in some cases made [her] want to 'respond' to the challenges / questions / techniques of their work."[167] Along these same lines, R. S. Gwynn defines "influence" in this way: "Love of a poet's work and memorizing his or her poetry comes first. Learning how the mechanics of certain poems work is another."[168]

THIS BE THE VERSE: POETIC REPLIES TO THE MOVEMENT

Marilyn Nelson describes her 1978 poem "Churchgoing" as her "one Larkin-influenced poem" and "the only evidence of her encounters with Larkin."[169] As this excerpt from Nelson's poem shows, it echoes Larkin's in many ways, from its title to its theme, its language to its tone:

> The Lutherans sit stolidly in rows;
> only their children feel the holy ghost
> that makes them jerk and bobble and almost
> destroys the pious atmosphere for those
> whose reverence bows their backs as if in work.
> The congregation sits, or stands to sing,
> or chants the dusty creeds automaton

In Larkin's "Church Going," the wry yet wistful speaker examines and repudiates traditional religious beliefs. In Nelson's "Churchgoing," the speaker initially approaches the subject in a similarly light way, depicting the bored, yawning Lutherans. Nelson's speaker asks herself "why I have come / to probe the ruins of this dying cult." As she sits through the Lutheran service, she yearns for the vitality and intensity that she associates with gospel music and African American churches, and mulls over the paradox of slaves who suffered at the hands of "Christian, slave-owning" hypocrites yet adopted their religion. She asks how these slaves could have "pitied the poor body of Christ!" while somehow ignoring the "hypocrisy" of their "owners," who subjected them to torments as harrowing as those suffered by Jesus. She speculates that "belief is given to the simple / as recompense for what they do not know," but decides that she'll "try to start / finding the black way back to what we've lost." Larkin's speaker is distant, seeing religion as little more than a set of rituals, the loss of which evokes nostalgia and some regret, but not deep introspection or grief. Nelson's speaker is "tormented in [her] heart." For her, religious faith merits serious consideration because people have suffered and died for it. And for her as an African American, it is inextricably intertwined with race: a battle of "fighting angels, one group black, one white."

Even if Larkin is an inspiration for many contemporary poets, including many New Formalists, his legacy as an artist is vexed by his personal characteristics as a human being. In her essay "Owning the Masters," Nelson alludes to Larkin's racism rather than his artistry: "How can I read Wallace Stevens without remembering that he asked, when Gwendolyn Brooks became the first Aframerican poet to be awarded the Pulitzer Prize, 'Why did they let the coon in?' What about Ezra Pound? What about Philip Larkin?"[170] Although Nelson mentions Larkin only in the context of a regrettably ugly side of his character, her familiarity with him is important, especially in the context of her essay, in which she addresses the question of African American writers' position in relation to the "white literary tradition." In addition, she suggests that writers can reply to and argue with poets like Larkin, Stevens, and Pound, engaging them in a contentious though productive conversation. Nelson's discussion is also valuable because she elucidates the influence of 'signifying' and how it allows "those . . . who come from traditions of oppression" to "own" the "Angloamerican tradition."

Nelson describes how Phillis Wheatley, an enslaved person who was also a renowned poet in eighteenth-century America, "found her voice within the oppressor's tradition because she had to sing." For Nelson, however, much of the poetry written in the twentieth century has lost its musical attributes. As she puts it, most "white poetry emulates speech, not song." Although she is reluctant "to become involved in the current debate between the so-called New Formalists (the singers) and the organic poets (the conversationalists)," she says that, nevertheless, "I hear the music more clearly, more compellingly, when I write with an ear to tradition: Hearing either the music of my people, or the rhyme and meter of the master's tradition." Something vital is lost, she says, when poets "play Hatfields and McCoys in the literary world," when they see tradition as "tribal and exclusive." Those proponents of "the literary separatism they called the Black Aesthetic," for instance, "threw out the baby with the bathwater. In their single-minded quest for a revolutionary poetry they paid a great personal and artistic cost."

Nelson says that "those of us who come from traditions of oppression find ourselves estranged from canonical texts," but she argues that it is wise, even mandatory, to "fight—against them and our arguments with them—to own" those texts. She describes how, as a young woman, Maya Angelou felt that Milton and Shakespeare wrote for her. Nelson states, "Maya is right: Shakespeare did write for her." Furthermore, she insists, "The Angloamerican tradition belongs to all of us, or should. As does the community into which the tradition invites us." Responding to Audre Lorde's statement that "the master's tools will never dismantle the master's house," Nelson counters:

> But why should we dismantle the house? . . . Why don't we instead take possession of, why don't we own the tradition? Own the masters, all of them. Wordsworth and Wheatley, Hughes, Auden. As we own the masters and learn to use more and more levels of this language we love, for whose continued evolution we share responsibility, the signifiers become ours. We must not stand, like trembling slaves, at the back door of the master's house.

Actively and deliberately "owning" the tradition allows writers to "escape the merely personal" and to engage "in dialogue with great thoughts of the past." Even if one wanted to resist those "great thoughts," the effort would be futile because of the very nature of language itself: "Other writers make our work possible; we write someone else's words." Poets benefit, argues Nelson, when they write "with an ear to tradition," for they are then able to "think and sing along with many other minds." Fully taking possession of the tradition, according to her, involves "the layering of meaning upon meaning," as described by T. S. Eliot in "Tradition and the Individual Talent."

As noted earlier, Nelson's views also encapsulate the notion of signifying as described by Henry Louis Gates. Because she is able to "hear the music more clearly [and] more compellingly" when she revisits various poetic forms and traditions—even those tainted by evils including racism, sexism, political extremism, xenophobia, and ethnocentrism—Nelson refuses to "stand, like [a] trembling [slave], at the back door of the master's house." The poetic music that she hears includes the music of "[her] people," and it also includes the music written by Shakespeare, Wordsworth, Hughes, Auden, and other "masters"—even when they have repellent personal views. Although Nelson is speaking specifically of relationships between African American poets and earlier generations of Anglo-European poets, signifying can be a way for all poets to fling open the doors to the "master's house" and benefit from the riches within. What's more, since signifying involves replying to, arguing with, imitating, mimicking, parodying, adapting, and reshaping various influences, it is a productive way to look at the relationships that the New Formalists have with the Movement writers.

In a 1996 discussion of her poem "Playground," Katha Pollitt does not use terms such as "signifying" or "argument," but both of these apply to the relationship between her own poem and one by Larkin:

> Behind my poem, of course, lies Philip Larkin's great poem "Afternoons," which is also about mothers in a playground. For Larkin, the mothers' plight, which he depicts with much tenderness and sympathy, is inevitable and quasi-biological: youth and freedom, love and beauty, last but a moment, then dreary old domesticity—so necessary to children but so unrewarding to men and women—takes over. It is nature—the heedless, demanding children, the next generation, the life force—that is pushing the mothers "to the side of their own lives."[171]

Given Larkin's reputation as a curmudgeon and a misogynist, it is worth noting that Pollitt admires the "tenderness and sympathy" in this "great" poem by Larkin. Despite her obvious attraction to "Afternoons," Pollitt wished to counter Larkin's deterministic depiction of motherhood: "In 'Playground,' I wanted to say that this process, which looks like nature, is actually social. The sadness comes not, as in Larkin's poem, because of something inevitable, but because of what needn't be, but is."

When Maura Stanton first read Larkin's poem "Aubade" in the late 1970s, she was "deeply impressed." In 1980, when she read several other poems by Larkin, she was so "knocked out by [his] work" that she studied his poems. She admired Larkin because he "spoke directly, honestly, colloquially and vividly—but in meter and rhyme." As she taught herself to write metrical poetry, Larkin "helped [her] do that but also keep in touch with natural, direct speech." She also "admired the way Larkin could be so brutally frank and direct, and yet sneak in a lot of lyricism and romantic stuff in a disguised way." Stanton, whose earliest poetry collections appeared in the 1970s, says that the poems from her middle period are "very much connected to Larkin." In her 1988 book *Tales of the Supernatural*, one poem, "Space," is written in a "direct imitation of the meter Larkin used in 'The Explosion.'" For Stanton, Larkin "still stands out . . . from the other Movement poets."[172]

Diane Thiel's encounters with poetry by Larkin and Gunn at Brown University "re-energized" her interest in writing formal poetry.[173] She explains that, since she "first read Davie in later years," he has had less of an impact on her than Larkin and Gunn. However, she "feel[s] a kinship with all three of these writers, particularly for their use of precise form, while also using free verse." More specifically, "[her] love of the epigram was partly influenced by Thom Gunn." When she first encountered Larkin, she "appreciated [his] facility with the lyric, and also his dark humor." It is thus not surprising that she has written a poetic reply to Larkin:

> I have always had a conflicted relationship with Larkin's work; while his form and often bleak portraits interest me, I often found myself in a dark mood after reading his poems, particularly his portraits of domesticity. I acknowledge this appreciation and wariness in the lines from "Bedside Readers":
>
> And Larkin, there's another to beware
> between the sheets, for all I like his form.

As Thiel describes them, there are extensive connections between her poem and two by Larkin: "I use Larkin's rhyme scheme and also iambic pentameter (as he does) in the poem, and respond to the two poems at length, echoing, in particular, Larkin's 'misery' which 'deepens like a coastal shelf.' I think it became a sonnet, though, to undercut the form. . . ." Despite its pessimistic theme, Larkin's "This Be the Verse," says Thiel, "makes [her] laugh out loud." In her own poem, she is taking a "jab at the poet" while also "simultaneously appreciating him with a humorous homage."[174] In "Bedside Readers," Thiel's speaker voices her doubts about men who keep poetry by Charles Bukowski at their bedside, then names Larkin as another dubious companion: "This be the verse to keep us all forewarned." When the speaker says, "A life with Larkin would have made me dive / straight off that rocky coastal shelf," she is alluding to the melancholy but humorous warning about parenthood that concludes "This Be the Verse":

> Man hands on misery to man.
> It deepens like a coastal shelf.

Get out as early as you can,
And don't have any kids yourself.

As "Bedside Readers" ends, Thiel's speaker issues her own warning, directly naming a poem by Larkin: "Unless you want a timely end, / Don't read your lover 'Talking in Bed' in bed."

As Molly Peacock lists writers who have had the most impact on her own poetry, she places Larkin alongside George Herbert, Elizabeth Bishop, Gerard Manley Hopkins, Shakespeare, Keats, and Dickinson. In graduate school, Peacock was "entranced" by Bishop and Larkin, and she continues to see these two, along with Herbert, as "central" among her influences.[175] When she "found Larkin in a Washington, D.C. bookstore in 1976 . . . [she] fell instantly in love" and "read every Larkin poem [she] could get [her] hands on." She "had respect" for Movement poets Gunn and Davie, but she "never read [them] over and over again" the way she read Larkin. She admires him "for his protean, entirely natural eight-line stanzas and gorgeous rhymes, for his grouchiness, his unshackled personality as expressed in his verse structures." Peacock even admires Larkin's adjectives: "Poor adjectives, they always get a bum rap, but Larkin's are always essential." Her involvement with Larkin's poetry has been surprisingly extensive and intimate. She says that she "found tapes in 1987 and listened to Larkin's voice, for a period of time between 1989 and 1991, in headphones as [she] went to sleep at night."

Given the connections between the New Formalists and the Movement writers, it is telling that, in his 1999 book *All the Fun's in How You Say a Thing*, Timothy Steele praises Larkin's "The Whitsun Weddings" and "Church Going" not only for their "lyrical grace" but also for their "thematic and argumentative richness."[176] Modernist and postmodernist poets tend to avoid outright statements that "telegraph" the main ideas of their poems. There are exceptions—Yeats's "That is no country for old men" is an apt example—but as Richard J. Gray puts it, "most modernist and postmodernist poetry . . . resists such pronouncements."[177] In contrast, Movement poetry is often characterized by its "essayistic" or "discursive" qualities.[178] In a discussion of the "new austerity" that arose in poetry after World War II, Michael Hamburger describes a poem by Pablo Neruda, saying that it is "akin to prose in its subordination of rhythm and imagery to argument."[179] This same description fits many poems by the Movement writers, who objected to what they saw as excessive metaphor and imagery. They leaned instead toward argumentative poetry consisting of aphoristic "thesis statements," supporting examples, reiterations of the main idea, transitional phrases, conversational asides, even instances of comparison and contrast.

Molly Peacock's early poetry suggests that she too has been inspired by this characteristic of the Movement writers; in poems such as "Things to Do," she is just as essayistic or discursive as any of them. Rachel Wetzsteon, who "loved" Larkin and Gunn when she first encountered their poetry in the early 1990s, says that she especially admires Larkin for "his ability to sustain LONG sentences over many lines; his last lines; his sly wit and marvelous melancholy; and how often he manages to combine them in a single poem."[180] Wetzsteon's description also fits many poems by Molly Peacock. For example, Peacock's "There's No Earthly Reason" is an argument, complete with "thesis statement," examples, and reiterations of the main point:

> There's no earthly reason to be horrified
> by the fact that we become like our parents.
> Hell, we imitated all their nonsense
> since we were born. We wanted to be, we tried
> to be all grown, all free. We did what we saw.
> We knew where the hand went on that hip,
> how the Lucky dangled from that lower lip

This poem, which argues that children are "the little whales / who swallowed [their parents] whole" and that "we are what we loathed / because of how we've chosen to be clothed," is a thematic mirror-image of Larkin's famous "This Be the Verse":

> They fuck you up, your mum and dad.
>   They may not mean to, but they do.
> They fill you with the faults they had
>   And add some extra, just for you.[181]

Peacock's poem is more than a mere echo of Larkin's; it is also an argument with his. In Larkin's poem, the parents damage the children. In Peacock's, the children do it to themselves: "we tie about / our bodies their lovely or ugly trappings." In Larkin's poem, the inheritance is always negative: "Man hands on misery to man." In Peacock's, the parental "trappings" donned by the children can be either "lovely" or "ugly." In a metaphor that is far more earthy and detailed than anything in Larkin's poem, Peacock's speaker returns to the Larkinesque idea that rejecting the "essence" of one's parents is, to put it mildly, difficult:

> What fails
> to get digested, the Jonah eye, or Jonah limb
> or knuckle, the part we took in but couldn't
> break down, the tooth of their essence in our dim
> interior, is what we puke up or pass out
> and what makes us free, the "them" we couldn't
> make into the "me."

Especially in the Confessional and post-Confessional atmosphere of the twentieth century, it is not unusual for poets to write about relationships with their parents. However, it is relatively rare for the resulting poems to be, in effect, argumentative or expository essays, as in these examples by Larkin and Peacock.

Peacock's "Our Room," which describes the speaker's attempts to help schoolchildren deal with the effects of growing up with an alcoholic parent, poignantly echoes one of Larkin's most haunting ideas: "The classroom becomes / oddly lonely when we talk about our homes." In other words, the children all have their own reasons to feel that, as Larkin puts it, "home is so sad." When I interviewed Peacock, she told me that "Home Is So Sad" was among her favorite poems when she wrote "Our Room" and that it still is.[182] Home may represent failure, as in another poem by Larkin, where home is "a joyous shot at how things ought to be, / Long fallen wide." In his "Poetry of Departures," the speaker comes right out with it: "We all hate home / And having to be there."

A sampling of Peacock's 1984 collection *Raw Heaven* further reveals the extent to which her early poetry features Movement traits. The poems often open with "thesis statements": "Summer is a chartreuse hell in the mountains" ("Old Roadside Resorts"); "Our homes are on our backs and don't forget it" ("Where Is Home?"); "Everything used to be symbolic" ("Violet Dusks"); "Islands are magical, like suns and moons" ("Islands in Our Eyes"); "Whoever loves a garden fears seasons" ("A Garden"); "The sadness that prevails among families / is the web of histories spun" ("The Web of Histories").[183] Blake Morrison describes additional quirks that the Movement writers adopted from William Empson, one of their idols: "The wit to which Movement poetry occasionally aspires consists less of ingenious metaphors, than of ambiguities, allusion, or, as can be seen in the following examples, clever-clever wordplays."[184] The three examples Morrison quotes are these: "He noticed no-one noticed him at all" (Gunn); "Which, when unfailing, fails him most perhaps" (Davie); and "The lesson is that breaking hearts must break" (Wain). In Morrison's terse assessment, "This feature of Movement poetry is one of its least attractive." Attractive or not, it also appears in Peacock's early poetry: "I'm afraid I'll be afraid of your voice" ("Afraid"); "To understand is to stand under the sky / of your own desires" ("The Sky Inside"); "The day's fun is a soft but clear / violet violence of were and we're" ("Next Afternoon").

NEW FORMALISM: THE NEW AND THE OLD

Theorists have amply demonstrated that *no* literary movement can ever be totally original. Indeed, says Frank Lentricchia, Ezra Pound's directive to "make it new!" did not mean that everything old had to be discarded; instead, it meant that writers and other artists should "make contemporary what is old."[185] According to Thomas Cable, the

New Formalists often "take pains" to distinguish themselves from earlier formalists, including Richard Wilbur, Anthony Hecht, James Merrill, and Howard Nemerov.[186] Some New Formalists freely acknowledge, however, that despite the name (which was, to some degree, foisted upon them), New Formalism is *not* new, except in relatively minor ways.[187] In a review of a collection by Mark Jarman, published in 2000, David Solway makes this very point. His review also draws an implicit connection between the New Formalists and a "totemic" poet who, as it happens, was a member of the Movement: "I would suggest that the epithet *new* is equally misleading, as it nearly always is. After all, what have totemic poets like Philip Larkin, James Merrill, and Richard Wilbur been doing for a generation and more if not precisely what the implicit manifesto behind the New Formalism so resonantly summons poets to attempt?"[188] In a review of *Rebel Angels* Richard Tillinghast makes a related point: "In the early 1980s a younger generation of poets, known as the New Formalists, re-invented the wheel, turning with delight to the pleasures of rhyme, discovering how meter and measured lines can discipline the poet into writing more concisely than he might have done without the stimulus of form."[189] Tillinghast's inclusion of Larkin in a list of the age's finest poets, in this same review, also implies that there is a connection between Larkin and the New Formalists: "Even after the supposed triumph of free verse, the most memorable poetry of our time—by writers such as Richard Wilbur, Philip Larkin, Robert Lowell, Seamus Heaney and Elizabeth Bishop—has remained notable for its formal elements."

In contrast, others, including critics generally sympathetic to New Formalism, have faulted this lack of newness. In "A Controversy Reignited: The Early 20th Century Vers Libre Debate as an Antecedent of New Formalist Criticism," Meg Schoerke suggests that the ideas in New Formalist criticism are "recycled."[190] The same has been said about New Formalist poetry. Remarks like David Lehman's, in his review of Mary Jo Salter's *Unfinished Painting* (1989), are common: "Salter makes us wonder whether there's really anything new in the new formalism. The virtues of her poetry are those of the formalism that prevailed a generation ago."[191] Similarly, in a 1986 review, Thomas Swiss asks, "How does one tell the 'new' formalists from the 'old' if all these writers are mining the same traditions, exhibiting the same manners?"[192] In *Unending Design: The Forms of Postmodern Poetry* (1991), Joseph M. Conte suggests that the "retrogressive New Formalists" should be called "Old Formalism Revisited."[193] In "Rebels Not Yet Angels" (1998), John Haines states that, despite its adherents' claims, the New Formalist movement is not a "revolution," although he acknowledges that it may be "a revival, yes; a renewal, if you like, or perhaps a restoration."[194] In the more dismissively titled "Rebels Without a Case" (1998), James Hatch asks, "How can working in forms that have been around for five hundred years or more be revolutionary?"[195]

Although this definition may not appeal to these critics, one meaning of the term *revolution* is a revolving or turning back to a starting point. As New Formalism involves a turning back to various starting points within poetry, it is clearly a revolution in this way. It is also revolutionary to defy the norms and doctrines of one's own time, even when such defiance involves returning to "forms that have been around for five hundred years." Also, as discussed in Chapter One, some poets and critics reacted harshly and downright hysterically to the New Formalists, as seen by the condemnatory terms they used, including "yuppie poets," "enemies of poetry," "piddling Pounds," "wimps," even "anti-Americans." To them, New Formalism must have seemed not only revolutionary but also deeply threatening.

The Movement writers and the New Formalists have reacted to such criticism in characteristically self-contradictory ways. In the very titles of their "manifesto anthologies"—*New Lines* and *Rebel Angels*—they have embraced the notion that a "revolution" must involve newness, novelty, experimentation. At the same time, and sometimes in the same documents, they have questioned it and rebelled against it. Writing in 1995, Dana Gioia insists that "sometimes refusing to be revolutionary is the most radical form of rebellion."[196] For Gioia, Larkin was just such a "rebel":

> The vivid articulation of the ordinary is in itself an exceptional act. To catch the unexpressed passions that brood under quotidian life is the most necessary of artistic accomplishments. In the age of experimentalism, cosmopolitanism, and abstraction, Philip Larkin . . . wrote the sort of poetry he himself desired—local, realistic, narrative, and formal. Consequently, every poem drew energy from a whole life, and even the simplest utterance bore the pressure of that particular life's dark and quiet passion.[197]

In the introduction to *New Expansive Poetry*, R. S. Gwynn states unapologetically that the New Formalists looked to models such as "Frost, Hardy, Jeffers, [and] Millay."[198] David Mason puts it this way: "The assertion that there's anything new about what my generation has done is just irrelevant. Novelty is not the point. Intensity of experience is the point."[199] In "Overcoming the Tic of Techniques," Dick Allen suggests that the "main early influences on Expansive Poetry" stemmed from the efforts of "poets born in the late 1930s and early 1940s . . . to combine what they felt were the best elements of poetry's warring camps in the 1960s—'Beat' and Academic."[200] Expansive Poetry, he says, borrowed freely, eclectically, and unashamedly, taking "its emphasis on content and subject and audience from the most politically and socially-oriented Beat Poetry, its use of colloquial language and natural speech patterns from William Carlos Williams." At the same time, acutely aware of "the scorn Academic Formalist poets heaped upon what they saw as the careless prosody of the Beats and Projectivist Verse poets, Expansive Poets took their form from the Academics, loosening it in the process." Although Expansive Poets adopted the formal predilections of the Academics, "they often discarded what they felt was an over-reliance on elitist, intellectual and New Criticism irony, wit, and classical allusions too often conveyed with a lack of emotion and passion."

Reviewing *Rebel Angels*, poet and critic Robert Phillips writes: "This is one of the things that *is* new about the new formalism: the fusion of earthy subjects with the unearthly lyric impulse."[201] German critic Franz Link says that the New Formalists differ from the "academic formalists" in two major ways: they "favor a more immediate rendering of emotions, a closer affinity to everyday speech and more popular subjects," and they "don't want to write 'workshop' poetry that is read by its practitioners only."[202] Making a similar argument, Robert McPhillips asserts that the "diction" of the New Formalists tends to be "colloquial rather than elevated" and that "cultural objects" in their poetry tend to be "indigenously American" artifacts.[203] Gioia, he says, "has perfected a quiet, colloquial, genuinely human voice . . . that is alien to the irony of the academic formalists and the frequent hysteria of the Confessional poets," adding that the "elegance" of a passage in one of Gioia's poems "doesn't rely on elevated diction, literary allusions, or an exotic setting."[204]

NEW FORMALISTS AND THEIR AMERICAN "MASTERS"

Since nearly all of the New Formalists are Americans, it is unsurprising that most of them name American poets and critics as their "masters." Direct personal connections between numerous New Formalists and other poet-critics further the likelihood that the older writers have influenced the younger ones. Dana Gioia, Robert B. Shaw, Rachel Hadas, and Mary Jo Salter studied with Robert Fitzgerald. Gioia and Salter also studied with Elizabeth Bishop. Timothy Murphy studied with Robert Penn Warren. Rachel Wetzsteon studied with John Hollander, and Annie Finch studied with Penelope Laurans as well as Hollander.[205] Salter and David Mason studied with Anthony Hecht. R. S. Gwynn studied with Miller Williams and James Whitehead.[206] Timothy Steele studied with J. V. Cunningham, a protégé and friend of Yvor Winters. This relationship, though indirect, is relevant nonetheless because criticism written by Winters inspired crucial Movement ideas.[207] Andrew Hudgins, Rita Dove, Maura Stanton, and Mark Jarman studied with Donald Justice (a former student of Winters), who is important not only as a poet and teacher but also as a link in the trans-Atlantic connections between the New Formalists and the Movement.

Richard Wilbur, in whom the New Formalists have found a "master" and a "compatriot," appeared with two nascent New Formalists, R. S. Gwynn and Paul Lake, in the 1977 special issue of *Mississippi Review* dedicated to "Freedom and Form."[208] As he describes what will be needed to help poetry recover from the damage caused by what he calls a "long . . . reign of error," Wilbur sounds like a precursor of the New Formalists. Coincidentally or not, he also sounds like the Movement poets:

> It will have to be said and proven, once more, that in art there is no joy without difficulty; that to be "natural" in art is not to blurt but to aim for perfection of utterance; that breadth and depth of vocabulary, good grammar and usage, the making of allusions, and the use of formal means are ways of achieving fullness and precision; that it is impoverishing to be incurious about the art of the past; that artifice is not necessarily cold; that high art is not necessarily pretentious; that to commit oneself to a form is far more daring than to be "free"; and that Whitman, God love him, is not the only possible touchstone.

THE MOVEMENT WRITERS: MENTORS, MEDIATORS, AND MODELS

Dana Gioia took two classes with Davie, whom he viewed as an "unofficial mentor."[209] Donald Justice served as Mark Jarman's teacher and thesis advisor, introducing him to Larkin's poetry and discussing its formal aspects with him. In addition, although Jarman was never one of Davie's students, they were colleagues at Vanderbilt University from 1983 until 1987. Jarman recalls many conversations with Davie about the appropriateness of using resources such as rhyme, meter, and form in American poetry. When he speaks of those forebears who gave young formalist poets "great hope," Timothy Steele often cites Larkin and Gunn. In *Missing Measures* (1990) and *All the Fun's in How You Say a Thing* (1999), he frequently mentions Yvor Winters and J. V. Cunningham, always favorably. Since Cunningham was one of Steele's teachers, it is unsurprising that Steele is sometimes called a "Wintersian."[210]

Although Davie is best known in the United States as a critic, a 1977 essay by Gioia (which I shall discuss later) strongly suggests that Davie's poetry, criticism, *and* teaching have influenced him. In a 1979 review of Davie's *The Poet in the Imaginary Museum*, Gioia describes Davie's efforts "to create a poetic style which kept the distinctively British sense of an audience and a tradition while acquiring the scope, the concentration, and the public-be-damned integrity of the American poetry he most admires."[211] He uses the word "groundbreaking" to describe four of Davie's critical books—*Purity of Diction in English Verse* (1952), *Articulate Energy: An Enquiry into the Syntax of English Poetry* (1955), *Ezra Pound: Poet as Sculptor* (1964), and *Thomas Hardy and British Poetry* (1972)—and lauds Davie's impact: "It is hardly surprising . . . that more than any other contemporary critic Davie has been the one who helped put British and American poetry back on speaking terms."[212] After listing several American poets whom Davie brought to the attention of an "initially suspicious and insular British public" and several English poets whom Davie brought to the attention of "chauvinistic American readers," he states emphatically, "if now very late in the seventies American and British poets are communicating on equal terms for perhaps the first time in history, it is as much due to Davie as to any other poet or critic living." Given Gioia's relationship with Davie, it is probably not coincidental that Gioia himself has endeavored to perform a similar function. As Kevin Bezner puts it, "No other American poet, it seems to me, has made such an effort at bringing current British and American poetry together."[213]

The "Donald Davie Issue" of *Sequoia*, in which Gioia's interview with Davie originally appeared, also features an essay by Gioia, in which he describes Davie as "not only one of England's greatest living poets" but also "its most brilliant and independent-minded literary critic."[214] He outlines Davie's poetic career, beginning with *Brides of Reason* (1955), "a brilliant collection of some thirty cool and ironic poems written for the most part in elegantly rhymed quatrains," and states that Davie has written "some of the best poems of his generation." Despite his initial image in the 1950s as "an unemotional, intellectual, and rational mind," Davie "gradually discovered a poetry capable of expressing the entire range of his own humanity—from tenderness to anger, from polemic to prayer."[215] In other words, Davie moved far beyond the narrowest Movement predilections. It is significant, though, that when Gioia lists ten of Davie's poems that most readers, himself included, would choose as their favorites, six date from the Movement period: "The Garden Party," "Remembering the Thirties," "Woodpigeons at Raheny," "Time Passing, Beloved," "The Mushroom Gatherers," and "Via Portello."[216]

Later in the essay, Gioia says that, as a critic, "Davie has probably exerted as much influence on the course of English poetry as any other writer in the past two decades. Two of his early books, *Purity of Diction in English Verse* (1952), and *Articulate Energy* (1955), soon became manifestos of sorts for British poets in the Fifties."[217] In Gioia's (minority) opinion, Davie's "most influential" critical book has been *Thomas Hardy and British Poetry*.[218] Although Davie's book was published in 1972, long after the dissolution of the Movement, it is in many ways a "Movement" document. Davie's thesis is that, for British poets, "the most far-reaching influence, for good and ill, has been not Yeats, still less Eliot or Pound, not Lawrence, but *Hardy*."[219] To Davie, Hardy's practice of "bow[ing] and retir[ing] at just the point where another poet would, for good or ill, advance and take us by the throat"—a rhetorical practice shared by many of the Movement writers—reveals "unaccustomed civility" and leaves readers "completely disarmed."[220] According to Davie, Hardy "is not 'great' because, except in *The Dynasts*, he does not choose to be."[221] A similar disdain for the "competition" of so-called greatness was also a defining characteristic of the Movement, as was Hardy's "modesty," to use Davie's term: "Major issues of national policy were among the matters that Hardy was too modest to concern himself with; and his modesty was that of the expert technician, imperious within his expertise, diffident or indifferent outside it."[222]

According to Davie, some may accuse Hardy of being a "cop-out" precisely because of his poetry's "neutral tone": "It begins to look as if Hardy's engaging modesty and his decent liberalism represent a crucial selling short of the poetic vocation . . . For surely the poet, if any one, has a duty to be radical."[223] Yet "Hardy, perhaps without knowing it, questions that assumption, and appears to reject it. Some of his successors in England, and a few out of England, seem to have agreed with him." The Movement writers are, of course, among these "successors." In his poem "Remembering the Thirties," Davie says, rather archly, that radicalism was not appropriate for his generation; instead, "a neutral tone is nowadays preferred."[224] Gioia himself has similarly called for "modesty" in poetry: "Sometimes the poetry we need most is written on a modest human scale—the voice of one human talking intimately with another with no grand gestures or heroic sweep."[225]

In Mark Jarman's view, Davie is "the most articulate Movement critic" and "one of the two great Pound scholars."[226] Jarman also admires Davie as a poet. In a 1988 collection of critical essays—which was dedicated to Davie—Jarman published "A Shared Humanity: 'In the Stopping Train' and 'The Whitsun Weddings,'" in which he compares poems by Larkin and Davie. (Davie's poem was first published in 1977, long after the Movement had dissolved, but Larkin's poem, first published in 1958, is a quintessential Movement poem.) Jarman states that "all of Larkin's strengths" are present in "The Whitsun Weddings," "including his love of and doubts about pastoral England: his eye for the telling image—those cattle, that hothouse, those canals—his extraordinary gift for the simple yet perfect imagistic phrase, 'the tall heat,' and even his way of pointing to a poem's central intelligence, the annoyed reference to 'the reek of buttoned carriage-cloth'."[227] According to Jarman, "The Whitsun Weddings" and "In the Stopping Train" have similar themes—"shared humanity" and "the perpetuation of custom"—though Davie's poem has also to do with "the Christian admonition, to love one's neighbor as oneself."[228] While he admires both poems, he credits Davie's with "greater symbolic and emotional resonance" than Larkin's.[229] For Jarman, "Davie's career is inspiring. But it is the religious vein running through his work that interests me the most at this time."[230]

Starting in the early 1980s, Jarman and Robert McDowell, co-editors of *The Reaper*, held Larkin up as an example of a poet whose poetry embodies "accuracy, at all costs," one of their "non-negotiable demands" for narrative poetry.[231] In light of the allegations that rhyme, meter, and various poetic forms are "un-American," it is telling that McDowell and Jarman offer a "British formalist" as a "master of form" from whom American poets should learn:

> Where more often than not a reader will have to grope for a structure where none exists, in Larkin's poems he is released from that task. He seeks and he finds. A master of form, like Larkin, is also freed from the anxiety that breeds inaccuracy. His poetry isn't guesswork; he doesn't say it unless it is so. How many contemporary American poets do the same? Not enough.

While Jarman and McDowell discuss a villanelle by Chase Twichell and a free-verse poem by James Galvin to illustrate their claim that *some* American poets are "master[s] of phrasing, of lines, of stanzas, of form itself," they give Larkin a prominent place in their essay. They also quote Larkin's "Sad Steps" in its entirety as an example of a poem in which the poet has "imagine[d] a distinctive self" and has also done "much more" than that: he has "unlock[ed] the jail of self."[232]

In the introduction to *A Few Friends: Poems for Thom Gunn's 60th Birthday*, the editor, Douglas Chambers, describes Gunn's "exacting energy, incantatory force, enacted choice, restless exploration of subject in form, humility of line and tone, celebration of risk, [and] affirmation of the physical world," saying that "these are the qualities singled out for praise in what the poets in this collection have to say about Thom and, more importantly, share with him in their poems."[233] According to Chambers, Gunn's poem "Touch" "is, of course, about touching, physical commitment, risk, but it is also about sureness of touch, poetic touch," and, in Chambers's view, the poems in this small anthology, which are deliberate "imitations" of poems written by Gunn, demonstrate that Gunn inspires "not mere imitation but that sort of touching." Throughout his tribute, Chambers suggests that Gunn—"O rare Thom Gunn, friend and inspiration!"—is a *model* for these poets.

In this same collection, Timothy Steele's tribute to Gunn similarly highlights the importance of this link between the Movement and New Formalism. For Steele, Gunn's "attempt to reconcile the contradictory impulses of modern verse" is "particularly significant."[234] Over the decades, he says, Gunn's "own free verse, and his essays dealing with Williams, Snyder, Eliot, Pound, and Bunting, have called attention to the resources and the achievements of the experimental tradition." As Steele notes, Gunn has embraced modernism—and, with that gesture, has decidedly extricated himself from the Movement—yet he has also availed himself of poetic resources that have existed for centuries and has continued to do "outstanding work in conventional measure," exemplifying "the timeless vitality of metre and rhyme." In his closing paragraph, Steele praises Gunn's poetry for "its sympathetic humanity and its observations of people."

In his tribute, Dick Davis says that he thinks of Gunn "as the best living British poet."[235] He admires Gunn for his "technique" and his "ability to use language persuasively," as well as his "intelligent sympathy with his subject matter that pervades everything he writes." Returning to Gunn's "technique," Davis praises it for its "clarity," its "lack of pretension and fuss," and its "exactness." Tellingly, Davis also notes the "humility" in Gunn's poetry. Davis doesn't bring up the Movement in this context, but most of the characteristics that he admires in Gunn were central to the Movement.

Since Gunn's Movement poetry is notoriously "tough" rather than "sympathetic," both Steele and Davis appear to be speaking of Gunn's later poetry—though the transformations in his poetry were becoming evident as early as 1957 and became quite plain in 1961.

The collection that Steele first encountered, *Selected Poems by Gunn and Hughes*, contains nineteen of Gunn's poems from collections published in 1954, 1957, and 1961. Several of them, including "On the Move" and "The Unsettled Motorcyclist's Vision of His Death," embody Movement characteristics and ideas, while others show the increasingly "sympathetic humanity" that Gunn developed as he severed his already tenuous ties with the Movement.[236] As Steele closes his tribute to Gunn, he quotes from *Positives* (1966): "Life should be a humane / Undertaking," and adds, "So should poetry. His has been. May he continue to write and to entertain and instruct us for decades to come."[237]

Reviewing collections by Davie, Gunn, and Ted Hughes in 1981, Paul Lake has almost nothing but praise for Gunn and Davie. Lake, a student in Davie's graduate poetry-writing class at Stanford, was among the earliest New Formalists. He does not label them as such, but the traits he commends in their poetry are characteristic of the Movement: "Donald Davie is a very different sort of poet from Ted Hughes, with more modest poetic aims and fewer visionary proclivities and pretentions [sic]."[238] Though Lake laments that in "too many of [Gunn's] poems, perhaps, the poet fails to give way to his passions" and that "occasionally, one wishes that Gunn would risk it all on one throw of the dice, go for broke, let loose," he maintains that "the form and language of [Gunn's] poems, which are formal, controlled, modest, and unaspiring," are strengths rather than limitations. Describing what he thinks would happen if Gunn did "go for broke, let loose," he reveals his own attraction to Movement values: "[He] would be like too many other poets—like Ted Hughes, for instance—who try to be grand and compelling in every poem they write, and so succeed in hardly any. No, one reads Thom Gunn for other pleasures. At his best, Gunn maintains a perfect balance between abandonment and self-control."[239] In this same article, Lake discusses Davie's "In the Stopping Train," pointing out several additional traits that typified Movement poetry: "ambivalence," "ironic distance," and skill with various formal resources, including "trisyllabic metrical feet" and "dactyls and trochees."

Commenting on Gunn's *Selected Poems: 1950–1975*, Lake says:

> Both early and late, he has written memorable poems. Moving from the early quasi-allegorical poems of his first volume (with their sometimes overly-clever language and forced rhymes) through the period of his study under Yvor Winters (when his poems sometimes took on his teacher's faults of an overly literary diction and stilted rhetoric) and into the period of his maturity, where he shook off his excesses and early influences and wrote more directly in his own manner and voice, Gunn has never failed to produce competent, rich, and satisfying poems.

Lake's appraisal of Gunn is entirely positive, except for his reservations about the poems in which Gunn is "attempting to throw off the constraints of formal verse," resulting in texts that strike Lake, paradoxically enough, as "artificially 'free' and open." These poems, he says, "don't seem to suit Gunn's talent, precisely because they deny him the opportunity to maintain that taut control which seems so philosophically, psychologically, and artistically right for him." Given Lake's ties with New Formalism, it is unsurprising that he prefers Gunn's formal poems, those characterized by "taut control," to his looser free-verse poems.

Like many other New Formalists, Andrew Hudgins vividly recalls his first encounter with the poetry of Larkin:

> I first read Larkin when a friend, back from England, gave me a Faber and Faber paperback of *High Windows* in the late seventies. I loved poems like "Church Going" and the one about the mine explosion. I don't think they had a lot of influence on me formally, but I was very much interested in the tonal shifts and how much intelligence was embodied in the way the poems contained both despair and humor in an uneasy balance.[240]

Hudgins goes on to say that he believes "a number" of the poems in his collection *The Never-Ending* are "reactions to reading and thinking a lot about 'Church Going' and 'The Whitsun Weddings,' though no one particular poem addresses any particular poem of [Larkin's]." When Hudgins became familiar with Davie's criticism, around this same time, his reactions were mixed:

> I loved his smart, combative style. I remember being both thrilled by his trenchant, take-no-prisoners attacks on William Carlos Williams and appalled by his not even seriously attempting to understand what Williams is doing. He was unsympathetic and reductive, but he raises thoughtful questions, questions that WCW partisans (and I'm sometimes one) have swept under the rug.

Hudgins says that when he read Gunn's *Moly* and *My Sad Captains*, also in the mid-1970s, "they didn't have much effect" on him: "The 'tough guy' poems were not very tough, and in fact silly and more than a bit inclined toward the sentimental." Though he admired Gunn's "technical skill," he felt that it sometimes came "at the expense of tension in the lines."[241]

Dick Allen cites the American poets Berryman, Bishop, Hall, Hecht, Kennedy, Lowell, Plath, Snodgrass, and Wilbur as those who have had the most influence on him. Nevertheless, Larkin's poetry has been "a constant inspiration over the years."[242] Allen first read poems by Larkin and Gunn in the late 1950s, at a time when the Movement writers were an "official" and well-publicized group. In the United States, the "war of the anthologies" raged at that same time, with the poets in *The New American Poetry 1945–1960* (edited by Donald Allen) flying the "avant-garde" banner and those in *New Poets of England and America* (edited by Donald Hall, Robert Pack, and Louis Simpson) hoisting the "traditional" colors. The first edition of *New Poets*, which appeared in 1957, includes poetry by Movement writers Amis, Davie, Gunn, Holloway, Jennings, and Larkin.[243] The second, published in 1962, includes these poets and adds Wain.[244] This is, again, the anthology in which Allen first encountered Gunn and Larkin. Noting the "extreme importance anthologies played in the formation of poetic consciousness in 1950s-1960s American poetry," Allen says that this particular one represented a major turning point for American poets. It also represented a major turning point for Allen, or, more precisely, it confirmed many of his existing ideas about poetry. Allen says that "in the late 1950s and early 1960s, we always thought of British and American poetry together" and that at Brown University, where he did his graduate work, "our degrees were in 'British and American Literature', not one or the other."[245] He adds that he has always been interested in "merg[ing] the best of what is characteristically known as formal British poetry and the free verse of American poetry. . . . Maybe I can say that for me Expansive Poetry didn't come from the Movement writers, but that British poetry . . . was always at my back."[246]

R. S. Gwynn, who began expressing "New Formalist" ideas at least as early as 1977, says that his primary influences have been formalist poets, though he also says that "every poet I have ever read is an influence in some sense of the term—often a negative influence."[247] Gwynn has been a "fan" of Larkin since graduate school:

> I loved the poems for their own sake, but I also loved the personality—or the strength of personality—that emerged from them. I don't think I was particularly surprised to learn from Motion's biography that he really wasn't a very nice man. Who could have doubted it? And so what?

A writer who considers herself or himself to have been influenced by another does not have to share the same tastes or predilections as the other writer, does not have to agree with the other writer, does not even have to *like* the other writer—or the other writer's work. Interest and engagement are the key factors. The parodist, for example, does not necessarily admire the work being parodied. As discussed above, Paul Lake, Marilyn Nelson, Katha Pollitt, Maura Stanton, Molly Peacock, and Diane Thiel have engaged in a variety of relationships with Larkin. Recent poems by David Mason, John Gery, Leslie Monsour, and Charles Martin, which I shall discuss later, also demonstrate textual and thematic relationships with the Movement writers.

In a 1979 review of Davie's *The Poet in the Imaginary Museum*, Gioia calls this collection "an important book containing some of the most penetrating essays on modern poetry written in the thirty years it covers."[248] He briefly outlines Davie's place in the history of the Movement, a "group of British poets who insisted on the continuing vitality of native literary traditions and on the incompatibility of modern experimentalism with English genius."[249] Davie "found himself in an ironic position," says Gioia, because he "gradually emerged as an apologist both for foreign poetry and for experimental writing."[250] In 1983, Gioia reviewed *The Shires*, saying that it "contains some of Davie's finest and most personal poetry," that it "is one of the most noteworthy and interesting books of English poetry published in the last ten years," and that it "marks a climax in the ongoing career of one of England's most important poets."[251]

Reviewing *The Poet in the Imaginary Museum*, Gioia compares Davie to Randall Jarrell, even though Davie "would probably not cherish the comparison": both of them "insist on seeing the poet as a member of society"; both "excel in close readings" but also "place the writer cautiously against his time and place before turning to the poems themselves"; and both "search the lives and backgrounds of authors for crucial clues to their writing."[252] The point of comparison that Gioia considers the most important is also pertinent to a discussion of the connections between the Movement and New Formalism:

> Most importantly, both of them refuse to write criticism only for other critics. They long for a mixed audience of poets, academics, students, and general readers, and if this audience still exists for poetry, it is largely due to efforts like theirs. Jarrell once asked for a type of criticism which would not only be intelligent and useful but also "sound as if it has been written by a reader for readers, by a human being for human beings." He would have approved of Davie. For Davie is a specialist who can speak to the general reader without condescension.

In Gioia's view, "virtually all of the essays and articles [in *The Poet in the Imaginary Museum*] remain engaging and approachable for all types of readers." He also says, "One of Davie's enduring concerns has been the relationship between the poet and his readers."[253] Gioia's emphasis on audience is especially telling for two reasons: first, it was a major emphasis of the Movement, and, second, Gioia himself has probably said more on this subject than any other New Formalist.

Larkin, says Gioia, has "absolutely" had an influence on him as a poet.[254] When he first encountered Larkin, along with American poet Weldon Kees, Gioia felt he had found the "two writers [he] had been looking for." Neither Kees nor Larkin, says Gioia, "is a genteel poet." They both "center their work in everyday middle-class experience," but they both "push their insights and ideas beyond the limits of comfortable middle-class taste." Larkin, who "revels in his bitter disappointment about life," is "very funny, but rarely in a polite way." In "The Old Fools," for instance, Larkin "describes the senile elderly in purposely disgusting terms," showing them "pissing themselves and drooling mindlessly, unaware of their own incontinence." Paradoxically, Larkin uses such "stark methods as a way of achieving a deeper level of compassion," even though "many readers will never work through the offensive elements to achieve that gentler insight." Kees, says Gioia, "is even angrier and more bitter. He loathes the modern world he lives in, but he sees no possibility of transcending it." This bitter pessimism is also present in Larkin, says Gioia. Both, he says, "are . . . stuck in the fallen world of everyday modern life." However, in a 1981 "Poetry Chronicle" (and again in a 1993 review), Gioia implies that Larkin transcends this "fallen world" to at least some degree, for there is a "visionary note underlying his best work".[255]

In the interview with Robert McPhillips discussed earlier, Gioia states: "My own poetry draws on two somewhat contradictory traditions. One part comes out of the heritage of Anglo-American writers like Auden, Hardy, Jarrell, Larkin, and Kees, a sort of novelistic . . . poetry."[256] He notes that some reviewers of his first book, *Daily Horoscope*, "linked me to the tradition of Larkin, Frost, and Hardy," something that he considered a "great and perhaps undeserved compliment."[257] Indeed, in an essay published in the same issue of *Verse*, McPhillips himself compares Gioia to several poets, including Larkin: "This still-young poet has left us, in two exquisitely wrought books of poetry, with enough evidence to assure us that he will continue to produce lyrics of the quantity and quality of such poets as A. E. Housman, J. V. Cunningham, Philip Larkin, and Donald Justice."[258] Critic Matthew Flamm explicitly—though unfavorably—compares Gioia to Larkin: "Once or twice Gioia attempts Larkin-style sketches of run-of-the-mill characters . . . but he lacks Larkin's feel for detail and his (grudging) sense of identification with the people he describes."[259] More positively, Andrew Swarbrick, writing for the *Oxford Times*, notes that Gioia's first book "drew admiring comparisons in America with Philip Larkin."[260] Swarbrick says that Gioia "has the same rather melancholic reflectiveness" as Larkin and that Gioia's poems "move between narrative and observation with something of Larkin's thoughtful probing." Swarbrick hastens to point out, however, that "Gioia is no imitator." As recently as 2004, this comparison makes yet another appearance. In a review of Gioia called "This Be the Prose," critic A. O. Scott alludes to Larkin's poem "This Be the Verse."[261] Then he says, dismissively, that Gioia's own "well mannered and well made" poetry makes him resemble "Philip Larkin without hangups, or Auden without the intensities of politics or religion."[262]

In a 1981 review of Kingsley Amis's *Collected Poems: 1944–1979*, Gioia contrasts Amis and Ted Hughes, saying that Hughes "writes about Man's Fate, [while] Amis discusses the fates of ordinary men," basing his poems not "on the ineffable enlightenment of private vision" but, instead, "on the shared perspective of common experiences . . . . Even when [Amis] strikes an apocalyptic note as he often does in his early work, the vision is ultimately tempered by common sense."[263] Gioia also contrasts Amis and Larkin: "Larkin may debunk romanticism in his poetry, but there is a visionary note underlying his best work. In contrast Amis never gives in to what used to be called 'the oceanic feeling.'" Ultimately, Gioia recommends the volume not only because Amis "demonstrates a lesson that is too easy to forget—that to write well about ordinary events takes extraordinary skill" but also because "those American readers who do not share [Amis's] anti-romantic assumption that intelligence, wit, form, and verbal ingenuity are the essentials of poetry" may find this volume to be a "mind-expanding experience." Several of these points coincide with ideas important to the Movement poets: valuing "common sense"; steering clear of phenomena that seem suspiciously "shamanistic"; writing poetry about "ordinary" people and "ordinary" events; bringing "intelligence, wit, form, and verbal ingenuity" to the center of poetry; and emphasizing "shared perspective[s]" resulting from "common experiences." Incidentally, these characteristics are also among the ones admired by Paul Lake and Dick Allen in their early reviews of Davie and Gunn.

In "The Barrier of a Common Language: British Poetry in the Eighties," Gioia, implicitly defying "most American readers," who are "not only unfamiliar with current British poetry but modestly proud of the fact," includes Larkin in his list of the "three older [English] poets whose work seems most guaranteed to survive," along with Basil Bunting and Robert Graves.[264] He mentions that Gunn has a "small but loyal" group of American followers, and points out that Amis and Davie are known in the United States, but "primarily for their prose." In "The Still, Sad Music of Philip Larkin," written in 1993, Gioia notes Larkin's widespread appeal, saying that "no British poet since Tennyson had simultaneously captivated both the literati and the common reader" and that Larkin "was the only living poet many of them knew by heart."[265]

In the 1970s and 1980s, according to David Mason, young American poets who wished to take advantage of various poetic traditions *needed* someone like Gunn as a "model of what the poet could be":

> I can actually remember editors telling me that rhyme and meter were not American techniques, or that I shouldn't use techniques like alliteration because they sounded artificial. Now, hardly anyone believes that such things were said to young American poets, but they were. Gunn, as an Englishman living in America, seemed a bridge to multiple possibilities for the art.[266]

Poetry seemed also to be such a solidly East Coast phenomenon that Mason sometimes wondered whether it was possible for him, a Westerner, to be a poet. "[Gunn] also influenced me by living in the West," says Mason, "proving it could be done. One didn't have to be an Easterner to have a life as a poet."[267]

Given Gunn's reluctance to be counted among the Movement writers, it is not surprising that he was reluctant to be thought of as an influence on New Formalism. In a 1989 interview with Gunn, Jim Powell comments, "In America recently literary journalists have begun to talk about something they call New Formalism."[268] Gunn bluntly dismisses it:

> New Formalism troubles me partly because, there, people might tend to identify me as one of its precursors. I'm not interested in encouraging such a school, because I think they should also be learning from people like Bunting and Pound and the other modernists.

As the interview continues, Powell says of the New Formalists, "It's a pretty narrow tradition they're committed to drawing on." Gunn agrees, "Yes, it's far too narrow a tradition," then says that when a New Formalist poet asked him to contribute to a magazine, he turned down the request and pointed out, "I've just written an article praising Ginsberg, and I think you should be reading him instead." Instead of "separating ourselves into armed camps," says Gunn, poets should "be fertilizing each other," moving toward "a tradition that's able to take account of the avant-garde and . . . the traditional."

In a review published a year later, Gunn made similar observations:

> The New Formalists and the Language Poets compete for our attention, but each group mirrors the other in the incompleteness of its ambitions. The first, complacency at its heart, has no interest in stylistic experiment, and the second scoffs at 'subject,' placing the term between quotation marks as if referring to some laughable affectation.[269]

Certainly, some associated with New Formalism appear to hold a narrow view of what constitutes "real" poetry, while others have been wrongly *accused* of holding such a view.[270] Gunn might have been surprised to learn that many New Formalists share his beliefs. Steele, who is often classed among the strictest traditionalists within New Formalism, expresses a cautious hope that American poets can develop a "healthy pluralism," providing "opportunities for all kinds of voices to be heard in American poetry, including the metrical voice."[271] As for the formal freedom he believes poets should have, Gioia says, in a letter to Franz Link, that he hopes "the available forms of contemporary poetry" will be expanded "to include all the traditional forms and genres as well as the Modernist mode."[272] Although he condemns "pseudo-formal poetry," Gioia states that he has "always worked in both fixed and open forms," finding that "each mode offered possibilities of style, subject, music, and development the other did not suggest, at least at that moment" and that "experience in each mode provided an illuminating perspective on the other."[273] Gioia believes that "fixed and open forms" can be valuable to all poets: "I find it puzzling . . . that so many poets see these modes as opposing aesthetics rather than as complementary resources. Why shouldn't a poet explore the full resources the English language offers?"[274]

In a 1987 interview, Gunn laments what he views as a divide between English and American poets:

> The English poets are still in love with meter and rhyme, and you don't get many of them writing good free verse. On the other hand, you don't get many Americans writing good meter and rhyme. There is a loss on both sides. . . . For a brief period, in the 1950s, they had been coming closer together and enriching each other, but they don't seem to be learning from each other at the moment.[275]

Gioia's passing mention of a salubrious period in the 1950s—when poets "had been coming closer and enriching each other"—may well be a reference to the Movement writers. Although Gunn was unimpressed by the New Formalists, many of them have tried to do exactly what he recommended. Marilyn Hacker, Julia Alvarez, Dick Allen, Annie Finch, David Mason, Dana Gioia, Kathrine Varnes, and others have also argued that English-speaking poets should learn from writers from around the world. Finch writes:

> In cultures where folk and oral traditions are still alive, where people still have their culture in their own hands, poetic form is often the furthest thing from elitist or reactionary—the decima tradition in Spanish-speaking countries, the slave ballad, the ghazal tradition in East Asia, and the cowboy ballad and rap form in the contemporary United States, are a few of the many forms that are people's forms.[276]

Gunn preferred not to be seen as a "precursor" to New Formalism, but Dick Allen states emphatically that Gunn "WAS a precursor."[277] David Mason, who admires Gunn "for his insistent freedom and range of subjects and forms," also insists that Gunn was a precursor "because he was lucid and memorable in both free verse and meter."[278] Gioia's view of Gunn is similar: "in an ideological sense" and in a "personal sense," he is most impressed by Gunn's insistence that he "did not have to give up free verse to write formal verse or give up formal verse to write free verse."[279] Since Gioia, Allen, and Mason themselves write (and advocate) both formal verse and free verse, their admiration for Gunn is unsurprising.

In the early days of New Formalism, Gunn admired poetry by at least two members of that group. In 1987, he wrote a blurb for Paul Lake's *Another Kind of Travel*, calling it a "clean and cunning book" and lauding Lake's efforts, in two particular poems ("An Apparition" and "South of the City"), "to grasp the ungraspable."[280] Several years before that, in 1981, Gunn reviewed Timothy Steele's *Uncertainties and Rest*, praising its "mixture of vitality and delicacy," in terms consistent with Movement ideals.[281] Although Steele's poetry is "about moments of sensation," these are "moments not beyond the understanding but, precisely, *of* the understanding; and they do not explode into ravings but surface calmly as composed reflections." He says of a Steele lyric that "without archness or anachronism it calls up the life of a whole tradition of love poetry."

In 1986, Gunn reviewed Steele's *Sapphics Against Anger*:

> Timothy Steele's poems are energetic at all points, and solid without being heavy. I can't think of any poet active in this country who writes stanzaic poetry so well. He speaks to me as a contemporary, and I never feel he has chosen to do so in meter for any other reason than that by doing so he can make his speech more forceful.[282]

By 2001, however, Gunn felt that Steele had "descended into the jocular, like the poems that used to be printed in humorous magazines of the nineteenth century."[283] He was also unimpressed by Gioia's poetry. Still, when I spoke with him in 2001 about his importance to Mason and to other young poets, Gunn said: "Well, of course one is flattered to be seen as an inspiration."[284]

PERSONAL CONNECTIONS

Timothy Steele knew Thom Gunn personally, first meeting him in 1973 to discuss a poetry chapbook that Gunn had been asked to write.[285] When Gunn served as the poetry editor of *Threepenny Review*, also in the 1970s, he "kindly asked [Steele] for work" and published "several poems that later appeared in *Sapphics Against Anger and Other Poems*."[286] Steele's ongoing respect for Gunn is clear. In 1989, he contributed to a poetry collection in honor of Gunn's sixtieth birthday. In 2004, shortly after Gunn's death, Steele said, "Though we weren't close, Thom was a friend. He was a very gentle man, despite the biker-rebel image he had in the poetry world. My feelings about him and his work are reflected in 'Vermont Spring' from *The Color Wheel*."[287] Steele's poem "Vermont Spring" is, in fact, dedicated to Gunn: "for T. G. on his 60th birthday."

As an undergraduate in the late 1960s and early 1970s, Dana Gioia attended several poetry readings by Gunn.[288] In 1975, Gioia audited Donald Davie's course on eighteenth-century literature at

Stanford University.[289] The following year, Gioia, John Gery, Vicki Hearne, and Vikram Seth took Davie's graduate poetry-writing course, thus establishing a direct link between the Movement and several founding members of New Formalism. (Paul Lake was Davie's student at a later date.) In the 1970s, Gioia saw Davie as his "unofficial mentor," and in 1991 he described Davie (who died in 1995) as "one of the great living literary critics."[290]

Davie and the other Movement writers had long since parted ways, but in the 1977 *Sequoia* interview conducted by Gioia (discussed in Chapter One), Davie revealed that he continued to have strong Movement leanings.[291] Richard J. Gray suspects, in fact, that Davie "took one route available to the expatriate: he became more 'British' the longer he stayed away."[292] As he became increasingly British, says Gray, Davie "actually reverted to Movement principles." If those principles were indeed central to Davie's "Britishness," it is logical to assume that they would also have been central to his classroom persona and that his students would have absorbed at least some of them from him. Such an assumption would be half right. Gioia says that Davie sought to *discourage* formal poetry but that, paradoxically, his efforts to do so *encouraged* several in the class to pursue their own forbidden interests:

> There was a sense, I think, among us [that] we were doing something slightly wicked. And yet very worthwhile . . . Donald Davie, a brilliant, wonderful man who seemed to radically revise his opinions with each decade, believed at this time that Americans should write in free verse. . . . There was a wonderfully ironic action in terms of literary history: that Davie, one of the key figures of the Movement, one of the leading formal poets of his generation, was trying to discourage this younger generation of American writers . . . from writing in form.[293]

Seeing the supposed impact of "literary fashion" on a critic and poet of Davie's stature, Gioia decided that he "had to write [formal verse] so well that it could convert the skeptics." At the same time, Gioia says, Davie encouraged both a "Poundian" and a "Wintersian" approach to poetry. Thus, while he endorsed freedom and experimentation, he also emphasized tradition and formal rigor.[294]

John Gery's impressions of Davie are similar to Gioia's. On the one hand, Gery says that Davie "had no difficulty taking 'formal poetry' and 'free verse' equally seriously."[295] On the other hand, much to Gery's surprise, Davie was "more interested in a meager experiment of mine in free verse where I had inverted the syntax of several colloquial American expressions" than he was in "an ornately designed lyric in the tradition of Donne" that Gery had also written. Although Gery has, "at best, a strained/restrained relationship with the New Formalist poets," he "certainly admire[s] several of the Movement poets." He often teaches works by Davie, Gunn, and Larkin, "sometimes to mixed reviews from students (esp. concerning Davie's notions of poetry and morality)." His comments about Davie reveal a strong and lasting admiration for his former teacher:

> I owe a great debt to Donald Davie not only as my teacher and as a model for my own teaching, but as a poet with a conscience and a poet committed to precision in expression. Davie has also been important to me in my work with Pound, again, as a teacher, as a critic, as a poetic influence. Davie's work on Pound has helped shape my fundamental thinking about Pound.

Paul Lake entered the Stanford University creative writing program with "no idea who Donald Davie was."[296] However, he enrolled in a number of classes taught by Davie and soon developed a high regard for him as a teacher and a critic. The first time Lake took one of his own poems to Davie's poetry-writing class, "Donald drew the attention of the other students to the work's formal properties." By 1980, when Lake and James Powell interviewed Davie for a journal called *Occident*, they both had an extensive acquaintance with his critical works, including *Purity of Diction in English Verse*, *Articulate Energy*, *Ezra Pound: Poet as Sculptor*, and *Trying to Explain*.[297] Lake says of Davie: "As it turned out, studying under Donald Davie and becoming a friend . . . was probably the single most important literary influence I've ever had—particularly on my teaching and criticism. To this day, Donald's voice and literary presence inhabit my literary consciousness."[298]

In a 1983 article, Harvey Oxenhorn discusses the creative writing program at Stanford, including at least one class taught by Donald Davie.[299] His description of Davie's teaching, coming from a student who did not become associated with New Formalism, provides an enlightening perspective on the classroom atmosphere experienced by those who did. According to Oxenhorn, "the Stanford programme . . . seeks to achieve range and variety by leading students to measure their own writing against that of acknowledged past masters." He adds that the poetry workshops at Stanford "tend to devote more attention to form and prosody than do most American workshops," motivated by the belief that "whether a poet works within a traditional genre, or out of it, or indeed reacts against it, a knowledge of that genre and of its conventions will help him define his subjects and focus his attitudes towards them." Oxenhorn avoids "indulging in the misrepresentations of Winters's poetic that have become commonplace" but notes that Davie's poetic was "considerably more flexible and pluralistic" than Winters's. Rather than entirely repudiating Winters, he "urged students to combine Winters's sensitivity to formal and moral values with a tone and language which reflected awareness of the time and place where they were being used." Another concern for Davie was that "'technique' matters [and] has moral implications, because technical mastery makes exactitude possible and because dishonest emotionalism and other kinds of fraud, in and out of poetry, thrive on imprecision." Davie's emphases show that he held onto Movement ideas: "Many of Davie's comments in workshop," says Oxenhorn, "seek to promote exactitude by directing extremely close attention to diction, syntax and meter in the students' poems." Davie also repeatedly made the point that "words have histories and metaphorical nuances to which good poets must be sensitive."

Most telling is Davie's emphasis on the necessity to be "fair" and "judicious." In class one day, having written "NO" across the top of a poem, Davie explained to the writer that it was unacceptable because of "what happened to the woman in the poem: 'It is not *fair*. You have abandoned your responsibility to *her*.'" Says Oxenhorn, "It is at such moments that a younger poet learns what all the talk of diction and syntax ultimately means." According to Gunn, Yvor Winters, from whom the Movement writers absorbed many ideas, was contemptuous of poets whom "he found betraying [poetry] by their slipshod writing, by their incoherent thinking, or by their use of it as an exercising ground for the ego."[300] In a 1977 interview conducted by Millicent Dillon, Davie voices a related idea: "I do not see why a poet in a poem should be absolved from the duty which we lay on ourselves and on others in other walks of life, of meaning what he says, of saying things which he will stand by."[301] Poetry that serves as no more than "a curious entrancing murmur in the background," he says, is an "insult [to] the memory of the Akhmatovas and Mandelstams and Pasternaks." Although Davie rejected some Movement stances, such as its "little Englandism" and its opposition to modernism, he did not surrender the interest in form, diction, syntax, emotional and intellectual balance, tradition, fairness, judiciousness, responsibility, and other matters that also characterized the Movement.

From 1983 until Davie's retirement in 1987, Mark Jarman was his colleague at Vanderbilt University.[302] Since New Formalism was already coalescing by 1983, with the publication of several poetry collections and poetic manifestos, Davie probably did not have an impact on the *formation* of Jarman's ideas about poetry. However, according to Jarman, Davie had an impact on their *refinement*.[303] In an interview published in *Image: A Journal of the Arts*, Jarman states that he and his contemporaries were "discouraged from writing meter and rhyme" in the 1970s: "There was a sense that one simply didn't *do* that."[304] At that time, even Jarman's teacher Donald Justice—"one of the masters of contemporary form"—wrote predominantly free verse, but upon seeing a "beautiful and moving and simple poem in tetrameter couplets" that Justice had written, Jarman "began to think that for some poets this is the way to write." Despite his attraction to rhyme and meter, Jarman says, "it took [him] a number of years, and also being colleagues with Donald Davie here at Vanderbilt, and his insistence that the forms of traditional English verse were evergreen," to become fully convinced that such traditions could work for American poets. As late as 1987, Jarman continued to tell Davie that "though traditional form may work for English poetry, the American language required something else," but Davie eventually helped to persuade him that "the forms of traditional English verse" were perfectly appropriate for American poets.

TEXTUAL CONNECTIONS

When I asked Robert McDowell which Movement poet, if any, he has read and admired over the years, he replied, "Larkin, of course, Larkin, and more Larkin."[305] Leslie Monsour believes current poets "owe a great debt to poets," including Gunn and Larkin, "who held the fort, so to speak, during the siege."[306]As early as her graduate school days, Molly Peacock was "entranced" by Larkin, and for her he is still "central."[307] When Annie Finch "first encountered Larkin in the mid-1980s," she was "delighted by his formal control and transparency."[308] She was also "very impressed" by Davie's criticism. Katha Pollitt says, simply, "I love Philip Larkin's poems."[309] In a 1990 review, Pollitt described Larkin's poetry as "delicate," "sharp," "endlessly interesting," "exact," and "surprising."[310]

In the late 1970s, David Mason met and interviewed Gunn, whom he saw as a "pivotal figure."[311] Even before that personal encounter, says Mason, "many of us looked up to him . . . as a model of what the poet could be, and what we were so often told we could not be—that is, he felt free to write in any verse form he chose and never restricted himself in terms of subject matter."[312] He also admires Larkin: "'Aubade' is one of several undeniable masterpieces Larkin left behind."[313]

When Rachel Wetzsteon first encountered Larkin and Gunn in the early 1990s, she "loved them both."[314] In an article that appeared in the *New Republic* after Wetzsteon's death, writer Adam Kirsch stated, "Her three books of poems—*Other Stars* (1994), *Home and Away* (1998), and *Sakura Park* (2006)—show a steady increase in mastery and feeling, as she took on the inheritance of Larkin and Auden . . . and made it her own."[315] In a 2015 article called "The Life and Death of Rachel Wetzsteon," author Con Chapman stated, "Wetzsteon took as her models two unlikely sources; Philip Larkin and W.H. Auden, taking the road less traveled—if at all—by female poets of her time."[316]

Vikram Seth, a student in Donald Davie's poetry-writing seminar in the mid-1970s, along with Dana Gioia, Vicki Hearne, and John Gery, feared that using traditional meter and rhyme "marked you as a fuddy-duddy," but he was reassured after his tutor, Timothy Steele, showed him the poetry of two predecessors: Frost and Larkin.[317] At that point, Seth decided that "writing in rhyme and meter," rather than causing one to become a "literary untouchable," allows one to "be very much of [one's] time, using patterns that had been used for centuries."[318] Steele himself says that young American poets with an interest in traditional poetic resources would have felt little hope in recent decades had it not been for a "distinct minority" of poets, including Gunn and Larkin.[319]

Dick Allen, who has been associated with New Formalism from the beginning, says that Wilbur, Bishop, and Larkin were among the writers that he and other poets kept in mind through the years "when, almost literally, a young poet, a poet born after the mid-1930s, could hardly get a rhymed and metered poem published . . . anywhere in America."[320] In a review written in 1974, Allen called Gunn a "poet of great technique, a master of rhyming and poetic pace, showing us one totally finished poem after another."[321] In *Moly*, he finds poems that he calls "masterful" and "perfect." The "emotion and meaning" throughout this collection, he says, "are never subjected to flashy effects." The poetry "does not at all excite," nor is it "intended to do so." Instead, it does something "much more difficult, so indicative of the work of a mature poet: it *satisfies* deeply." Since most of the poems in *Moly* bear little resemblance to Movement poetry, Allen's attention to Movement traits—the poetry's technique, its finished qualities, its lack of "flashy effects," its tendency to satisfy rather than excite—is noteworthy.[322]

In "Philip Larkin: A Stateside View" (1976), Robert B. Shaw surveys *High Windows, The Less Deceived, The Whitsun Weddings, Jill,* and *A Girl in Winter.* In addition to noting the "formal perfection" of Larkin's poetry, he commends Larkin for his "tenacity" in "maintaining standards of craftsmanship whose rigour seems enhanced by an infrequency of publication."[323] Shaw also praises the "wondrously expressive imagery or scenic description" in such poems as "The Less Deceived" and "The Whitsun Weddings" and says that "Larkin's moments of affirmation seem totally felt, and are as moving as they are rare." Although the review is not entirely positive, Shaw admits that "Larkinolatry is an easy condition to succumb to. I have suffered bouts of it myself."

In "The Confinement of Free Verse" (1987), Brad Leithauser includes Larkin in his list of poets who have composed "magnificent sonnets" since T. S. Eliot questioned in 1917 whether "the sonnet was still practicable."[324] In a 1990 article, Rachel Hadas describes Larkin and Elizabeth Bishop as "diverse, skilled, and original."[325] In a review also published in 1990, Andrew Hudgins states that Larkin has written "great" and "important" poems.[326] As Hudgins speaks of the "weary pessimism" in Larkin, his admiration for the older poet is clear: "He looks us in the eye as if to say with a sorrowful shrug, 'Isn't that the way the world is?' And so beautifully is the melancholy song sung, we agree before we entirely know what we are agreeing to."[327] Writing in 1993, Gioia characterizes Larkin as "one of the century's four indisputably great poets born in the British Isles," alongside Hardy, Yeats, and Auden.[328]

Gioia's admiration for Gunn, Larkin, Davie, and Jennings has endured for decades. In a recent email, he mentioned that he has loved the poetry of Elizabeth Jennings for forty years but has only now written an article about her.[329] As he put it, "It finally began to bother me that she has become so forgotten—perhaps in the U.S. never known at all." Reviewing Gunn's *Games of Chance* in 1982, Gioia describes Gunn as "a very versatile writer both technically and thematically."[330] In a discussion of his "poetic heroes" in a 1995 interview, he cites Elizabeth Bishop and Philip Larkin as "important influences who reinforced [his] sense that poets should be slow to publish."[331] Gioia believes that Larkin has influenced him "mostly as a poet" and Davie "mostly as a critic."[332] In fact, in a 1997 interview, he says that several critics, including Davie and Winters, have "shaped [his] literary sensibility as much as any imaginative writers" have.[333] Interviewed in early 2000, he again includes two Movement poets among his favorites: "Auden is perhaps my favorite poet except for Shakespeare, and I love Larkin so much that I have much of his work by heart. . . . I also admire Thom Gunn and Dick Davis, two superb British poets who live in the U.S."[334] Gioia says that he "admire[s] many poems by Davie, Gunn, Amis, and Jennings" but that he deems Larkin "without a close second . . . the best of the Movement poets."[335] Larkin, he says, "represents a sort of gold standard in contemporary poetry—accessible, funny, and yet both profound and sadly expressive."

Steele's admiration for Gunn and Larkin has been similarly enduring. In 1989, twenty years after he first encountered their work, Steele praised both, calling their poems "widely known and rightly treasured."[336] In 1994, his wholly positive assessment of Gunn appeared in the *Oxford Companion to Twentieth-Century Poetry in English*. Larkin and Gunn are also cited several times in Steele's 1999 study of prosody, *All the Fun's in How You Say a Thing*: Larkin is a good model for poets who wish to write "broken-backed or clipped pentameters"; his "Whitsun Weddings" and "Church Going" are examples of poems that "combine lyrical grace with a thematic and argumentative richness that we customarily encounter only in much longer poems or in such prose forms as the essay, short story, or novel"; his epigrams are "outstanding"; his "Merlin in the Cave" is an "excellent recent poem" using the "rhyme royal" stanza; and his "Words for Some Ash" is an "outstanding [poem] written in catalectic trochaic trimeters." Steele also recommends criticism by Davie, and by Yvor Winters, himself a major influence on Movement ideology.[337]

The affection for Larkin has clearly continued, as illustrated by two poems that appeared in 1999 and 2006. Charles Martin's "Just a Smack at Larkin" was published in the Hudson Review in 1999.[338] The second line is an especially effective echo of "This Be the Verse": "They tucked you in, your mum and dad . . . ." In an email, Martin described his motives in replying to Larkin's poem: "I wanted to write a poem that would be as absolute in its conviction as his was. I think that, probably, both of us were right."[339] In 2006, David Mason published "Larking for Larkin," a poetic reply to Larkin's poem "Toads," which describes work as a "toad" and asks, "Why should I let the toad work / Squat on my life?"[340] In Mason's poem, the poet speaks ironically to himself, saying, "Suffering always felt better when it was brief / and picturesque," then admits that his younger self was "at least pretending / you knew how to shoulder Mr. Larkin's toad / and all that dread descending." In a recent email, Mason pointed out that the "you" in the poem, "is of course me, remembering my younger self and the sort of work I used to do."

CHAPTER 4

Verse Craftsmanship, Plain Language, and New Austerity

> *Of course, in the older generation, even though they were a distinct minority, Wilbur and Larkin and Kennedy and Bowers and Gunn—and, to mention a few others, Turner Cassity, Henri Coulette, Charles Gullans, W. D. Snodgrass, and Helen Pinkerton—were all writing beautiful formal poems, and that gave all of us who were younger and interested in form, great hope.*[341]
>
> —*Timothy Steele*

Remarkably often, descriptions of the Movement writers could apply equally well to the New Formalists.[342] When the Movement writers were an active group, they implicitly characterized themselves in the same dramatic way that Lewis Turco would later characterize the New Formalists: as "verse craftsmen" battling "priest-poets" or "prose shamans."[343] The Movement writers might also have thought that Felix Stefanile's description of Dana Gioia's early poetry would nicely suit theirs: "citizen-poetry—and not the poetry of some new shamanism . . . or for that matter of ponderously mystical stones that glow in the sun."[344] The Movement writers justified their own reliance on rhyme, meter, and other poetic resources in the same way John N. Miller justifies Timothy Steele's: "Poetic tradition, thus recalled and created, brings to mind our endangered traditions of civility, sociability, and human settlement."[345]

Describing the attitude embodied in their poetry, the Movement writers used terms similar to those later used by Franz Link, who said that Dana Gioia's poetry presents a "stoic attitude toward life, accepting its limitations."[346] The Movement writers and the New Formalists may be united by their weaknesses as well as their strengths (or, at times, *perceived* weaknesses and strengths). In J. D. McClatchy's view, the "discipline and prejudice" characteristic of Yvor Winters can lead to poetry that seems "pinched and crabbed, neither heartfelt nor mindful of the expressive and emotive extremes poetry can deftly accommodate."[347] Although McClatchy says Steele's poetry is neither pinched nor crabbed, he sees in it some of the limitations of Winters's poetry. Comments like McClatchy's—and harsher ones—were directed against the Movement writers, who were themselves Wintersians. Writing in the early 1960s, John Press said that the poetry of many 1950s writers, including those in the Movement, was often "hard-boiled," "facile," "erudite," "pedantic," and "arid."[348] Press also alleged that these younger poets had "withdrawn from the public world." John N. Miller sees the same problem in Steele's poetry, in which, he says, the "larger public or social issues of our time exist only as a vague ambience, never seriously defined or confronted."[349]

The Movement writers were praised—and criticized—for doing what Mary Kinzie notes in Steele: he "cultivates restraint as a mechanism for the release both of wit and feeling."[350] Kinzie regrets, however, that Steele's poetry tends to be "laconic, when every fibre in the poems strains toward tears." Variations on this observation have come up repeatedly in connection with both groups. Alan Brownjohn admires the reticence in Larkin's "Ambulances": "Reticence, as a quality, is about at the same time possessing, yet withholding, the features of extremity. . . . Larkin touches the theme of mortality in a grave, fine, genuinely understood way."[351] Brownjohn also admires poems by Elizabeth Jennings that "sometimes register acute personal suffering but never go beyond a proper reticence."[352] Fred Chappell admires the "telling reticences" in Mark Jarman's poem "The Home."[353] Peter Russell, reviewing Gioia's first two books, *Daily Horoscope* and *The Gods of Winter*, praises the "very containedness and distancing with which [Gioia] treats heart-rending or unspeakable suffering and sorrow."[354] But Matthew Flamm is not impressed: "Gioia is too well behaved—the decorousness of his writing . . . keeps experience at a distance."[355] Even worse, John Press says that the irony often seen in 1950s poetry is there to "conceal the absence of deep feeling."[356] Neil Corcoran criticizes the "often too constrained and corseted decorums" of Davie's early poetry, but he says that, thanks to "Pound and the American model" of poetry, Davie moves beyond these decorums.[357]

Gioia's admiring comments in a 1983 review of Steele's *The Prudent Heart* suggest that there are Movement-like qualities in Steele's poetry. He does not mention the group by name, but *all* the qualities he lists are characteristic of the Movement:

> [Steele's] work announces no brave new ideology. It projects no compelling persona. What one notices instead is a carefully cultivated sensibility flawlessly translated into words. There is no urgently prophetic tone, just the voice one educated person might use in talking with another. Steele believes he can command the reader's attention by writing well about ordinary things.[358]

As suggested by this review, the two groups share strikingly similar ideas about the nature and purpose of poetry itself, as well as the proper role of the poet. Gioia affirms the practice of "project[ing] a carefully cultivated sensibility" rather than a "compelling persona"; he praises Steele for "writing well about ordinary things" rather than attempting to be a "prophet" or bearer of a "new ideology." Similarly, in a review of *Daily Horoscope*, Gioia's first collection, J. D. McClatchy calls him a poet of "sure skill" who "could well become our silver-tongued elegist," especially if he "challenge[s] his skill with greater risks."[359] McClatchy sounds much like John Press, who in 1963 offered tentatively hopeful praise for the Movement writers and other 1950s poets: "It is, after all, better to misuse than to abandon intelligence, and those who master a technique have acquired an instrument on which they may come to play good tunes."[360] Although McClatchy does not mention the Movement, his observations further highlight the parallels between the two groups. His description of *Daily Horoscope* would fit, say, "The Whitsun Weddings" or "In the Stopping Train": "This is a poetry of the suburbs, 'the saddest places,' and of the commuter." McClatchy feels that a "strong undercurrent of melancholy" unifies Gioia's poems. Larkin's poetry, especially, has been described in exactly this way. Many poems in Gioia's collection, McClatchy notes, are "set among mortgages, insomnia, ennui, and small complaints, 'the useless insight, the unbroken dark,' an unnerving familiarity—a loneliness that blurs." The second half of this description fits many poems by Gunn and Davie, and the entire passage is practically tailor-made for Larkin.

According to McClatchy, the poems in *Daily Horoscope* are not a "conversation with song" but are instead a "conversation with speech," a notion that was *central* to the Movement. McClatchy notes that Gioia writes in a "middle style [that] suits the directness of some of his poems." This description calls to mind "the new austerity" identified by Michael Hamburger, in his 1969 book *The Truth of Poetry*:

> The new anti-poetry . . . arose from an acute distrust of all the devices by which lyrical poetry had maintained its autonomy. For the new anti-poets it was not enough that poetry should be as well written as prose. It should also be capable of communicating as directly as prose, without resort to a special language mainly distinguished by its highly metaphorical character.[361]

For these poets, says Hamburger, "The invention of metaphors and similes was felt to be a luxury, a self-indulgence, if poetry could do without such personal linguistic accretions."

Gioia's "middle style" and the directness of his writing could be said to continue the "new austerity" embraced decades earlier by the Movement writers. An aphoristic line of Gioia's poetry that McClatchy quotes—"these insufficiencies make up the world"—could easily have come from a poem by Larkin.[362] It recalls one of Larkin's favorite themes: life consists of little more than boredom, annoyance, disappointment, fear, and loneliness, followed by deterioration and death. The "sparkling armada of promises" for which "we" wait in

Larkin's "Next, Please" will "leave us holding wretched stalks / Of disappointment." In his poem "Dockery and Son,"

> Life is first boredom, then fear.
> Whether or not we use it, it goes,
> And leaves what something hidden from us chose,
> And age, and then the only end of age.

Larkin's "Poetry of Departures," which Gioia vividly recalls encountering in the 1970s, bluntly says, "We all hate home / And having to be there." As seen earlier, Gioia has suggested that his first encounter with this poem was a transformative experience, leading him to see Larkin as "not merely a master but a confidant."[363] The term "insufficiencies"—which almost summarizes the Movement view of life—also appears in Davie's "Hawkshead and Dachau in a Christmas Glass," a characteristically Movement poem: "Some mooning hobo, by inhuman fires / Of stars or moon, may, glancing in the glass, / Observe his insufficiencies."[364] Gioia's poetry differs from that of the Movement, however, in its suggestion of a longing for transcendence, "another world . . . / behind the ordinary."[365] Larkin, especially, would likely have scoffed at the very notion.

Even one of McClatchy's negative comments about Gioia—"Melancholy plus energy can add up to bitterness"—could just as easily be used to describe Larkin. Indeed, it fits Larkin far better than it does Gioia. McClatchy's assessment of a weakness in *Daily Horoscope* also resembles criticism often leveled against Movement poetry: "There is a good deal of gentility throughout *Daily Horoscope*; poems that might be tragic are only sad, and witty ones sometimes merely winsome." McClatchy goes on to say that the "very skill that makes these poems so rhythmically alert, formally varied, and emotionally poised seems simultaneously to inhibit them." Press's criticism of the Movement writers (and other 1950s poets) is similar: they tend to "display a self-awareness which all too frequently hardens into a crippling self-consciousness," and their "carefully cultivated tone of conversational ease, especially when combined with the employment of strict verse-forms, at times degenerates into affectation and mannerism."[366] Even worse, according to Press, "In the very act of writing a poem they seem to ask themselves whether it is critic-proof, whether it is vulnerable to rigorous analysis or to mockery, whether they have been guilty of unpardonable emotion or unregulated enthusiasm." Press's observations are harsher than McClatchy's, but both clearly feel that the poets in question are overly studied, self-conscious, and restrained. In this context, Michael Hamburger's description of the "limits" that were central to the poetry of the "new austerity" comes to mind once again.[367] Richard J. Gray speculates that the poetry of the Movement writers and the New Formalists "*thrives* on limits."[368]

In a discussion of several collections by Steele, Kevin Walzer invokes the Movement writers indirectly when he says that Steele's poetry is written in "a plain language that descends from Ben Jonson and John Dryden to Robert Frost and Yvor Winters."[369] He finds in Steele's first book, *Uncertainties and Rest* (1979), an "impressive range of subjects, tones, and forms." Rather than writing the "short-lined, imagistic free verse" that typified American poetry in the 1970s, Steele uses "various structures of meter and rhyme" in his "discursive, even essayistic investigations of abstract topics." His poetry "finds beauty and joy where others might overlook them, maintains a steady, calm tone, and depicts these concerns in clear language cast in traditional modes." Steele is also interested in "the natural world" as well as "human character." Unlike the Romantics, however, the Movement writers tended *not* to be attracted to nature. "As an alternative to a wild and depopulated outdoors," Blake Morrison says, they "offer cheerful and populated interiors—the living room, the teashop, the pub."[370] Although Steele often writes about nature, he shares the Movement attraction to urban settings and human-made artifacts, not as foils for "unspoiled" nature but for their own sake.

Walzer uses the terms "discursive" and "essayistic" to describe Steele's poetry. These traits are central to Movement poetry. Morrison describes how, under the influence of "Logical Positivism," the Movement writers wrote poems that "would proceed, or would give the impression of proceeding, by logical argument."[371] To be sure, "discursive essayistic investigations" like those found in Steele and "logical argument[s]" like those found in Movement poetry can be problematic: abstract, prosaic, earthbound. As Morrison emphatically states, "Poetry *should* be something sublimer than thinking, and the Movement's failure to recognize this was to be one of the limitations of its programme."[372] In the context of Walzer's review, there are two important differences between Steele and the Movement writers: his impressive range of tones as opposed to their limited range, and his interest in nature *as* nature as opposed to their general lack of interest in the natural world.[373]

Although John Lucas ultimately says that the New Formalist anthology *Rebel Angels* "ought to be on the shelves of anyone who cares about poetry," his review is pertinent, ironically enough, because of what he dislikes about the book.[374] In addition to lamenting the "enervate dullness" and "bookish smell" that, in his opinion, permeate the collection, Lucas devotes an entire paragraph to a criticism of Movement traits that he sees throughout. He chides one poet for using a phrase, "bodied forth," which "comes from a poem written by Philip Larkin some fifty years ago," and he is exasperated by the "hesitations," "qualifications," and "dithering binaries" throughout *Rebel Angels*:

> The Movement poets of the 1950s were rightly criticized for giving house room to ersatz ratiocination: an on-the-one-hand-but-on-the-other sort of balance, the presumed decorum of which, far from being intellectually daring, was merely habitual, the dithering binaries of the tame and the just. Well, consider the way in which in *Rebel Angels*, words like "yet" and "odd" are used to indicate sudden check to the thought, as in "Odd, how his genius courts expectancy," or "Yet time yields shape and history."

In 1980, Morrison noted a related habit in the Movement writers: "Movement poetry contains an unusually large number of arguing connectives—words like 'for', 'still', 'yet', 'because', and 'so'."[375] John Press expresses his impatience with the tendency:

> The practice of scattering here and there such empty phrases as 'of course', 'I'm afraid', 'it seems', in so far as it is not just metrical padding, appears to be a vaguely reassuring gesture intended to show that these highly intellectual poets want their readers to relax and feel at home in a genial atmosphere.[376]

For Davie, this habit hinted at the "craven defensiveness" of the Movement writers, including himself.[377] Morrison offers a muted defense of the tendency, saying that "allow[ing] hesitations and qualifications into a poem is in a sense more honest than to pretend they do not exist."[378]

Whether this tendency is vaguely reassuring or dithering, craven or honest, it appears throughout *Rebel Angels*.[379] Rafael Campo's "For J. W.," which describes how difficult it can be for a man to express romantic feelings for another man, fits the pattern: "I knew, / Or thought I knew, exactly how I felt." The speaker in Gioia's "Counting the Children" says, "I gave up those vigils years ago. / My daughter's seven now, and I don't worry—/ At least no more than any father does." In two other poems by Gioia, variations on the phrase "I suppose" add a Movement-like hesitancy to the speakers' tone. In "The Red Hat," by Rachel Hadas, the speaker's self-correction would fit into a typical Movement poem: "Now our son / officially walks to school alone. / Semi-alone, it's accurate to say." The speaker in Andrew Hudgins' "The Hereafter" suddenly undercuts his own musings about mortality: "For so long I have thought of us as nails / God drives into the oak floor of this world, / it's hard to comprehend the hammer turned / to claw me out. I'm joking, mostly." In Mary Jo Salter's "What Do Women Want?" the speaker says that "an unbagged beverage" in the pockets of a homeless woman "looks like a flask of vodka," then immediately says, "But no, it's dish- // washing liquid!" The woman's "dirty secret," as it turns out, is "not to miss / the thing that . . . well, it's hard to say; but what / she'd want, if we were given what we want." Although hesitations, asides, corrections, and equivocations like these are common in twentieth-century poetry, they are *characteristic* of the Movement. Those New Formalists who have close connections with the Movement writers may well have absorbed this tendency from them.[380]

CHAPTER 5

Poetry

Oddly—and wrongly—neither Gunn nor Larkin was included in any college English course I took; I came to them later. . . . I loved them both.[381]

—Rachel Wetzsteon

CLARIFYING THE FOCUS

Since Davie, Gunn, and Larkin are the most prominent members of the Movement, and since Gioia, Jarman, and Steele are among the most prominent "founding members" of New Formalism, I shall focus my attention on poems by these six writers. Because there are many excellent poets and critics in both groups, the choices were difficult. The Movement might never have existed had it not been for Robert Conquest, who edited *New Lines*, the first collection of Movement poetry. Elizabeth Jennings and D. J. Enright rebelled, early on, against the limitations and restrictions of Movement ideology.[382] English critic Neil Powell classes Jennings among "the most important English poets of the late twentieth century"—as important as Gunn and Larkin.[383] Among the New Formalists, Charles Martin is an award-winning writer, whose range extends from "translations of the classical Roman poet Catullus to offbeat, quirky modernist and surrealistic works in the style of Franz Kafka, Theodore Roethke, Matthew Arnold, and Alfred Lord Tennyson."[384] David Mason is also an award-winning poet, as well as a "deft essayist and critic."[385] The late

Rachel Wetzsteon, a "poet of keen insights and wit," wrote poetry described as "hard-edged yet sinuous, rich with feeling yet unsentimental."[386] In the early days of New Formalism, Marilyn Hacker was, in Annie Finch's words, among the "courageous and lonely forerunners."[387] Finch herself was among those who pushed New Formalism to evolve and expand, especially in its attitudes towards poetic form, international poetry, postmodernism, and gender. A list of contributions made by the Movement writers and the New Formalists, which would take pages, might show just how difficult the selection process was. Nevertheless, since I am writing about the *formative* influence of the Movement writers on the New Formalists, it makes sense to limit the focus to these six writers: Philip Larkin, Donald Davie, Thom Gunn, Dana Gioia, Mark Jarman, and Timothy Steele.

DANA GIOIA AND THE MOVEMENT

When Dana Gioia became acquainted with Larkin's work in the 1970s, he then began, "systematically," to read work by other Movement poets, especially Gunn and Davie.[388] Although much twentieth-century poetry deals with the theme of "what to make of a diminished thing," as stated in Frost's "Oven Bird," the Movement writers, especially when they were an "official" group, came close to *specializing* in it. "The Burning Ladder," the opening poem in *Daily Horoscope*, Gioia's first book (1986), depicts a decidedly "diminished" version of the biblical Jacob, who climbs a burning ladder and wrestles with a powerful angel. In Gioia's poem, Jacob never wrestles with an angel or climbs "the ladder / burning in his dream." He does not even see a "real" burning ladder, blazing in the night sky, obviously sent by God, but merely sees his ladder in a dream. Instead of "ris[ing] / like a flame to join / that choir," this poor Jacob "slept / through it all," doing no more than "shivering." In the poem, Jacob is incapable of acting because "gravity / [is] always greater than desire." Exhaustion and gravity tether him to the earth, sap him of "desire," turn him from a human into a "stone / upon a stone pillow," and make him powerless to fulfill God's grand plans for him. Jacob also, perhaps, represents a poet who aspires to greatness but finds his artistic desire unable to counter the gravity that holds him down. Interpreting the poem as autobiographical, Franz Link says, "'Gravity' keeps [Gioia] within the limits of his everyday world; yet, his poetry tries to catch glimpses of the world Jacob saw in his dream."[389]

"The Burning Ladder" has intriguing connections with Gunn's poem "Lazarus Not Raised," which takes an equally diminished look at a biblical figure.[390] Although Jesus offers this dead man a second chance at life, Lazarus as depicted by Gunn cannot—or *will* not—muster sufficient energy or gumption to accept. Summoned from the comfort of death, Lazarus chooses at first to indulge in an untaxing mental activity, "ambl[ing] at an easy pace / In childhood fields imaginary and safe." But "the miracle [has] not yet taken place." Somehow, although conscious enough to reminisce, Lazarus is still dead. Even the miracle itself is diminished: it is a "scheduled miracle," no longer the spontaneous act it appears to be in the Bible, inspired by Jesus's grief and his love for Lazarus. Gunn's narrator makes it clear that Jesus's offer of grace is not a blessing to be appreciated. Rather than rejoin his loved ones, Lazarus chooses to "disregard the nag of offered grace" and to remain a corpse: he "blinked and shook his head / Then sank again, sliding without a trace / From sight." Inertia and a lack of desire keep Lazarus buried, distended and decomposing in his grave, "to take slime on the deepest bed / Of vacancy." He evidently cannot muster the will to be fully present. Or, as a perverse way of exercising his human will, Lazarus *deliberately* refuses to return to life. In this sense, he resembles the title character in Gunn's "The Unsettled Motorcyclist's Vision of His Death," who stubbornly rides through "walls of rain" toward his own death but prides himself, even as he sinks into the marsh, on "being what I please." As he refuses the miracle and chooses death, Lazarus vanishes into vacancy, leaving not even a trace of himself. In addition to this stubborn willfulness, the other important factor in his refusal appears to be his fear, combined with a strange anger, caused, presumably, by the disruption of his peaceful death: upon his face, briefly, is a "terrified awakening glare"—a telling contrast with the "greasy placid face" he possessed earlier in the poem.

The "failure of nerve" depicted in both poems represents an interesting philosophical difference: while Jacob fails because of forces beyond his control, Lazarus seemingly fails *deliberately.* This detail calls to mind the Movement insistence that it is wiser and safer—on a personal, national, and international level—to maintain a "self-induced and stubborn loss of nerve," as Davie puts it in "Creon's Mouse." In fact, Davie's poem asserts that "no one must be daring anymore." In the Movement view, failure is not necessarily failure at all. Gioia returns to the same issues in a wryly humorous poem called, bluntly, "Failure" (2001):

> Why not consider it a sort of accomplishment?
> Failure doesn't happen by itself. It takes time,
> effort, and a certain undeniable gift.
> Satisfaction comes from recognizing what you do best.

The language, the confiding tone, and the mocking claims that failure is a "beautiful" child, daily becoming "more gorgeously like you," as well as an "accomplishment" in which you can take a "special pride," are Larkinesque. Gioia ends the poem by suggesting that failure is a sign that "you" have tried your best: "You only fail at what you really aim for." While Gioia's poem contains a tongue-in-cheek bravura that Larkin's ironically titled "Success Story" does not, the ideas in the two poems are nearly identical:

> The explanation goes like this, in daylight:
> To be ambitious is to fall in love
> With a particular life you haven't got
> And (since love picks your opposite) won't achieve.
> That's clear as day. But come back late at night,
>
> You'll hear a curious counter-whispering:
> Success, it says, you've scored a great success.
> Your wish has flowered, you've dodged the dirty feeding,

> Clean past it now at hardly any price—
> Just some pretence about the other thing.

Ambition is dangerous and unwise, as suggested by Larkin's metaphor of unrequited love. Although he eventually makes it clear that failure isn't *really* the same as success, he also suggests that the mind is capable of persuading "you" into believing "you've scored a great success."[391]

For the Movement writers, the very existence of failure and its inevitability were among the reasons never to aim high, but they might have approved of Gioia's humorous look at failure. In 1982, interviewer Robert Phillips noted that Larkin's favorite subjects appear to be "failure and weakness."[392] Gioia's poem could almost have been inspired by Larkin's answer: "A good poem about failure is a success."[393] The philosophical views underpinning their thinking are, however, quite different. Gioia jokingly suggests that failure is an accomplishment in itself—that it is, in fact, a sign of great ambition—but he still believes that ambition is vital. In contrast, the Movement writers often suggest that ambition is too risky to bother with. Blake Morrison and others have suggested that cultural and historical factors contributed to the Movement writers' distaste for ambition. Primary among those were the smoldering ruins of World War II, which vividly demonstrated the destructive and deadly results of unchecked ambition. The New Formalists, in contrast, grew up at a chronological and geographical distance from such lessons. Their America takes pride in its optimistic, "can-do" attitudes and its Horatio Alger stories of ambitious types who doggedly work their way to the top.

Another major difference between "The Burning Ladder" and "Lazarus Not Raised" is that Gioia places the blame on a human being and on natural forces, whereas Gunn goes much further, not only questioning the powers of a frail human but also implicitly questioning the powers of Jesus, despite his divinity. A later (and quite compassionate) poem titled "In Santa Maria del Popolo" expresses a related idea: for most people, there will be no life-altering moment of revelation, no "wide gesture of the lifting arms," as seen in Caravaggio's depiction of St. Paul. Most people are "too tired for more than this /—For the large gesture of solitary man, / Resisting, by embracing, nothingness." If even Jesus lacks what it takes to save a human from "nothingness," the sole option—a paradoxical one—may be to resist it by passively yielding to, as Davie puts it, a "self-induced and stubborn loss of nerve." Gioia may have rejected such nihilistic ideas because they go against his own beliefs, or he may simply have found them uninteresting or irrelevant. Despite these differences, "The Burning Ladder" and "Lazarus Not Raised" share a number of particular details, and they are very close thematically. Both illustrate the resigned belief that life-saving miracles, superhuman gestures, and larger-than-life mythologies are not feasible. Although this type of resignation frequently appears in twentieth-century poetry, it utterly *permeates* Movement poetry. In short, Gioia's "The Burning Ladder" may be both a reply to and an argument with Gunn's "Lazarus Not Raised."

Gioia's poem may also be a response to "Jacob's Ladder" by Donald Davie. Despite its title, Davie's poem has almost nothing to do with Jacob's story; instead, it is about sex, the human will, and aspirations and failure.[394] The two lovers in Davie's poem have "agreed we would not mount by those / Platonic ladders planted on the heart." The "Platonic ladders," evidently, represent the "minds that abide the body and its throes, / Reluctantly, and only for a start." Although they agree to avoid these ladders, the two nevertheless "ascend" the one that the speaker calls "Jacob's." Of course, even if the biblical Jacob's Ladder was firmly planted on the ground, it reached, daringly and ambitiously, all the way to Heaven. The "Jacob's Ladder" in Davie's poem, in contrast, is sensible—a quality much admired by the Movement writers. Although it extends to orgasmic heights, it does not involve emotional or intellectual risk, as would a ladder reaching to the "peaks." Somehow, the two lovers can climb this ladder "without . . . knowing any sense of strain," and even when they have climbed so high that they must breathe "upland air," they remain in "habit's level pastures": "We want, and yet we do not want, the skill / To scale the peaks that others tell us of . . ." Endorsing such limited aspirations, again, was central to the Movement writers, who insisted that *actively* choosing to be *passive* wards off hardship and struggle—even conflict, war, and defeat.

The similarities between Gioia's poem and Davie's are limited yet interesting. The differences are more numerous—and more interesting. Both poems are about the failure to reach the "peaks." Gioia's is about a person who, apparently, aspired to such peaks once upon a time, but who is now so exhausted and so "sick / of travelling" that he has lost his ambition and his strength. In contrast, the lovers in Davie's poem consciously *decide* to fail. Their failure is a result of an internal force, "the will," whereas in Gioia's poem, the failure of the main character is determined by natural forces that cannot be overcome by a mere human, especially not one so worn out that he is "a stone / upon a stone pillow." Davie implicitly argues that it is best not to expend too much energy, not to aim too high. Gioia's idea is quite different: one *should* aim high, but one must also realize that the limitations of this world may hold one back. As seen earlier, *if* Gioia had Davie's poem in the back of his mind as he wrote his own, he was evidently not attracted to the Movement notion of deliberate failure. The small similarities between "Jacob's Ladder" and "The Burning Ladder"—and the larger thematic differences between the two—make Gioia's poem seem like a somewhat prickly response to Davie's.

"View from the Second Story," another early poem by Gioia, may well be a response to Larkin's "Waiting for breakfast, while she brushed her hair."[395] The speaker in Larkin's poem looks "down at the empty hotel yard," only to see wet cobblestones that "[send] no light back to the loaded sky." Outside, although it is morning, it is so misty and dark that "rooms [are] still burning their electric light." At first, the speaker thinks, "Featureless morning, featureless night." Suddenly, though, he decides that his gloomy thought has been a "misjudgment," that the mist is "wander[ing] absolvingly past all it touch[es]," and that the electric lights are "pin-points of undisturbed excitement." Then he turns and kisses the woman who shares his hotel room, "easily for sheer joy tipping the balance to love." Unfortunately, his doubts aren't completely resolved. What will the "tender visiting," which is currently "fallow as a deer or an unforced field," demand of the speaker? Will this "tender visiting"—perhaps representing the speaker's muse—insist on having everything its own way? Will it "refuse to come" until he is alone, requiring him to send his lover "terribly away"? Surrounded by unpromising things, then suddenly surprised by promise, then just as suddenly overcome with doubts, the speaker remains undecided as the poem ends.

In Gioia's "View from the Second Story," the speaker looks out the window and sees that "the winter sky [is] a bright grey / against the windowpanes." He sees lights "coming on / in all the other houses," but in his own room, he sees "only weak sunlight from the rain-streaked glass / dissolving in the shadows of the furniture." A dark cloud seems to loom over the relationship in this poem, as the unnamed "You" is "in the bedroom, sleeping, or crying," and the speaker wonders whether he is "afraid to look." Despite his uncertainty about her state of mind (and his own), he feels "how easily the room"—maybe the room in which he is standing, or maybe a room in which a painful argument has taken place—"comes back again." He remains where he is, almost paralyzed, "at the wide window / looking for something beyond the dark rows / of winter trees and houses . . . / waiting, listening to the rain while the air which seemed / invisible turns gradually to black."

Although Larkin's poem is set at the beginning of a day and Gioia's at the end, a meditative speaker in each poem looks out an upstairs window and sees gloomy, wet darkness. In each, the speaker notices the lights in someone else's room, whereas his own is dark. In each, the speaker seems solitary, though he is not alone. In each, the speaker is contemplating a troubled relationship. Unlike Gioia's, Larkin's speaker appears, at least briefly, to feel some hope. At the same time, Larkin's speaker is contemplating the necessity to send away his lover, whereas Gioia's speaker has not reached that point. The weather, which mirrors the speakers' feelings in both poems, evolves from gloomy to promising in Larkin's, whereas in Gioia's it never grows brighter; in fact, it "turns gradually to black." Both poems are highly Romantic, filled with immense, inchoate yearnings. In each, as noted above, the speaker is waiting for something. The speaker in Gioia's is waiting for something momentous, which he seems to hope will materialize "beyond the dark rows / of winter trees and houses." In what appears to be a typical Movement debunking of Romanticism, Larkin's speaker is prosaically "waiting for breakfast."

Larkin's poem doesn't, however, entirely resist Romantic impulses. The "tender visiting" in the poem seems somehow supernatural, even shamanistic. In addition, the misty sky acts as a stereotypically Romantic pathetic fallacy, reflecting the speaker's sudden feeling that his "lost lost world" has been restored to him. In Gioia's poem, the sun and darkening sky act similarly, reflecting the fear and sadness felt by the speaker. It is important to note that Larkin's poem first appeared in *The North Ship* in 1945, several years before his association with the Movement and its distaste for "Romantic" gestures. Interestingly, in 1981, five years before he published his first collection, *Daily Horoscope* (in which "View from the Second Story" appears), Gioia approvingly pointed out a tendency in Larkin that could be said to appear in this poem: "Larkin may debunk romanticism in his poetry, but there is a visionary note underlying his best work."[396] As Larkin's poetry tends to focus insistently on *this* world, a world populated largely by drooling "old fools," mothers "loud and fat," "crooks and tarts," children with "shallow violent eyes," "uncle[s] shouting smut," and boys "puking" in the "Gents," Gioia's praise for the "visionary note" in Larkin's best work is both significant and surprising.[397] The visionary note in this particular poem resonates briefly, as the speaker feels "sheer joy tipping the balance to love." An even more visionary note is struck, of course, by the "tender visiting" and all that it represents.

In a review of *Daily Horoscope*, Robert McDowell says that "The Room Upstairs" "echoes Frost."[398] A dramatic monologue, written in blank verse, with a speaker who recounts an emotional event in his life, Gioia's poem does resemble one of Robert Frost's dramatic monologues. In even more ways, however, it echoes Larkin's "Mr Bleaney."[399] In Larkin's poem, a talkative landlady shows a potential tenant an unpromising upstairs room and tells him a bit about the previous lodger, Mr Bleaney, including the fact that he lived in that one room "till / They moved him"—perhaps until he was transferred by his firm, perhaps until he died. She outlines a brief biography of Mr Bleaney, including "what time he came down" in the mornings, what sorts of dietary quirks he had, and where he went for his holidays. As the landlady affectionately describes him, she implies that, by taking her "bit of garden properly in hand" and encouraging her to buy a television set, he had made himself a valued part of the household. As Bruce Martin puts it, "despite the shabbiness of his surroundings, Bleaney loved and was loved."[400] To the speaker's way of thinking, though, Mr Bleaney "egged her on" until she bought a "jabbering" television. As he looks around the room, listens to the landlady's overly familiar chatter, and notices how scrappy the "bit of garden" is, he assumes that Mr Bleaney's life was limited and pathetic. The fact that he lived in a single room in someone else's house—not a terribly nice house at that—signifies failure in itself. The room even lacks space for the belongings often considered essential to a meaningful life (books, photographs, mementoes).

In a moment of rather grand Yeatsian questioning, the speaker wonders whether Mr Bleaney "lay on the fusty bed / Telling himself that this was home," unable to "[shake] off the dread / That how we live measures our own nature." Did Mr Bleaney feel "pretty sure" that "at his age having no more to show / Than one hired box" meant "He warranted no better"? Immediately, as if rejecting such philosophical questioning, Larkin has his speaker, practically in mid-question, say, simply, "I don't know." And, with that, the poem ends. The speaker has good reason to be asking these questions, not only about Mr

Bleaney's life but about his own: he has, after all, just moved into the same "hired box" in which Mr Bleaney lived, surrounded by diminished things, perhaps because he could never overcome a Prufrockian—or Larkinesque—failure of nerve. Indeed, the fact that he never moved until some unnamed "They" moved him suggests a thorough passivity. Despite the characteristic Movement undercutting of the speaker's questions, they are there nonetheless. His effort to shrug them off, ironically, increases their power, because he so clearly wishes to avoid them and because he appears destined to suffer the same fate as Mr Bleaney. Indeed, his own fate will probably be worse, for he seems utterly uninterested in making himself a "loved" part of his new household.

Both the similarities and the differences suggest that "The Room Upstairs" is a response to "Mr Bleaney." Gioia's poem begins the same way as Larkin's. In this case, the landlord invites the potential tenant to "come over to the window for a moment." The landlady in Larkin's poem does not invite the speaker to look out the window, but he does anyway and sees "a strip of building land, / Tussocky, littered." In Gioia's poem, the potential tenant sees a "dust-brown" hill "without trees" nearly as forlorn-looking as the scene in Larkin's, but, in this case, the hill is the only feature of the natural landscape that has not been disrupted by humans. Both owners talk about previous occupants of the room, but instead of dwelling on minor matters such as dietary peculiarities and favorite holiday destinations, the landlord in Gioia's poem discloses his passionate attachment to his former tenant.[401]

In telling the story, he reveals his deep regret for having missed a romantic opportunity with this tenant, David, a "clever, handsome boy / Who thought he was a poet." On a mountain-climbing expedition, David was battered while rescuing a female friend who had become paralyzed with fright halfway up a steep slope. After taking a shower, he dropped his towel and showed his landlord the cuts, bruises, and rope burns covering his back. As David stood there, the landlord "felt like holding him" but did not because he "couldn't bear it." Tragically, David later died in a mountain-climbing accident in Europe. The very night of his death, he again visited the landlord—but only in a dream. Frightened at first, because "there was nothing in [David's] body now, / Nothing but the voice that spoke to [him]," the landlord told David to "go away." Instead, David said, "But I've come back to you. / I'm cold. Just hold me. . . ." This time, he did what he wished he'd done earlier: he took David in his arms and held him. Then, in the dream just as in life, the young man "slipp[ed] silently away / Like snow between [his] fingers, and was gone."

Both poems, to a great degree, are about limitations and failure. In Larkin's, as the potential tenant looks around the grim little room, he detects hints of a life surrounded by diminished things and held back by fear. The landlady seems not to think of Mr Bleaney's life in terms of failure, but the potential tenant, who soon becomes an official tenant, clearly sees it in those terms and, furthermore, seems destined to live an even sadder version of the same life. Similarly, in telling his own intimate story, again to a stranger, the landlord in Gioia's poem reveals a lifetime of loneliness and regret caused by his own long-ago failure of nerve. One rhetorical difference between the two poems, which contributes to a thematic difference, is that Larkin's poem, unlike Gioia's, reveals the speaker's thoughts. Gioia allows the landlord to engage in philosophical questioning without authorial interruption or ridicule. Gioia's poem is also far more emotional than Larkin's, and it indulges in a Romantic occurrence that is unimaginable in "Mr Bleaney": the heartrending visit of the ghost of David. True, he appears in a dream, but both his appearance and his disappearance are ghostly. The Movement writers would likely have dismissed it as "shamanistic."

All the characters in Larkin's poem—from the landlady to the absent Mr Bleaney to the speaker himself—are depicted negatively. When *Selected Letters of Phillip Larkin, 1940–1985* was published in 1992, his prejudices, including anti-academicism, misogyny, homophobia, class snobbery, racism, xenophobia, and ethnocentrism, were thoroughly documented.[402] In a 1993 review of Andrew Motion's *Philip Larkin: A Writer's Life*, Gioia catalogues Larkin's hatreds:

> If he hated immigrants, trade unions and the Left, he also despised children, marriage, bachelors, family life and the consolations of religion . . . He loathed the proprieties of middle-class life equally with the squalor of the poor. . . . He disliked continental Europe as much as the Third World. Above all, he hated himself—his face, his body, his "filthy family," and his "bloody sodding awful life."[403]

Speculating that Larkin may have suffered from what the Elizabethans termed "misanthropy and melancholy, hatred of humans and incurable depression," Gioia suggests that there may have been valid psychological reasons for his negative depictions of these characters and others. At the same time, as Richard J. Gray points out, the narrator in Larkin's poem resembles the cynical and defensive characters often appearing in novels by Graham Greene.[404] It is impossible to determine whether Larkin's negative depictions of various characters stem from melancholy, from misanthropy, from his admiration for "less deceived" novelists such as George Orwell and Graham Greene, or from a combination of factors. What is clear is that Gioia presents his characters far more compassionately than Larkin does his.

Another major difference between the two poems involves social class. Larkin's touches on class *differences*.[405] His speaker appears to consider himself superior to the lower-middle-class landlady, whose house and garden are obviously humble and whose conversation focuses on a sorely limited range of topics.[406] In contrast, although Gioia's poem reveals nothing about the potential boarder (except that she or he is an extraordinarily patient listener), it depicts the landlord as urbane and almost aristocratic: he laments the overdevelopment of the surrounding area, mentions that he designed his own large and undoubtedly expensive house, and points out his long-term affiliation with a local university. The landlady in Larkin's poem rents a room presumably because she needs the money, while the landlord in Gioia's poem rents because he desires the company. The issue of social class is not overtly explored in Gioia's poem, possibly because the *listener's* thoughts are never revealed or possibly because the subject is less interesting to Gioia than it was to Larkin. In fact, social class tends to be less interesting to American poets than to many English ones, perhaps especially the defiantly "middlebrow" Movement poets. Indeed, Americans tend to avoid the very *idea* of class distinctions. Although Gioia proudly claims a working-class background, Paul Breslin has aptly noted that the New Formalists, including Gioia, "are inclined to take white middle-class life too readily as the universal, as 'the' established culture."[407] In this instance, however, Gioia may simply be more interested in failure, lost opportunities, and loneliness than he is in class issues.

Gioia's poem "In Cheever Country" is reminiscent of two poems by Movement writers: Davie's "In the Stopping Train" and Larkin's "The Whitsun Weddings."[408] While some of the similarities may be superficial, others are far deeper, and they all suggest a textual relationship between Gioia and his elders. "The Whitsun Weddings," the first of the three to be published, is set on a warm, "sunlit Saturday." It is not surprising, therefore, that the speaker mentions the uncomfortable aspects of the train journey, from the "hot" cushions to the "reek of buttoned carriage-cloth." Nonetheless, the narrator seems serene: "all sense / Of being in a hurry [is] gone." Outside the window, he sees a landscape both like and unlike the one in Gioia's poem. In both poems, the landscapes are ordinary, rather than sublimely Romantic, but the landscape in Larkin's poem, in which pleasant sights and smells intermingle with unpleasant ones, is more active and, in some ways, uglier. As the train "ran / Behind the backs of houses" and "crossed a street / Of blinding windscreens," the speaker "smelt the fish-dock." Soon the train passes a more pleasant sight, "wide farms," populated with "short-shadowed cattle," but these are followed immediately by "canals with floatings of industrial froth." The "smell of grass" intermittently "displace[s] the reek of buttoned carriage-cloth." There is also the sight of the "river's level drifting breadth . . . , / Where sky and Lincolnshire and water meet." Inevitably, though, "the next town" seems bound to be "new and nondescript, / Approached with acres of dismantled cars."

Although, for a while, Larkin's speaker continues with his reading rather than noticing the people boarding the train and standing on the station platforms, he soon notices that many of the groups are wedding parties. His interest is awakened, and from then on he pays more attention: "Struck, I leant / More promptly out next time, more curiously, / And saw it all again in different terms." The girls saying goodbye to their newlywed friends, are "grinning and pomaded" and dressed "in parodies of fashion." Despite these snobbish characterizations, the speaker briefly sympathizes with them: he notices that the young women seem bereft, "as if out on the end of an event / Waving goodbye / To something that survived it." This sympathetic view is short-lived, and he returns to unflattering terms to describe the wedding parties that he sees at one station or another:

> The fathers with broad belts under their suits
> And seamy foreheads; mothers loud and fat;
> An uncle shouting smut; and then the perms;
> The nylon gloves and jewellery-substitutes,
> The lemons, mauves, and olive-ochres that
>
> Marked off the girls unreally from the rest.

As Mark Jarman puts it in a 1988 essay on "The Whitsun Weddings" and "In the Stopping Train," "the catalog of Larkinesque caricatures . . . is smugly satirical."[409] All the while, despite his snobbishness, the speaker is paying close attention to these other lives, becoming involved and gradually returning to the sympathy he briefly felt earlier.

The speaker notes that "a dozen marriages got under way" in a very short time, and he thinks about the implications of what he has seen. As he and his fellow passengers look out the windows, the speaker assumes that "none / Thought of the others they would never meet / Or how their lives would all contain this hour." Even if they never know each other, they are connected by their distant yet shared activities and by the very fact that they have all *existed* together in this same hour. Such a warm, humane view is surprising and touching, especially coming from one who earlier could see only the "seamy foreheads," the apparently awful "perms," and the "jewellery substitutes."[410]

The narrator of Davie's "In the Stopping Train," who seems deeply frustrated with himself, is so involved in Prufrockian self-interrogation that he often speaks of himself in the third person.[411] He chides himself for a number of supposed shortcomings, including his tendency to be a man of "art" and "language":

> He never needed to see,
> not with his art to help him.
> He never needed to use his
> nose, except for language.

As he ponders the names of flowers and the meaning of terms such as "stopping train" and even "love," he seems to have run out of patience with himself. He can name all the varieties of flowers, but he can "identify hardly any." His life has consisted mostly of the "dance of words," it seems, rather than first-hand or communal experiences. According to Jarman,

> "The Whitsun Weddings" and "In the Stopping Train" touch on the same two subjects, but Davie would have been far more interested in "shared humanity" than in "the perpetuation of custom" . . . The "shared humanity" that must mean something has been glossed in numerous ways throughout the poem, as Davie responds to his possible carriage mates, to the remembered wisdom of grown-ups, to the traffic outside the train, to his wife and daughter, to the enviable position of [Australian poet] Judith Wright who speaks for her nation, and to himself.[412]

Jarman's interpretation seems apt, for the speaker in Davie's poem pays close attention to his own insight about "shared humanity," which "surely, / surely . . . means something." As he ponders this concept, the moment is so intense that he "pummels his temples." He even chides himself because, unlike Judith Wright, he speaks only for himself.

Davie's speaker eventually seems to undercut his own insights, however, by saying that the man on whom the poem has focused is "not / our chap, but another." This "chap"—apparently an alter-ego or doppelgänger for the speaker himself—has a "foolish beard" and an "uncertain mouth." He has already proven his foolishness, in fact, by taking "some weird girl off to a weird / commune, clutching at youth." As the poem ends, the speaker implicitly ridicules the emotional "bother" experienced by this "chap":

> Dear reader, this is not
> our chap, but another.
> Catch our clean-shaven hero
> tied up in such a knot?
> A cause of so much bother?
>
> He knew too few in love.

Although the self-questioning in which the speaker and his alter-ego have engaged seems to have been cut short, this final observation that "he knew too few in love" bears examining for what it says about shared humanity: the speaker himself *knows* people but fails to *love* them adequately. According to Jarman, "The reproach implicit in this line is a Christian one." The speaker interacts with no one on the train. To Jarman, this is precisely the point: "Davie's concerns as a Christian are the salvation of his soul and the fellowship of his fellowmen. It makes sense that as a Christian poet he would be distressed by the self's interference with these aims, especially as it uses language to obstruct them." Jarman's implication—that a number of obstacles interfere with our ability to interact in meaningful ways with others and with the world in general—strikes me as correct. Still, an emphasis on fellowship and shared humanity is central not just to Christianity but to many religious, philosophical, and ethical systems. Both "The Whitsun Weddings" and "In the Stopping Train" deal, in large part, with the need to love one's neighbor—even if that neighbor possesses an "uncertain mouth," is "loud and fat," insists on wearing "parodies of fashion," or sports a "foolish beard."

Kevin Walzer says that Gioia's "In Cheever Country" is distinctive because of "its tone of quiet celebration" of the happiness that can be found in middle-class life.[413] More typically, in Walzer's view, American poets "attack the problems of middle-class life, either loudly (W. D. Snodgrass, Anne Sexton) or with a quiet whine (Stephen Dunn, Jonathan Holden)." Although this poem does not "whine" about middle-class life, it does not glorify that life, either: "Gioia's speaker arrives home to a quiet happiness, despite his consciousness of the costs—physical and spiritual—of the system in which he is employed." Robert Peters, who accuses Gioia of writing "Easy Listening Poetry," scoffs at the claim that this poem has any depth: "In his attention to the towns he travels through, he sounds like an American Betjeman, intent on pointing out the obvious in comfy five-line stanzas."[414] Donald Atkinson, too, fears that Gioia will become "*le Betjeman de nos jours* by the new readership we are all supposed to covet."[415] Although Peters and Atkinson obviously see Betjeman as more of a sentimental skeleton in the closet than a worthy ancestor, it is interesting that they invoke him in connection with Gioia, since the Movement writers, especially Larkin, admired Betjeman. Resemblances to Betjeman notwithstanding, "In Cheever Country" calls to mind "The Whitsun Weddings" and "In the Stopping Train," not only because all three are set on trains but also because they all focus on the musings of a more or less ordinary person riding through a more or less ordinary setting and coming to sudden insights about himself and his connections to fellow humans.

The speaker in Gioia's poem, who is riding through "Cheever Country"—suburban Westchester County, New York, where John Cheever set many of his stories—looks out the train window at streams, forests, rivers, "leaf-swept yards," "smooth parkways," the "County Airport." Perhaps because this landscape is ordinary, not edgily urban or sublimely Romantic, the speaker muses that "no one takes [it] too seriously." Instead, it is characterized by the almost-comical fantasy of its earlier inhabitants, who refused to accept the reality of the setting: "defiant pergolas, a shuttered summer lodge, / a shadowy pavilion framed by high-arched windows / in this land of northern sun and lingering winter." The setting is also characterized by the suburban developments that have arisen since the days of those wealthy residents. Even the supposedly poetic town names borrowed from Cheever's stories—"Clear Haven, Bullet Park, and Shady Hill"—seem intended to serve "as a talisman against the commonplace," which is evidently determined to pervade everything. As the speaker wryly puts it, "There always seems so much to guard against." Suddenly, as he continues to look out the window, the light changes, "and the passengers / standing on the platform turn strangely luminous." In a moment of almost prayerful gratitude, the speaker says, "If there is an afterlife, let it be a small town / gentle as this spot at just this instant."

As the train moves on, the speaker sees evidence of former wealth, embodied in ruins much like those admired by the Romantics: "Marble staircases climb the hills where derelict estates / glimmer in the river-brightened dusk." Of "these palaces the Robber Barons gave to God," some have been converted into "convents" and some into "orphanages," while still others "are merely left to rot." Whatever the case may be, "splendor in ruins is splendor still," says the speaker, who entertains a fantasy of standing on the grounds of an estate like these. In a passage that greatly troubled critic Greg Kuzma—who accused Gioia of being obsessed with money—Gioia's speaker describes the "huge factories" where the "Robber Barons," in the late nineteenth and early twentieth centuries, made their fortunes:

> Somewhere upstate huge factories melt ore,
> mills weave fabric on enormous looms,
> and sweeping combines glean the cash-green fields.
> Fortunes are made. Careers advance like armies.
> But here so little happens that is obvious.

Reading this poem, a person who is at all interested in social and economic justice might well make several observations. The workers who did all the labor in these "huge factories" undoubtedly lived in tiny, squalid cottages, while the owners accumulated fortunes and lived in splendor. The workers would have had few, if any, leisure hours, while the owners spent time in their "balustraded gardens above the river." And the workers had few, if any, opportunities to escape the noise and pollution of the factories and the river, while the owners retreated to their vast estates, which were, not coincidentally, "above" all of that grimy reality. Gioia's speaker makes no such observations. He says only that "each detail warns it is not so difficult / to make a fortune as to pass it on" and that "it is wonderful to imagine standing / in the balustraded gardens above the river." His sympathies appear to lie entirely with the factory owners and their heirs. Regrettably, as noted by Kuzma, Gioia's poem does gloss over the lives of the workers who were (and still are) exploited by factory owners like these.[416] At the same time, though, the poem is making the Movement-like suggestion, which is also characteristic of Romanticism, that structures such as mills and machines such as sweeping combines are worthy subjects for poetry, every bit as worthy as cathedrals, castles, rustic farms, and sublime landscapes.

The last line of the passage quoted above is intriguing: "Here so little happens that is obvious." Even in a noisy factory, even in the middle of "cash-green fields," and certainly in an ordinary suburban landscape, life can be subtle, can be worthy of contemplation. Many poets have been conditioned to view such "ordinary" lives and surroundings as unpoetic, but Gioia's poem counters that stereotype:

> And this at last is home, this ordinary town
> where the lights on the hill gleaming in the rain
> are the lights that children bathe by, and it is time
> to go home now—to drinks, to love, to supper,
> to the modest places which contain our lives.

By suggesting that such places are worthy of poetry, Gioia has entered Movement territory. Many poems have been written about the challenges and the humiliations of blue-collar and working-class lives—and the dignity that can be found therein—but both the Movement writers and the New Formalists have implicitly argued that suburban and white-collar lives are also worthy subjects.[417] Gioia's poem is, at least in part, challenging prevalent stereotypes about poets and about worthy subjects for poetry—stereotypes that, two decades earlier, the Movement writers themselves challenged.

The poems by Davie, Larkin, and Gioia are not, of course, exactly alike.[418] The speakers in the poems by Larkin and Gioia focus on their surroundings and (eventually) pay close attention to their fellow commuters. Davie's speaker, so immersed in his own thoughts that he might as well be alone, notes that he will "have his flowering gardens / to stare at through the hot windows," but since he says nothing further about them, it seems that he does not pay attention to them. Also, rather than noticing other passengers or bystanders, he only hopes that there will "not for pity's sake / be a crying child in the carriage." He eventually notices the "chap" on the train with him, but that chap seems to be an alter-ego of sorts rather than a separate individual. The speakers in Gioia's and Larkin's poems do not examine themselves from the outside the way Davie's speaker does, nor do they wrestle with feelings remotely like his: of having made mistakes, of "going mad," of hating his fellows, of being a "gross egotist," of needing to be "punished." As Jarman succinctly puts it, "Existential anxiety is not present in 'The Whitsun Weddings.'"[419] The same could be said of "In Cheever Country."

Although Gioia's decision to set his poem on a train may simply reflect his own experience as a white-collar executive living in suburban New York and commuting to New York City, it could also have been influenced by "The Whitsun Weddings" and "In the Stopping Train." The thematic similarities are especially intriguing. In Larkin's poem, the speaker suddenly has a compassionate insight into those people who are boarding the train and those who are seeing them off.

They are not, he realizes, merely laughably "common" people with dreadful perms, brash synthetic wardrobes, and coarse vocabularies. Instead, they are participants in an almost mystical human rite. In Gioia's poem, the speaker suddenly sees the passengers on the platform as more than workaday commuters. They become "luminous" representatives of the beauty and peace to be found in seemingly ordinary lives. In Davie's poem, the speaker mentally wrestles with the things that separate human beings from each other: miscommunication and misunderstanding, violence, "the dance of words," "recklessness," "gross egotis[m]." Even the act of thinking divides humans. Although the speaker has no epiphany like the ones in the poems by Gioia and Larkin, he seems determined to believe that there is a "shared humanity" among people. From settings to themes, it seems highly likely that Gioia's poem was inspired by Davie's and Larkin's. Jarman feels that "'In the Stopping Train' is in part a response to 'The Whitsun Weddings'."[420] I believe that "In Cheever Country" is a response to both of them.

Gioia's "California Hills in August" may be a response to Davie's "Low Lands," which describes the "uncertain" beauty of the fens of Cambridgeshire, England:

> I could not live here, though I must and do
> Ungratefully inhabit the Cambridgeshire fens
> And the low river delta we pass through
> Is beautiful in the same uncertain sense.

The speaker goes on to compare the river delta to a snake, "its serpentine iridescence / Of slow light spilt and wheeling over calm / Inundations, and a snake's still menace / Hooding with bruised sky belfry and lonely farm." The metaphor creates a vision of a landscape that is beautiful and brooding, vulnerable and threatening. Contradictions like these meander through the poem, in much the same way that a river meanders through the countryside (and a snake meanders along the ground).[421] The poem concludes:

But a beauty there is, noble, dependent, unshrinking,
In being at somebody's mercy, wide and alone.
I can imagine a hillborn sculptor suddenly thinking
One could live well in a country short of stone.

Gioia's poem also opens with the description of a setting—a sharply contrasting one—that many would find impossible to appreciate:

I can imagine someone who found
these fields unbearable, who climbed
the hillside in the heat, cursing the dust,
cracking the brittle weeds underfoot,
wishing a few more trees for shade.[422]

All around, the speaker describes the landscape: all around are "twisted shapes of black elm, / scrub oak, and chaparral," along with "thistle, foxtail, golden poppy." To someone unfamiliar with the terrain, the desert trees might well appear to be dead, the desert flowers nothing more than weeds, "and yet how gentle it seems to someone / raised in a landscape short of rain." Befitting the stereotypes about the western United States, the landscape is independent, prickly, and downright ornery. Gioia's poem could be described as a refraction of Davie's. The two settings are exact opposites: one wet, the other dry; one fertile, the other seemingly barren; one flat, the other hilly; one largely domesticated, the other wild; one dependent on humans, the other scornful of them.

If, in fact, these two poems are related, cultural and geographic factors may help explain the contrasts between them. England has been at the mercy of humans for at least two millennia, while many parts of America remain relatively undomesticated. Also, given the density of its population and the longevity of its history, England probably stresses community and cooperation more than America does, which may add another dimension to the phrase "being at somebody's mercy." Yet the speaker calls the landscape "wide and alone," suggesting that, for him, it is still desolate, perhaps because he feels he does not belong there. America's stress on rugged individualism may help explain the attraction that Gioia's speaker feels to the independence and aloofness of the dry California landscape. In America, where cultural, political, and religious teachings frequently stress self-determination and independence, most people would be unlikely to sense any beauty in "being at somebody's mercy." Although there are risks involved in imposing biographical information onto literary texts, the differences may also stem in part from the poets' own circumstances. Having grown up in Northern England, Davie himself might well share the hillborn speaker's feeling that he "ungratefully inhabit[s]" the flat fen country of Cambridgeshire. The poem's sense of unease may also result from the contradictory nature of the landscape itself—or, more likely, the speaker's contradictory reactions to it: it is simultaneously tamed and as menacing as a snake; it is abundant with vegetation and equally abundant with "sleek and lissom" rats; it is beautiful, but only in an "uncertain sense"; and it is flat, leading to tedium for those who are hillborn. In contrast, having lived in the dry hills of California, Gioia would understand his speaker's sense that this landscape is "gentle," although it may seem unwelcoming, even dead, to those who are accustomed to lusher, greener landscapes.

Differences like these do not, of course, foreclose the possibility that Gioia's poem is, in effect, a revision of Davie's, in the sense of "re-seeing" it. Both poems describe landscapes that have an "austere beauty" of their own, one that is difficult for others to appreciate. There are even similarities of phrasing: Gioia's poem opens with "I can imagine someone," while Davie's closes with "I can imagine a hillborn sculptor." It is worth noting that, in an essay published nearly thirty years ago—before New Formalism began to coalesce as a movement—Gioia included "Low Lands" in his list of Davie's ten best poems.[423]

Gioia's "The Homecoming" is a dramatic monologue filled with images of religious fanaticism and outright violence.[424] Since Gioia has long admired poets such as Browning, Frost, Robinson, and Jeffers, who specialized in dramatic monologues, they were undoubtedly among the inspirations for this poem. "The Homecoming" also contains beguiling echoes of a poem by Larkin and one by Davie. In its theme and in several of its details, it is reminiscent of Larkin's "Home is so Sad." Granted, the situations in the two poems are not the same. For one thing, while there is not even a hint of violence in Larkin's poem, Gioia's speaker is an escaped convict who graphically describes his violent past and cold-bloodedly kills his foster mother. Nevertheless, there are striking parallels between the two. The personified family home in Larkin's poem sits, quiet and unchanging, as if hoping to win back whichever member of the family was "the last to go." When it becomes clear that the home is "bereft / Of anyone to please, it withers so" and has "no heart to put aside the theft // And turn again to what it started as, / A joyous shot at how things ought to be, / Long fallen wide." In Larkin's poem, "home" does not represent love, nostalgia, or a warm refuge in a cold world; instead, it represents sadness and failure. The house in Gioia's poem, which has also remained unchanged in the years since the foster son left it, unquestionably represents sadness, failure—and worse. As he said when interviewed by Gloria Brame, Gioia vividly remembers his first encounter with "Poetry of Departures." Since Gioia found this poem so inspiring that he saw Larkin as a "master" and a "confidant," the poem's theme would certainly have resonated with him. For the foster son in Gioia's poem, home truly is "so sad," and it is far worse than that: it is like prison, like hell, and there is no escaping it. For good reason, then, he would hate "having to be there."

The physical characteristics of the homes also merit a closer look. Whereas Larkin's inventory of items in the parlor is fairly sketchy—"the pictures and the cutlery. / The music in the piano stool. That vase"—the description in Gioia's poem is detailed and lengthy. Otherwise, the parlors in these two poems are eerily similar. As the foster son waits for his foster mother to return home, he "passe[s] the time remembering / what it was like to grow up in this house":

> This little parlor hasn't changed a bit
> in twenty years. Those china figurines
> along the mantelpiece, the ivory fan,
> the green silk pillows puffed up on the couch
> were sitting in exactly the same place
> when I first came. And that pathetic print
> of Jesus smiling by the telephone—
> even the music in the piano stool.

Notably, "the music in the piano stool" is specified, in exactly the same words, in both poems.[425] It may even be significant that Gioia has chosen to give the foster home a "parlor" in the first place. Such a small, formal room used almost exclusively to greet guests may be common in older American houses, but it is far from universal, and in the United States the term "parlor" tends to be used less often than "sitting room" or "living room." These similarities may simply represent both poets' efforts to create an old-fashioned—and somewhat suffocating—ambience. However, it is useful to return to the interview with Gloria Brame, in which Gioia says he feels a "physical thrill of excitement and delight" when he first encounters a "really splendid new poem." The very first example that he gives to illustrate his point is Larkin's "Poetry of Departures," leaving little room for doubt: the echoes of Larkin in a large number of poems by Gioia—including "The Homecoming"—must be more than coincidence.

Throughout his childhood and adolescence, the speaker in Gioia's poem was terrorized by his foster mother. Although she may have meant well, she was a fanatic, and her religious teachings contributed, ironically, to his downfall:

> She told me years ago how everyone
> would either go to Heaven or to Hell.
> God knew it all, and nothing you could do
> would make a difference. . . .

Because her teachings offered no hope of redemption, he believes he is doomed, and damned. It is easy to see why he would think so. From his earliest years, he has been rejected:

> She raised me, but she wasn't family.
> I don't know how she first got custody,
> except that no one really wanted me.
> My father disappeared when I was three.
> I don't remember him. Then the next year
> my mother took off, too. . . .

The evening that he escapes from prison and returns to his former home, he looks into his old bedroom, where he sees evidence of a new foster son, letting him know that he is not only forgotten but also replaceable. Also, much like the house in Larkin's poem, his room, in all its grimness, has remained frozen in time:

> I knew the room. It hadn't changed at all.
> The air still stunk from every grudging meal.
> The blistered paint, the battered bed and desk
> still moaned about the cost of charity.

Even as an adult, he would probably feel devalued by the fact that he has been replaced, especially since the foster mother hasn't bothered to change the bedroom from the way it was. She appears to be more faithful to her furniture and her knickknacks than to these young human beings. The charity she offered was "grudging" and came with a "cost," or at least it seems that way to the poem's speaker. This woman is the only person who has ever tried to help him, but, tragically, her efforts have failed. About the new foster son, the speaker thinks, "He had the wisdom of the unloved child / who knew he had been damned by being born." The speaker believes that the same description also applies to him.

After he has murdered his foster mother, the speaker in Gioia's poem momentarily feels "radiant," "invincible," "strong," and "free."

Although the similarity may be coincidental, these adjectives sound like those used by Gunn in some of his early poems, in which action, even violent action, is a positive thing. The speaker in "Lerici" contrasts those who "[fall] submissive" with those who "make gestures with arms open wide," expending "muscle" and "breath" up to the very instant they are conquered by death. As the speaker lauds the "strong swimmers, fishermen, explorers" who "dignify death by thriftless violence—/ Squandering with so little left to spend," it is clear that he prefers those who, even in dying, are more than a "minor conquest of the sea." In "A Mirror for Poets," the violence of the Elizabethan era contributed to the discovery, for poets, of "Arcadia, a fruitful permanent land." The "red-coat soldier" in Gunn's "Incident on a Journey" says that his own violence "made [him] wise":

> No plausible nostalgia, no brown shame
> I had when treating with my enemies.
> And always when a living impulse came
> I acted, and my action made me wise.
> *And I regretted nothing.*

The murderer in Gioia's poem seems similarly invigorated by the violence he has committed. He soon remembers, however, that he is doomed: "I had come home, and there was no escape." This view, like the one seen in Larkin's poem, goes against all the affectionate clichés about "home sweet home." For Larkin, "home" is not like that at all. For the young man in Gioia's poem, home is as bad as Hell:

> That night I knew that I would go to Hell,
> and it would be a place just like my room—
> dark, suffocating, with its door shut tight,
> and even if my mother were there too,
> she wouldn't find me. I would always be alone.

The mother to whom he refers is apparently his biological mother, whom he has seen only once, at a distance, since she abandoned him.

Unlike Odysseus, who is recalled by this passage, this young man won't even be able to try to put his arms around his mother. His imaginings, while filled with exasperating and self-serving rationalizations, take the very concept of doom to a hopeless new level. There has never been any comfort for this young man, and there will be none.

The inextricable connections between the foster mother's grudging charity and the young man's acts of horror suggest the possibility that this poem may also have been inspired by Davie's "Homage to William Cowper." Although this poem, an *ars poetica* and condemnation of certain types of poetry, does not deal with themes even remotely similar to those in Gioia's, it refers to domestic matters in oddly ominous ways:

> I too have sung the sofa and the hare,
> Made nightmare ride upon a private air
> And hearths, extinguished, send a chill for miles.

In the last stanza, in which he is criticizing "most poets," the speaker presents an image of violence invading a supposedly safe setting and preying on a helpless creature:

> Most poets let the morbid fancy roam.
> The squalid rat broke through the finch's fence,
> Which was a cage, and still was no defence . . .

Home is supposed to be a safe place, yet in these poems by Davie and Gioia, the "morbid fancy roam[s]," making it anything but safe. The foster mother in Gioia's poem has provided the foster son with a home, but it is a "dark" and "suffocating" place. What's more, each time she lectures him about Hell, she threatens him with what might be called eternal violence. After years of such teachings, he becomes much like the "squalid rat" in Davie's poem, attacking and murdering innocent animals, then a prison guard, then, finally, his own elderly foster mother. The house in Gioia's poem is also "a cage, and still [is] no defence." For years, it caged the foster son, but it offered him no defense against his foster mother's teachings or against his own wicked urges. As he waits for his chance to kill her, he paces through the house like a frustrated animal in a cage. And at their final meeting, the house which is also a cage offers no defense for the foster mother.

It is tempting to think that Gioia may have been inspired by the last line of Davie's poem: "For Horror starts, like Charity, at home." Such a breathtakingly negative view defies the comfortable teachings with which most of us grow up, yet Gioia's poem perfectly illustrates Davie's twist on the old adage. Admittedly, the argument I am positing here is tenuous. Still, if Gioia was familiar with "Homage to William Cowper" when he wrote "The Homecoming," he may have consciously or unconsciously remembered some of the images, especially the last line. It is possible that "The Homecoming" is an intriguing and surprising response to these two poems by Larkin and Davie (and, in passing, to the suggestion in Gunn that violence can be empowering). In its graphic depiction of a number of killings and in its focus on a fundamentalist, hellfire-and-brimstone Christianity, however, Gioia's poem is different from these others. It could thus be described as a thoroughly American refraction of the poems that seem to have inspired it. America is, after all, far more religious—and, paradoxically, far more violent—than England.

MARK JARMAN AND THE MOVEMENT

Mark Jarman has admired the poetry of Larkin and Gunn since his days as a college student, and for several years he had a close working relationship with Davie, whom he calls "the most articulate Movement critic" and "one of the two great Pound scholars."[426] His comments about Gunn are also telling: "Partly he fascinated me because he wrote about California, where I was from. . . . When I was learning to write, I imitated him a lot." Surprisingly, Jarman—who characterizes himself as a narrative poet more than a formalist—says he was also attracted to Gunn because of his use of "ingenious verse forms, like rhyming syllabic verse." The Movement writers did not write treatises arguing for the importance of storytelling, but their *poetry* suggests that they may have valued it nearly as much as the "Expansive Poets" have done.

The impact of the Movement may be less noticeable in Jarman than in Gioia, but there is extensive evidence that Jarman has strong personal and textual ties to Davie, Gunn, and Larkin. Jarman himself says that people have commented on the resemblance between his poem "My Parents Have Come Home Laughing" and Larkin's "Coming" (which itself echoes Hardy's "The Darkling Thrush"). As a "laurel-surrounded" thrush proclaims "It will be spring soon, / It will be spring soon," the speaker in "Coming" is carried back to his memories of childhood, which he characterizes as "a forgotten boredom." The beauties of the "longer evenings" and the optimistic song of the thrush make him feel puzzled yet hopeful, "like a child / Who comes on a scene / Of adult reconciling, / And can understand nothing / But the unusual laughter, / And starts to be happy." In Jarman's poem, which is set in Scotland, the speaker's parents return home after "a feast for Robert Burns." Somehow, the child knows that they have been laughing all the way home, although he does not know why.[427] After a "giggling" discussion about whether they should place a telephone call to the United States, the parents eventually tire and lose "the strength to keep laughing." Soon, the speaker says, "I hear, as their tired ribs / Press together, their bedroom door not close / And hear also a weeping from both of them / That seems not to be pain, and it comforts me." When the child in Larkin's poem "comes on a scene of adult reconciling," he "can understand nothing," but the "unusual laughter" causes him to "be happy." Similarly, the child in Jarman's poem does not understand his parents' lovemaking, but the "weeping" that accompanies it "comforts" him.

Over the years, religious belief in general and Christianity in particular have been central to Jarman.[428] Doubt has also been important. Jarman's "Comparisons of Wonder," Larkin's "Faith Healing," and Davie's "The Evangelist" deal with these issues in similar ways.[429] Jarman's poem, which appears in a 1981 collection called *The Rote*

Walker, opens with a description of a home for disabled children and adults. "My father," says the speaker, "took me to meet the boy / of bandages, of folded, flaccid arms." This boy's only means of communicating appears to be "whistling through his throat," and his lack of control over his "functions" requires him to wear a "urine flask." While at the home, the speaker also sees "the grown children / with beards and breasts like costumes, / their Halloween cakewalk of pathos." When he subsequently reads about miracles in the Bible—"*the blind saw immediately, / the maimed were healed instantly*"—he is "filled with wonder." His recollection of the handicapped people he has seen, however, makes him view these stories of miracles as "shrewd tales," designed to sell a doctrine:

> This is how you lose your simplicity.
> When the preacher says, "But we will cross over,"
>
> you know there are complications.
> You know that every escape clause
> is always the heart of the matter
> unlike those bedded, braced, blanked out here
> who knew or never knew
> and crossed over into this life.

Given the reality of life for the people in the institution, the speaker can't help feeling that there must be an "escape clause" in the preacher's assurance that "we will cross over." If these people couldn't even cross over into this life, it seems unlikely that we will cross all the way over to Heaven. For the speaker, the preacher's promises, as well as the Bible itself, are equivalent not only to deliberate fictions ("shrewd tales") but also to dubious legal documents. Those who believe them have not yet lost their "simplicity." It is notable that he doesn't think of an "escape clause" as a minor part of such documents; it is "always the heart of the matter." This young man wants to believe, as demonstrated by his Bible readings and prayers, but he is struggling.

Larkin's "Faith Healing" describes an event at which a dark-suited, silver-haired evangelist with a "deep American voice" calls people forward, lays his hands on them, and prays for them. For some reason, all the people who come "to his voice and hands" are women, "Moustached in flowered frocks." After their brief time with the evangelist, they are "exiled // Like losing thoughts." While some "go in silence," others "sheepishly stray, not back into their lives / Just yet." Others stay where they are, "twitching and loud / With deep hoarse tears, as if a kind of dumb / And idiot child within them still survives / To re-awake at kindness." The descriptions of the women nearly obliterate any evidence of sympathy, but there seems to be a bit:

> In everyone there sleeps
> A sense of life lived according to love.
> To some it means the difference they could make
> By loving others, but across most it sweeps
> As all they might have done had they been loved.

They have come to the evangelist searching for the missing ingredient that would, they believe, fulfill them, but their longings are incurable. In fact, "all" is "wrong," and all are overcome with sorrow:

> An immense slackening ache,
> As when, thawing, the rigid landscape weeps,
> Spreads slowly through them—that, and the voice above
> Saying *Dear child*, and all time has disproved.

"That," says the speaker, "nothing cures." No healing—of the body or of the spirit—takes place. The speaker, especially, remains "rigid," unconvinced. After all the prayers and tears, the only "voice above" comes from the evangelist: it is merely a human voice, not a Heavenly one.

In a discussion of "Faith Healing," Bruce Martin says, "Characteristically [Larkin] fastens our attention not on the phoniness of the healer or the stupidity of the faithful, but on the psychological significance of what happens to them, a significance universalized in the final stanza."[430] I believe Larkin "fastens our attention" on *all* of these things. As mentioned above, his speaker demonstrates sympathy as well as empathy, but these are counterbalanced by his egregiously unflattering descriptions of the women.[431] In addition, the description of the evangelist drips with doubt. He treats the women like children, demanding to know, *"Now, dear child, / What's wrong."* Even this ostensibly sympathetic question is phrased as an impatient command, lacking the expected question mark.[432] Without waiting for them to elaborate on "what's wrong," he "goes into a prayer," after which he "abruptly" grabs each woman by the head. He actually dares to get bossy with God, "Directing" him "about this eye, that knee." After spending "twenty seconds" with each woman, he shoos her away. Since Larkin himself was notoriously prejudiced against "foreign" countries, the "deep American voice" of the evangelist makes him seem questionable, a slick con artist deceiving these naïve English women thirsting for faith in a predominantly secular society. Larkin's speaker also compares the women to "losing thoughts," to straying sheep, and to "dumb" and "idiot" children who are desperate for "kindness." Incidentally, although these metaphors are patronizing and insulting, they come directly from Judeo-Christian teachings. Throughout the Bible, people are sheep who must be watched over, led about, and told what to do, and to enter the kingdom of Heaven, they must become children.

Davie, like Enright and Amis, was raised in a Nonconformist religious family. In England, Baptists were (or are) known as "Nonconformists" and "Dissenters" since they did not belong to the Church of England. They tend to question the elaborate rituals, hierarchical structure, idolatry, and certain doctrines of Anglicanism, such as infant baptism. Since, in their view, even children are sinful creatures who are doomed to hell unless they are "saved," they also have little patience with the joyful and supposedly "heedless ways" of childhood as described by Dylan Thomas and other poets. Ironically, then, a Movement-like sense of *doubt* is central to the *faith* in which Davie grew up. His poem "The Evangelist" depicts a Baptist preacher much like the "faith healer" in Larkin's poem:

> 'My brethren . . . ' And a bland, elastic smile
> Basks on the mobile features of Dissent.
> No hypocrite, you understand. The style
> Befits a church that's based on sentiment.
>
> Solicitations of a swirling gown,
> The sudden vox humana, and the pause,
> The expert orchestration of a frown,
> Deserve, no doubt, a murmur of applause.

All of this suggests that the people in the congregation are being manipulated—by the evangelist, perhaps by religion itself. The performance of the evangelist "Deserve[s] . . . a murmur of applause." Even the "sudden vox humana" of the musical instrument (an organ) is merely a clever imitation of the human voice, perhaps intended to sweep up the congregation in the emotion of the moment. The speaker, who is far too detached to be moved by the preacher, the sermon, or the music, notes that, throughout the congregation, there are "tides of feeling." His metaphor dehumanizes the multitudes surrounding him, stripping them of their volition and making them as thoughtless as the ocean responding to the pull of the moon.

When he remembers that "Bunyan found a place for wit," the speaker seems to be trying to persuade himself that faith and intelligence can coincide. However, since he immediately drops the subject, he may be implying either that he doesn't accept such a juxtaposition or, just as likely, that no one else in the congregation would care about it. He confesses that his resistance to the preacher's sermon is, in part, a defense mechanism: "Yes, I am more persuaded than I think; / Which is, perhaps, why I disparage it." When some unknown "you" points out that the evangelist is "patently sincere," the speaker retorts, "Because he is so eloquent, you mean? / That test was never patented, my dear." The Movement's deep distrust of language—their insistence that eloquence has nothing to do with sincerity or honesty—is shown here. As suggested by Blake Morrison, Michael Hamburger, and others, the Movement writers had good reason to see language and eloquence as dangerous, given what they had witnessed in the years before and during World War II. The speaker then describes the situation in terms that can best be described as paradoxical:

> If, when he plays upon our sympathies,
> I'm pleased to be fastidious, and you
> To be inspired, the vice in it is this:
> Each does us credit, and we know it too.

The evangelist's eloquence is itself paradoxical, as it has one impact on the speaker and an entirely different one on the unnamed "you." And somehow, simultaneously, in the speaker's estimation, each tendency is a "vice" and "Each does us credit."

These three poems are by no means identical. Whereas Jarman's speaker seems to have a great deal of sympathy for the characters described in his poem, Larkin's does not. That said, though, Jarman's speaker has little sympathy for those who offer religious doctrines filled with "escape clauses"—or, perhaps, for those who accept the doctrines. Also, when he describes the adults in the institution, the speaker's language seems Larkinesque, tinged with grotesque humor: the mentally handicapped adults are "grown children / with beards and breasts like costumes," drifting aimlessly along "their Halloween cakewalk of pathos." For Larkin's speaker, the trusting Englishwomen are little more than "idiot child[ren]," whom he describes as "Moustached in flowered frocks." Davie's speaker says almost nothing about the people in the congregation, pointing out only their involuntary "tides of feeling." While the speaker in Larkin's poem goes into extensive detail about the physical characteristics and words of the evangelist and the reactions of the women who have come forward to be "healed," the speakers in the poems by Davie and Jarman pay more attention to the debate going on in their own minds than they do to the preacher or the congregation. Larkin's speaker is utterly unpersuaded, whereas Davie's and Jarman's speakers are, to some degree, stirred by what they hear and see. Biographical facts, one suspects, underlie these differences: Larkin was skeptical about religion, while Davie and Jarman were (or are) believers.

Nevertheless, the poems are similar in their handling of religion, preachers, belief, believers, doubt, miracles, promises. The evangelists in all three poems, it could be said, are telling "shrewd tales" and making promises with undisclosed "escape clause[s]." Jarman's poem even ends with a hint of the "clever-clever wordplay" that Blake Morrison has described in the Movement writers:

> You know that every escape clause
> is always the heart of the matter
> unlike those bedded, braced, blanked out here
> who knew or never knew
> and crossed over into this life.

Larkin's poem features no such "clever-clever" plays on words, but, as seen above, Davie's does, in a passage that makes the speaker sound smug and patronizing:

> You round upon me, generously keen:
> The man, you say, is patently sincere.
> Because he is so eloquent, you mean?
> That test was never patented, my dear.

The parallels among these three poems become especially noticeable in the *way* they deal with their subjects. In all three, the speakers are not simply people reading scriptures or listening to sermons; they are detached *critics* appraising *performances* or *texts*. Although such an approach may be typical of modernism, it may also be one more piece of evidence that Jarman's poem is echoing, responding to, and arguing with those by Larkin and Davie.

Jarman's poem "Greensleeves," which appears in *The Rote Walker*, also seems to respond to a number of Movement poems.[433] In "Greensleeves," the speaker meditatively describes memories and the "oblique" ways they often come to us:

> So much comes to mind
> from the side, like the dust
> down blades of sunlight.
> Memory shows a morning
> of all the family together,
> palpable through the years—
> but only as elbows and cups.

The speaker seems to say that memory has great power, enabling us to retrieve the past, intact and "palpable." But he immediately undercuts his own observation by saying that the members of the family appear "only as elbows and cups," suggesting that memories tend to appear in fragments and that our recollections are sometimes dominated by oddly irrelevant items, even absurdities. This remark, especially in its anti-climactic juxtaposition of images and tones, sounds much like Larkin's description of photography, in "Lines on a Young Lady's Photograph Album," as "Faithful and disappointing!" For Richard J. Gray, this passage in Jarman's poem is a "very evocative [and] precise way of describing the fragmentary nature of memory—especially memories from childhood."[434] He adds that the passage "strikes [him] as very 'novelistic' in the best sense."[435]

Jarman's speaker goes on to say that we are determined to recall the past and that in our efforts to do so we resemble archaeologists—or ghosts: "We haunt / our own lives, posing, // or scan our portraits / squinting into the glare of the background." The reference to "posing" calls to mind the first line of Gunn's "Carnal Knowledge": "Even in bed I pose." It also evokes a line from Gunn's "A Plan of Self-Subjection," in which the speaker says, "In sex do I not dither more than either / in verse or pose . . . ?" Furthermore, several of Gunn's poems feature *doppelgängers* who "haunt" the lives of his characters.[436]

As Jarman's speaker suggests, we may even hope to discover that "a guardian secret attends us." The past is notoriously difficult to capture: it often turns out that one thing or another, whether a house, a favorite "scrap of melody," or a beloved relative, is simply "Not there, / not there anymore." But the past doesn't always vanish. Alone somewhere, evidently the family home, the speaker discovers that he can still play a sequence of "five notes" on the piano:

> A scrap of melody,
> it is the one piece
> I ever played well; my heart
> is still in it, too.
> It is possibly this
> that I mean. So much meant
> to be lost is saved.

The last sentence, which is notably Larkinesque in its wording, reverses the usual pessimistic perception of memory. The speaker seems to have had the sudden insight that we sometimes remember things we don't expect to remember—and even things we'd rather not remember. He does not elaborate on how he feels about this, but his statement that his "heart / is still in" the piece he plays on the piano suggests that, at least in this instance, he is grateful.

The speaker in Larkin's "Lines on a Young Lady's Photograph Album" addresses the "young lady" whose photographs prove to be "Too much confectionery, too rich" and cause him to "choke on such nutritious images." He catalogues the images—which are, interestingly enough, almost like the fragments that later appear in Jarman's poem—including the child in "pigtails, clutching a reluctant cat," the "sweet girl-graduate," and "the disquieting chaps who loll / At ease about your earlier days." He also meditates on photography itself:

> But o, photography! as no art is,
> Faithful and disappointing! that records
> Dull days as dull, and hold-it smiles as frauds,
> And will not censor blemishes. . . .

Because photography captures everything, it "overwhelmingly persuades / That this is a real girl in a real place." Something about photographs, the speaker suggests, is inherently sad. Immediately, though, in a Movement-like change of direction, he says that it may not be photography at all that "leaves us free to cry." We may cry simply because we are looking at "*the past*": "Those flowers, that gate, / These misty parks and motors, lacerate / Simply by being over." Seemingly relieved yet aching with self-indulgent loneliness, the speaker says that, even if the young lady shares her future with someone, she will, in these photographs, remain in "a past that no one now can share." That past "holds [her] like a heaven," and she lies "Unvariably lovely there," becoming "Smaller and clearer as the years go by."

As pointed out by Blake Morrison, George Orwell's "determination to be 'less deceived'," along with a number of his other concerns, "played a crucial part in shaping the Movement's political identity."[437] Since Larkin's "Lines on a Young Lady's Photograph Album" originally appeared in a collection called *The Less Deceived*, it comes as no surprise that it takes a "less deceived" look at memory. Jarman's "Greensleeves" takes a similar look at this subject, as does "Between Flights," in which the speaker questions the reliability of memory and the accuracy of recollections about childhood:

> You won't need to make up a story about us.
> If you have overheard us, then you know
> The one we're telling each other will do.
> It's about an everyday catastrophe
> That makes us wonder if our childhood
> Was all we thought it was. . . .

The "everyday catastrophe[s]" and other occurrences of childhood often become somewhat blurred in our recollections. This blurring may even, at times, be a deliberate effort to avoid the realization that childhood was not "all we thought it was." In "I Remember, I Remember," Larkin's speaker takes a non-nostalgic look at childhood, describing all the things that did *not* happen as he was growing up in

Coventry, his hometown. He didn't invent "blinding theologies" of any kind; didn't receive revelations from "an old hat"; didn't know a "splendid family," with muscular boys and bosomy girls, to whom he could turn when he "got depressed." He didn't go with a girl into the "bracken" and "go through with it," causing everything to become "a burning mist." His "doggerel" wasn't published in the local paper, and the mayor's "distinguished cousin" didn't speak in awed tones of the speaker's unrecognized talent. Although Coventry was not the idealized hometown often seen in poetry, the speaker doesn't wish "the place in Hell"; he admits, with an implied sigh, that "Nothing, like something, happens anywhere." Even more skeptically, Larkin's "Reference Back" suggests that memories are worse than pointless:

> Truly, though our element is time,
> We are not suited to the long perspectives
> Open at each instant of our lives.
> They link us to our losses: worse,
> They show us what we have as it once was,
> Blindingly undiminished, just as though
> By acting differently we could have kept it so.

Davie's "The Garden Party" also touches on the subject of memory, suggesting that, if one's youth involved "prigs" who lived lives of "moneyed ease" while one lived a life of deprivation, one may be better off staying in the present, for "theirs is all the youth we might have had," and "it's too late to learn to tango now."

Although Jarman's poems lack what might be seen as the sourness of Larkin's and Davie's, his musings on memory are otherwise much like theirs. Jarman's 1990 poem "The Home" might be described as kinder and quieter than Larkin's "The Old Fools," but the shared characteristics suggest that Jarman's poem may be a response to this one, as well as several others.[438] Larkin's poem somehow manages to be simultaneously humorous, disgusting, and threatening. The first stanza has an ominous tone because the speaker poses one urgent question after another:

> What do they think has happened, the old fools,
> To make them like this? Do they somehow suppose
> It's more grown-up when your mouth hangs open and drools,
> And you keep on pissing yourself, and can't remember
> Who called this morning? Or that, if they only chose,
> They could alter things back to when they danced all night,
> Or went to their wedding, or sloped arms one September?
> Or do they fancy there's really been no change. . . .

The question that ends the stanza is both frightening and bleakly funny: "Why aren't they screaming?" As seen in Chapter Two, Dana Gioia has argued that, paradoxically enough, "The Old Fools" demonstrates compassion by being honest about the infirmities of elderly people. Although it is derisively harsh, it may seem somewhat sympathetic, in part because, beginning with the second stanza, Larkin shifts from third- to second-person pronouns to describe the sudden and explosive deterioration that will, he says, occur at death. The use of "you" also serves to remind readers that they will "break up" in the same way:

> At death, you break up: the bits that were you
> Start speeding away from each other for ever
> With no one to see. It's only oblivion, true. . . .[439]

Even before death "you" are only "bits" waiting to "Start speeding away from each other." The "first signs" that the final "oblivion" is approaching are "Not knowing how, not hearing who, the power / Of choosing gone." Contributing to the sympathetic tone are the speaker's attempts to imagine what it is like to be old: "Perhaps being old is having lighted rooms / Inside your head, and people in them, acting." Although "you" "can't quite name" these people, each one represents a "deep loss restored." All the time they also live beneath "Extinction's alp, . . . never perceiving / How near it is." For the young, this "peak" is also always there, but for the old, it is "rising ground."

As he answers another series of urgent questions that end the poem, Larkin's characteristic use of "we" only adds to the sharpness of his answer. "We" shall do more than *imagine* what it is like to be an "old fool":

> . . . Can they never tell
> What is dragging them back, and how it will end? Not at night?
> Not when the strangers come? Never, throughout
> The whole hideous inverted childhood? Well,
> We shall find out.

This humorously bitter yet somehow compassionate poem forces readers to face the kind of old age that most people fear, which involves little more than loss and indignity ending in a ghastly obliteration. "Heads in the Women's Ward," published around the same time (1972), does much the same thing in its depiction of doomed elderly women lying in hospital beds, but it is unrelieved by even the grim humor of "The Old Fools." "Ambulances" (1961) deals with a similar idea: the inevitability of illness, weakness, and death, all of which represent "the solving emptiness / That lies just under all we do." As onlookers catch a glimpse of the "wild white face" in the back of the ambulance, they sympathize, saying, "*Poor soul,*" but the poem suggests they are sympathizing just as much with themselves. "Aubade" touches on many of these issues in even more frightening detail.

Larkin's "The Building," which contains many of the same ideas, begins as a riddle of sorts, never using the word "hospital" and only mentioning "a kind of nurse" in the fourteenth line, at the end of the second stanza. The building appears to have been designed in an effort to "correct" some "error of a serious sort," but this is an error that, clearly, cannot be corrected. As visitors climb the stairs, "their eyes / Go to each other, guessing" what has gone wrong. They are "quiet" because of "This new thing held in common": illness, disability, suffering, death. A vast divide separates those inside the hospital from the outside world, where people go blithely about their daily lives on "short terraced streets / Where kids chalk games" and where "girls with hair-dos fetch // Their separates from the cleaners." In grim contrast, those "unseen congregations" lying upstairs in the building, whether female or male, old or young, "know they are going to die. / Not yet, perhaps not here, but in the end, / And somewhere like this." These people represent all of us, no matter who we are, for we will all die "in the end." Surprisingly, the hospital represents the possibility of transcendence, something that rarely comes up in Larkin's poetry. Unsurprisingly, though, Larkin suggests that such transcendence—which, paradoxically, involves "struggle"—is not possible:

> . . . That is what it means,
> This clean-sliced cliff; a struggle to transcend
> The thought of dying, for unless its powers
> Outbuild cathedrals nothing contravenes
> The coming dark, though crowds each evening try
>
> With wasteful, weak, propitiatory flowers.

Jarman's "The Home," which may be a response to a number of the poems described above, depicts a convalescent or nursing home that will soon be replaced by a new structure. This poem involves riddles, much like "The Building." It never identifies the mysterious "committee representing the Committee" who are visiting. The poem specifies that there are three of them, and that is all: no names, no titles, no distinguishing characteristics. The first woman they encounter in the hallway is also introduced in a playful, almost riddling fashion. She is "nearly bald" and so "small" that she must look up at them. She is "neatly attired," and her "rosy scalp and sparse white hair / Looked fresh." Through such details the reader is led to believe that she is an unusually alert elderly patient. She also, like some of the people who *are* patients, "would be glad to leave" the deteriorating building with its cold concrete floors. Eventually, though, we learn that she is a member of the staff. Larkin would likely have approved of Jarman's depiction of this woman, not only because her identity comes as a surprise but also because she fits one of his favorite themes: especially in settings such as these, the healthy and the ill are in the same predicament, surrounded by disease, shadowed by death. Just as the "nearly bald" woman and the "committee representing the Committee" in Jarman's poem are stripped of the details that would normally identify them, the visitors to the hospital in Larkin's poem are stripped of individualizing details:

> . . . Humans, caught
> On ground curiously neutral, homes and names
> Suddenly in abeyance; some are young,
> Some old, but most at that vague age that claims
> The end of choice, the last of hope; and all
>
> Here to confess that something has gone wrong.

In both poems, all "know they are going to die, / Not yet, perhaps not here, but in the end, / And somewhere like this."

Of the nursing-home residents in Jarman's poem, there are evidently three categories: those who "Do not wish to move," those who "do not know what is happening," and those who "will be difficult to move." This humorously pessimistic classification system makes Jarman sound much like Larkin, who might have called these the three main categories of humanity in general. In another touch of Larkinesque pessimism, even the manager's mother is a resident in the home:

> Mother, the manager whispered, won't you be glad
> To leave here? She snored a little.
> Mother's asleep, he said. But she will be glad.

Although she can't speak for herself, she is ostensibly one of the few residents who "will be glad" to leave. The wryly absurd non-response of the mother could have come straight from a poem by Larkin, where parents and children seldom have much to say to each other. The "conversation" between mother and son in Jarman's poem resembles, for instance, an exaggerated reversal of the conversation in "Reference Back," in which a son has supposedly come home for a visit, but sits alone in his room, playing "record after record, idly," and "Wasting [his] time at home." His mother, at the other end of the "unsatisfactory hall," can apparently think of nothing to say to him except "*That was a pretty one*," in response to one of his records. He does not bother to answer.

Jarman's poem is most revealing about a resident named John, who lives in a "big room" with a limited view of the garden through "chinks in the hedge." His room also has noisy plumbing, stubborn window cranks, and "terribly dry" steam heat:

> There wasn't much to the room.
> His bed near the window, a desk,
> And the massive TV draped with lace
> And covered on top with photographs.

In some ways, his room resembles the "hired box" in Larkin's "Mr Bleaney":

> . . . Flowered curtains, thin and frayed,
> Fall to within five inches of the sill,
>
> Whose window shows a strip of building land,
> Tussocky, littered . . . .
>
> Bed, upright chair, sixty-watt bulb, no hook
> Behind the door, no room for books or bags. . . .

Although John's room is an institutional setting, it seems fairly homey, furnished with a few items that make it a meaningful place, whereas Mr Bleaney's room has no such belongings. Also, although the poem does not specify why, it turns out that John is one of the residents who "wants to stay." In that way, John is also like Mr Bleaney, who obviously wanted to stay in his bare, utilitarian "hired box," for he never left it until "They" moved him.

As Jarman draws a vivid picture of the blatantly institutional kitchen and dining hall of "The Home," he continues to sound like Larkin:

> Two huge female cooks and two
> Whip-thin serving women worked up
> A batch of chipped beef for dinner.
> All this will change, of course.
> Seated among the twenty or so tables,
> The manager pointed to pictures on walls,
> Mostly oblongs of oily twilight,
> Sepias, faded earth tones.
> These will go, too, the manager said.
> We want friendly, vivid colors.

It is easy to imagine an annoyingly optimistic do-gooder and modernizer in a Larkin poem saying, "We want friendly, vivid colors" (just as it is easy to imagine one of Larkin's speakers sarcastically recommending the "Lemon, sapphire, moss-green, rose" of "The Large, Cool Store" or the "lemons, mauves, and olive-ochres" of "The Whitsun Weddings"). Even the language in the above passage hints at a close textual connection between the American poet and his English elder. The "unspeakable wives" in Larkin's poem "Toads" are "skinny as whippets," while the "serving women" in Jarman's poem are "Whip-thin."[440] Also, as Jarman's "huge female cooks" and "Whip-thin serving women" chat with each other about the "batch of chipped beef" they'd recently "worked up" for the old dears at the nursing home, their language sounds slightly off to Americans, who would probably say they'd "prepared" or "cooked" or "fixed" the chipped beef. Jarman may have picked up expressions like "worked up" while living in Scotland as a youth, but it is also possible that he absorbed them while reading Larkin, his "favorite" Movement poet, whom he admires enough to have memorized some of his poems.

In Jarman's poem, when the committee members visit the building site for the new nursing home, they see that "the vast green of a cemetery" is next door. As a *memento mori*, it could hardly be more obvious. The manager in Jarman's poem has, however, "persuaded" himself that the cemetery "resemble[s] a golf course / And offer[s] the peace of a golf course." He may hope that he will in this way convince himself—and the residents—that the location is not as tasteless and ominous as it seems, but euphemistic thinking will not change the fact that they will be living next door to a large expanse of earth with dead people buried in it—and, presumably, plenty of room for more.

TIMOTHY STEELE AND THE MOVEMENT

Timothy Steele has said that the "beautiful formal poems" written by poets including Larkin and Gunn "gave all of us who were younger and interested in form, great hope."[441] He has also clearly been interested in some of the Movement writers' subjects and themes. "Coming Now," from 1983's *The Prudent Heart*, echoes so many poems by Larkin that it could be described as an homage to him. I shall focus on its parallels with "Coming," "Going," "Love Songs in Age," "Aubade," and "Dockery and Son," though it also calls to mind "Mr Bleaney" and "Reference Back." Steele's poem, set at the end of summer, opens with the description of a storm, in which the "wind is always from the North, churning / The lake to a frenzy, wave on wave crashing / Against the rocks in wild frothy explosions. . . ." Larkin's poetry seldom, if ever, describes such tumultuous weather, but apart from a few slight differences like this one, a strong argument can be made that Steele's poem is a reply to a number of poems by Larkin.[442]

Midway through "Coming Now," as the speaker listens "to the waves and wind-thrashing trees," he comes to a Larkinesque realization. As is often the case in Larkin, regret is a mandatory component of growing older and looking back over one's life:

. . . And where I lie
I know that to age is not so much to sense

Time passing as to hear, in wind, histories
Of prospects and hopes irrevocably gone,
Of affections undermined by reticence

And virtues conceded to weakness or to chance.

These lines could have come from any number of poems by Larkin. What's more, "reticence" was especially important to the Movement writers. In their work, it was often presented as a virtue, while in Steele's poem it results in the "undermin[ing]" of "affections." Steele's poem may represent a "trans-Atlantic refraction" of the Movement view. In the cultural stereotypes, if not in reality, Americans scarcely value reticence, while the English are known for it. Steele himself seems to have ambivalent feelings towards reticence, however, for he presents it as a positive value in other poems.

"Coming Now" also echoes Larkin's "Going," in which the speaker watches the "evening coming in / Across the fields" and observes that it "lights no lamps." It seems "Silken," like a coverlet, but "When it is drawn up over the knees and breast / It brings no comfort." In Steele's poem, similarly, although the "soundings of the darkness" are "beauty itself," they are "Ceaseless and uncomforting." In addition, though the echo may be coincidental, the title of Steele's poem is almost identical to Larkin's "Coming," whose speaker also quietly watches as dusk approaches: "On longer evenings, / Light, chill and yellow, / Bathes the serene / Foreheads of houses." Larkin's poem is fairly optimistic, for the singing thrush inspires the speaker to "[start] to be happy." Steele's speaker, in contrast, fails to feel even such hesitant happiness. As he listens to the waves, wakes to a new morning, and moves through his day, he is filled with fear and dread:

. . . Toward dawn I sleep, then wake to day. The fire lit,
I read and work. But altering as the light

Alters with the hours, I can feel coming now
A massive presence, an accumulation
Of time and loneliness, long in gathering,

> Which, like the wind's deep rising over water,
> Will rise about me till I hear it always,
> Steady and full, till I do not hear it at all.

In almost every way—the language, the rhythms, the situation, the firmly asserted pessimism, and, especially, the melancholy yet apprehensive tone—Steele's closing stanzas are virtually identical to the opening lines of Larkin's "Aubade":

> I work all day, and get half drunk at night.
> Waking at four to soundless dark, I stare.
> In time the curtain edges will grow light.
> Till then I see what's really always there:
> Unresting death, a whole day nearer now,
> Making all thought impossible but how
> And where and when I myself shall die.[443]

The last stanzas of Steele's poem, quoted above, also sound very much like the closing lines of "Dockery and Son":

> Life is first boredom, then fear.
> Whether we use it or not, it goes,
> And leaves what something hidden from us chose,
> And age, and then the only end of age.

For Steele's speaker, the "accumulation / Of time and loneliness" will end only with death, when he will "not hear it at all." Although the view in Larkin's poem is even grimmer, the ideas are remarkably similar. One slight difference between the two poems, which may stem from differing attitudes toward audience in England and the United States, is that the speaker in Larkin's poem speaks for all of "us," while the speaker in Steele's speaks only for himself. The Movement writers' use of "we," which seems intended to be inclusive but can sometimes be coercive, has been noticed by a number of critics, including Blake

Morrison. Steele, in contrast, does not appear to assume that all of "us" share the same fate or the same fears as his speaker.[444]

In a 1984 review, Gordon Harvey explicitly connects the two poets, calling Larkin "One of Steele's models."[445] He praises "Coming Now" as one of the "two most accomplished pieces" in *The Prudent Heart.*[446] Describing the "power" of the closing stanza, Harvey says that, nevertheless, it has its limitations:

> This has power enough to make one wish it took on more. The last line, for instance, might have supported two senses: one no longer hears the accumulation of time and loneliness after death; but also, more interestingly, though the accumulation is increasingly present in the heart, with age one is habituated to its presence. But the poem . . . means unblinkingly to face the fact that to age is to feel regrets and loneliness at the thought of death. So qualifiable is this "fact" by experience, though, including the experience of Steele's other poems, that the brooding seems indulgent—especially in a young man.[447]

Harvey evidently suspects that the speaker and the poet are the same person—and he evidently has little patience with young poets who regret measuring out their lives in coffee spoons. Nonetheless, we might recall that "The Love Song of J. Alfred Prufrock" was also written by a poet in his early twenties.

In his discussion of Larkin's "Love Songs in Age" and Steele's "Old Letters," Harvey suggests that Steele's poem is the stronger of the two:

> Where Larkin's "Love Songs in Age" simply laments the gap between promise and eventuality, Steele considers both the nature of promise and the way in which knowledge of it might influence one's actions in the present. And Steele's is a fuller style, incorporating into a conversational medium both sensory sharpness and moral firmness ("too given to the self," "because of vanity").[448]

Larkin's poem describes an elderly woman who has saved "her songs" for decades, until, one day, "in widowhood / She found them, looking for something else." As she plays the songs, which once "ushered in" such things as "the unfailing sense of being young" and "that certainty of time laid up in store," she finds that they still make such promises, along with all the promises typically associated with love. She has learned, however, that these, in particular, are lies:

> The glare of that much-mentioned brilliance, love,
> Broke out, to show
> Its bright incipience sailing above,
> Still promising to solve, and satisfy,
> And set unchangeably in order. So
> To pile them back, to cry,
> Was hard, without lamely admitting how
> It had not done so then, and could not now.

The straightforward pronouncement that opens Steele's poem is, as Harvey implies, Larkinesque. It is also much like the aphoristic "thesis statements" found in many Movement poems (and avoided in much modernist and postmodernist verse):

> Old letters are reproaches, mute petitions
> Unlosable in some desk drawer
> Or attic box. . . .
> they speak of
> Now-jettisoned ambitions
> And insecurities which passed for love,
> And document not times when we were stronger,
> But rather climates favorable to
> Illusions not illusions any longer.

The closing line of the stanza also calls to mind a number of Movement poems. Larkin's "Deceptions," about a young woman who has been drugged, raped, and "ruined," has little in common with "Old Letters," but there may be a thematic connection nonetheless. Addressing the young woman, Larkin's speaker says, ". . . you were less deceived, out on that bed, / Than he was, stumbling up the breathless stair / To burst into fulfillment's desolate attic." Gunn's "To Yvor Winters, 1955," touches on a similar idea, as it stresses the necessity to "learn the false from half-true premisses." The wording and the underlying concept are alike: the best one can hope for, in a corrupt and deceitful world, is to have "Illusions not illusions any longer."[449] Additionally, as discussed earlier, the Movement writers were fond of what Blake Morrison calls "clever-clever wordplays." Gunn's "Legal Reform," for instance, ends with this assertion: "For law is in our hands, I realize: / The sentence is, condemned to be condemned." His description of the human-made beauties of a city—"Indifferent to the indifference that conceived her"—is similar. "Tamer and Hawk" ends with a description of the paradoxical relationship between the tamer and the hawk: "Through having only eyes / For you I fear to lose, / I lose to keep, and choose / Tamer as prey." A notoriously aphoristic and self-contradictory assertion ends "On the Move": "One is always nearer by not keeping still."[450] In Davie's "Garden Party," the speaker says, "I shook absurdly as I shook her hand." The speaker in "Hypochondriac Logic" asserts that the hypochondriac "thinks pain to be / More real as more illusory" and goes on to say "So argue all men who have thought / A truth more true as more remote. . . ." The closing lines of Larkin's "Talking in Bed" may be among the best-known examples of this trait:

> . . . Nothing shows why
> At this unique distance from isolation
>
> It becomes still more difficult to find
> Words at once true and kind,
> Or not untrue and not unkind.

For better or worse, Steele's closing line resembles all of these. Other New Formalists also seem to be attracted to these ways of playing with language to create ambiguity or paradox. When the narrator of Gioia's "His Three Women" (1986) says that it is "maddening to have / A constant woman constantly in mind," his remark sounds as if it could have come from a poem by Gunn, Larkin, or Davie. The narrator also says that "There is every reason he should love her / Except that love will never come from reason." Jarman's "Ascension of the Red Madonna" (1981) ends with an oxymoronic image that would fit perfectly in a Movement poem:

> . . . everyone wants
> what she wants, for her to be gone,
> out of the world, out of those
> flamboyant windows where light,
> the photographer's blinded plate,
> appearing as nothing is everything.

While oxymoronic and paradoxical phrases can be found in poetry written throughout the centuries, the Movement writers may well have helped inspire Gioia, Jarman, and Steele to include "clever-clever wordplays" such as these in their poetry.

In "Coming Now" and in "Old Letters," looking back on life does not always result in a feeling of satisfaction, accomplishment, or joy; it may merely lead one to see "how much of life's gone wrong." Both poems are also permeated with pessimism and resigned acceptance. Larkin has been criticized for similar tendencies—and worse. In an otherwise positive review from 1976, Robert B. Shaw, who is often associated with New Formalism, criticizes Larkin's tendency to push many of his poems toward "downbeat conclusions":

> There are times at which one feels that the dooms of Larkin's characters have been unduly and insistently contrived. . . . Recurrently annoying is the busy stage-managing by which Larkin will lull the reader into a false security only to pull the rug out from under him in a last stanza, or a last line. 'Love Songs in Age', for instance, relies heavily on this tactic.[451]

To Shaw, "The tone of such downbeat conclusions is mannered and tenuous: while an admirer hears restrained, ironic sympathy, the sceptic detects a note of submerged *schadenfreude*."

Although Gordon Harvey asserts that Steele's "Old Letters" is stronger than Larkin's "Love Songs in Age," he says that, unfortunately, Steele's poem fails to live up to its promise: "One wants the anticlimactic banality of the last two lines to be deliberate, an implicit reminder that something vital is missing from a life lived just wishing decently to get through."[452] For Harvey, the almost willful defeatism that ends the poem weakens it:

> So, likewise to return the letters finally
> Back to wherever they belong,
> Is to admit how much of life's gone wrong
> Because of vanity and discontent,
> And is as well to envy
> Those who refuse to hunger for event
> And who accept the wisely-unbegun,
> Just wishing decently to get through life
> And trying not to injure anyone.

Whether the "anticlimactic banality of the last two lines" is intentional or unintentional, the suggestion embodied in them is characteristic of the Movement. As in the poem "Lerici," Gunn often suggested that the best way to live—and die—was "with arms open wide." In contrast, Larkin and Davie often argued for a restrained and supposedly sensible approach. Larkin's "Born Yesterday," which is dedicated to Kingsley Amis's daughter Sally (and may itself be a reply to Yeats's "Prayer for My Daughter"), consists of wishes that the newborn child will grow up to become "ordinary," possessing, "like other women, / An average of talents: / Not ugly, not good looking."[453] Anything "uncustomary" would only "pull you off your balance." In "Success Story," Larkin warns that ambition is as futile as unrequited love. The two lovers in Davie's poem "Jacob's Ladder," as seen earlier, *choose* to limit themselves and refuse "To scale the peaks that others tell us of." In "Creon's Mouse," a definitive "Movement" poem, Davie condemns "daring":

> If too much daring brought (he thought) the war,
> When that was over nothing else would serve

> But no one must be daring any more,
> A self-induced and stubborn loss of nerve.

It is enough, the Movement writers often say, to "accept the wisely un-begun," to try to move through life gently and "decently," without risking failure and without hurting anyone. Just as Gioia seems to have been attracted to the theme of failure in many of Larkin's poems, Steele may have been attracted to the Movement's pessimistic view of life and its limitations. However, just as Gioia adapts their view of failure to fit a more optimistic perspective, Steele emphasizes the need to be considerate, quiet, and accepting rather than the need to give up before one even starts. As discussed elsewhere, the differences may stem, in part, from biography and history. Steele grew up at a generational and geographical distance from the difficulties witnessed (and endured) by the Movement writers in England during and after World War II.[454] Also, the cheerful optimism seen in the United States is different in tone and attitude from the strength and resilience that have characterized England over the centuries. These are generalizations, of course, but to varying degrees, they are also truths.

Steele's poem "Sapphics Against Anger," first published in 1984, ends with a meditation on the "good life," which sounds much like the sort of life the Movement writers would have endorsed:

> Better than rage is the post-dinner quiet,
> The sink's warm turbulence, the streaming platters,
> The suds rehearsing down the drain in spirals
> In the last rinsing.
>
> For what is, after all, the good life save that
> Conducted thoughtfully, and what is passion
> If not the holiest of powers, sustaining
> Only if mastered.

The "good life" is comfortable, domestic, as quiet as a "post-dinner" kitchen. The only "turbulence" is in the kitchen sink. This "good life" is even "rehears[ed]," perhaps in the sense that actions are not taken before they are considered carefully and practiced mentally. Such a life is "Conducted thoughtfully." Passion is part of this life, and it is "the holiest of powers," but it is "sustaining" only if it is "mastered." This last idea would fit neatly in "To Yvor Winters, 1955," in which Gunn says that Winters, his teacher and mentor, "keep[s] both Rule and Energy in view, / Much power in each, most in the balanced two: / Ferocity existing in the fence / Built by an exercised intelligence." Steele's speaker also hopes that, if he becomes "Angered," he will "be near a glass of water" and will "think of Silence." This is a poem about control, mastery, restraint—all of which were central to the Movement philosophy. Steele's interest in these issues has extended throughout his career as a poet.[455] In "Hortulus" (1994), the narrator humorously describes a male bird who might benefit from exercising some Movement-like restraint:

> Her suitor squawks and waves his wings about
> In angry-plaintive-pleading-lover style.
> Too great an ardor is a common blunder:
> She sees him through an unromantic lens
> And all but asks him, *Can't we just be friends?*

As he listens to the "harangue" of the overly passionate bird—which surely also represents overly passionate poets—the speaker wishes that he could offer a piece of advice: "*Woo clemently.*" Larkin and Davie—but probably not Gunn—would have offered the same advice, to intemperate birds as well as intemperate poets (and others).

Steele's "Vermont Spring" (1994) features the dedication "for T. G. on his 60th birthday."[456] In an email interview, Steele said, "My feelings about [Gunn] and his work are reflected in 'Vermont Spring' from *The Color Wheel*."[457] This poem's description of a forest on the verge of springtime contains hints of Movement thinking: "If April mixes memories and desires, / Here it blends beauty with austerity."[458] The phrasing of this line calls to mind the "new austerity" described by Michael Hamburger, and forty years earlier, the Movement writers argued for the value of poetry that "blends" exactly these two extremes.[459] Steele's poem says that "time will deepen talent into art" and that the person who is blessed with such a "gift" will be fortunate: "Lucky the man who, coming to that gift, / Retains this vernal tang of mind and heart." The Movement writers advocated precisely this balance between "mind and heart." In a 1971 letter to *The New Statesmen*, for instance, Conquest quotes Gunn's assertion that the Movement writers were "only writing in the tradition . . . lasting from Chaucer to Hardy, that a poem should balance the emotion with the intellect." (Again, Hardy is often seen a forebear of both the New Formalists and the Movement writers.) When I spoke with Conquest in 2001, he emphasized that this balance was the *main* priority of the Movement.[460]

According to Douglas Chambers, the editor of *A Few Friends: Poems for Thom Gunn's 60th Birthday* (1989), Gunn exemplifies "sureness of touch, poetic touch."[461] The poems in this collection, he says, show that "Thom has inspired . . . not mere imitation but that sort of touching." Two of the three poems by Steele in *A Few Friends* "reply" to poems by Gunn. "Decisions, Decisions," concerns free will and the necessity to define oneself existentially by "choosing, choosing," despite the awareness "That time may claim those choices with its own / Inevitable air of history."[462] Such existential self-definition and inevitability were central themes in Gunn's early poetry, as in "On the Move," where "Men manufacture both machine and soul." Humans—though the poem focuses only on men—are "self-defined, astride the created will." Steele's version is, in effect, a less testosterone-driven way of expressing these very ideas.

In Gunn's early poems, nature was merely an unthinking obstacle: "Much that is natural, to the will must yield." His later poems implicitly endorse empathy rather than force. "Considering the Snail," which mentions the "power . . . at work" in nature, begins by questioning whether animals move with purpose just as humans do:

. . . He [the snail]
moves in a wood of desire,

pale antlers barely stirring
as he hunts. I cannot tell
what power is at work, drenched there
with purpose, knowing nothing.
What is a snail's fury?

The speaker concludes that the snail's "deliberate progress" is probably driven by "slow passion." Blake Morrison says that even though this poem is "Movement-like in its attempt to dignify a small object," it shows a "greater responsiveness to the natural world than most Movement poems" and that "Gunn might legitimately see this as a more 'humane' poem than his early ones," even though it is concerned with a "non-human world."[463] Steele's "Dependent Nature," which also originally appeared in *A Few Friends*, contrasts creatures who know nothing of the "gap between the longed-for and the real" with those who recognize these "disparities." It implies that "the worker"—a bee—does not know why she "settles on a blossom to her taste," just as "the sweetpeas, climbing on their net," do not know why they grow and spread as they do. This innocence may be an advantage, for, unlike humans, they do not suffer from "sad mirth" and do not need to "shield themselves from a regret / Of the dependent nature of their power." In "Considering the Snail," the onlooker does not understand the snail's motives; in "Dependent Nature" the creatures themselves do not understand them. In both, the speaker seriously—not at all dismissively—ponders the motives of beings usually considered "inferior," and muses on the mysterious "power" found in animals.

"Small Lives," which appears in *Sapphics Against Anger* (1986), may also be a response to "Considering the Snail." (Both poems—Gunn's and Steele's—may be responses to Marianne Moore's "To a Snail.") In Steele's poem, the speaker watches a fly and a "pill bug." Confessing that he does not know why "such small lives so fascinate," he sees something in them that he also sees in himself: ". . . a responsive impulse moves my gaze, / An impulse I can see in them as well."

In the case of the fly, which has become both "dazed" and "tired" in its explorations of "the oddly solar weather / Inside a lampshade," the "impulse" seems to be curiosity. In the case of the "pill bug," scooped up in a "shovelful of peat," it seems to be fear. In both instances, the "impulse" echoes the "slow passion" in "Considering the Snail," in which something more than mere instinct is driving a supposedly lowly creature.[464] In each poem, the speaker also recognizes the "slow passion" or the "impulse" as something that he, as a human, shares.

In "From a Rooftop," Steele finds beauty in an urban setting, something the Movement writers also valued.[465] Here, even the humble rooftops of skyscrapers are beautiful, with their "gravelled tar / Where glassy fragments glitter" serving as a "measure of the intermediate worth / Of all the stories to the morning star / And all the stories to the morning earth." The buildings serve as a transition, that is, between the beauty of human-made objects and the beauty of nature. Similarly, in a discussion of Steele's "Near Olympic," Kevin Walzer points out that "Steele finds surprising beauty in the mixture of human relics and struggling nature."[466] Although Gunn, in his poem "In Praise of Cities," sexualizes the city in a way that Steele does not, these two poems resemble each other, not only in their focus on objects that most would consider unappealing and rundown, even sordid, but also in their suggestion that "the work of man" is "loveliest":

> She presses you with her hard ornaments,
> Arcades, late movie shoes, the piled lit windows
> Of surplus stores. Here she is loveliest:
> Extreme, material, and the work of man.

Though set in a poor Los Angeles neighborhood, where "the poorer families" live in "one-time motels," Steele's poem lingers lovingly on the beauty and serenity to be found there. In Gunn's case, the "work of man" manifests itself in "hard ornaments," while in "Near Olympic," it does so in the kind of nature the speaker finds in this urban setting—not lush forests, raging torrents, or awe-inspiring mountains, but nature domesticated, nurtured, and controlled by humans. And, to him, it is beautiful. He lists examples of the natural bounty in this "neighborhood of nurseries / And of good gardeners," from the "Sweet corn and yellow squash" to the "bonsai." Sadness and hopelessness exist here, but they intermingle with joy, which is found in the exuberant children, the abundant vegetation, and even the "flame-painted . . . Mustangs and Chevelles."

"The Wartburg, 1521–1522," which also appears in *Sapphics Against Anger*, depicts the thoughts of Martin Luther as he "broods" in a garden. Here, Luther is neither the fiery orator railing against the idolatrous excesses of the Catholic Church nor the subversive critic secretly nailing the Ninety-Five Theses to the cathedral door. Instead, he is cowed, hiding out, biding his time walking in a garden and thinking spiritual thoughts. He is a diminished figure, suffering at least temporarily from a failure of nerve. This Luther is ever-devout, however, believing that everything in the world can be read in a theological sense, "like clues from which may be inferred / Imperatives of the Almighty's word" and that "nature veils . . . a master plan": a hare being "savage[d]" by a pair of dogs, for instance, represents "frail Man," and the two dogs represent "the Pope and the Devil." When he has occasional doubts, he trusts that God has "arranged" the world so that "even doubt / Is simply a predestined mood." The poem's narrator sees things more skeptically: Luther "justifies" and "works out" his beliefs, using his intellect to interpret the world and *make* it fit what he believes. As Luther leaves "The garden where he broods," the narrator emphasizes that the situation is less certain in his own mind than it is in Luther's:

> Even this last scene's ambiguously spliced:
> The bridge creaks down, he rides across;
> His mount's as humble as the mount of Christ;
> And, see, out there above the Schloss,
> A widening band of chimney smoke is curled
> Vaguely downwind, toward the modern world.

The diction hints at a skeptical viewpoint. A scene in a film that is *spliced* has been cut, edited, and modified to eliminate what doesn't fit and to make it say what its editor wants it to say. The narrator might say that Luther is usually such an editor but that, here, some other editor—whoever that may be—has not created a tidy and unambiguous "scene" that can be easily interpreted to fit God's "design." While a determinedly devout soul might interpret the "chimney smoke" as a symbol of God's presence, the narrator sees it as, simply, smoke. "The modern world" is waiting, unavoidably, "downwind." Luther's kind of faith will not survive much longer.

Most tellingly, Steele's poem is an "essayistic," almost analytical discussion of Luther's beliefs. It forcefully states a thesis, contains supporting examples, and employs comparison and contrast. It also uses "arguing connectives" much like those for which the Movement writers were criticized: "Odd, how his genius courts expectancy, / And views life as a text it's read" and "Yet others, seeking God in all they see, / Not finding Him, will claim He's dead. . . ." John Lucas, as seen earlier, criticized the New Formalists for the kind of "on-the-one-hand-but-on-the-other sort of balance" and "dithering binaries" found throughout Movement poetry.

Steele's "Mockingbird" (1984) and Gunn's "Patch Work" (1992) may represent a surprising inversion of the expected relationship between an older poet and a younger one.[467] That is, Gunn's poem may be an answer to Steele's. Both are about the song of the mockingbird and its combination of artistry and imitation. Both are also about poetry. The mockingbird does not have a song of its own; it derives its music from other birds, quoting snippets of their calls and constantly combining and recombining them in an ever-changing musical collage.[468] As Steele describes it, the mockingbird "does his imitations all day long. / Appropriating every voice he hears." This "singer" demands attention—and deserves it—for, "astonishingly shifting vocal gears," he "chirrups, trills, and whistles" in a virtuosic performance. Yet he is no more than an imitator. If Steele's judgment is applied to poets, he is clearly expressing some approval of the persistence, boldness, and "virtuosity of tone" of those who, like the mockingbird, brilliantly imitate others, but that approval is limited, to say the least. The speaker disapproves of such poets for a number of reasons, including their imitative behavior. If they receive inadequate "notice," they engage in a "hectoring barrage." Their "manner" is "pertinacious." They perform "erratically," "tirelessly," and "crazily" to produce "inflated noise." They steal "words" from "smaller, lesser" poets, then use those "words" to "refute" those very same poets. The speaker pities the mockingbird, for "the sequences he invents / Are born of urgent pathos, in this sense: / For all his virtuosity of tone, / The singer has no note which is his own."

Although the poem depicts mockingbirds—and the poets who resemble them—in condescending and critical ways, it also, intentionally or not, depicts the way that creativity works, according to many modernist and postmodernist theorists. In their view, artists and writers can never be truly original; the language and the ideas that they use are "always already" present, not unique to them. Steele's poem implicitly argues with this viewpoint. In addition, it calls to mind the notion of "signifying," as described in Chapter Two. The mockingbird's songs represent signifying because of the way he irreverently steals phrases from others—the "real" songbirds—then creates new melodies by rearranging and otherwise toying with these "stolen" phrases. Whether or not Steele has ideas like these in mind, it is clear that his poem is not, to put it mildly, a positive view of poets who do nothing more than imitate or steal from others.

Gunn's "Patch Work" opens with an implicitly derogatory description from "the bird book," which states that mockingbirds are "common" and "conspicuous," but the poem questions those terms. It offers a much more positive view of mockingbirds—and hence the poets who resemble them—than that offered in Steele's poem. Granted, Gunn specifies that the mockingbird is "Suburban," presumably suggesting that it is ordinary, by no means exotic or rare. It also lacks soaring ambitions; instead, it "sweeps at a moderate height." Just as in Steele's poem, this bird is an imitator, even a thief, singing a "repertoire of songs that it has heard /—From other birds, and others of its kind," and "has recombined" the songs of other birds. Here, however, when the bird takes these songs, they become "its own." The "sexual longings" that the bird expresses contribute power to the song, "almost" allowing it to "[mount] to / Fulfilment that does not destroy / The original." The longings also "give / . . . muscular vigour to a note so strong." Gunn sees the mockingbird as a creative figure motivated by many of the same urges as human artists. Its "plangent notes" and its "trills" are "Lifted upon the wing / Of that patched body, that insistence / Which fills the gardens up with headlong song." Gunn shares Steele's view of the mockingbird as noisy and insistent, but, unlike Steele, he does not see these traits as negative. Instead, for Gunn, the bird is a determined little artist living in a "patched body" and working with limited resources, yet still producing "muscular" notes and "headlong song." Even if it is a clown, a ragamuffin, and a musical plagiarist, it is still an artist.

Gunn suggests that the mockingbird's songs are "derivative," and he overtly labels its "sexual longings" as such. Most poets and other artists would be insulted by this term, but Gunn does not necessarily see "derivative" as in insult. In fact, in an essay called "Adventurous Song," he says that Robert Duncan was "proud to call himself a derivative poet."[469] Here Gunn takes what might be seen as a postmodernist view of creativity: artists may try to conceal their "debts," but they are inevitable. Although he compares the process to cannibalism, such artistic borrowing is, for him, simply a fact:

> We are all, of course, derivative, but most of us try to cover up our debts when we are aware of them, and to present our work as self-sufficient and self-originating. We are warned by the example of . . . Theodore Roethke, who acknowledged "I take this cadence from a man named Yeats," but took it without adding enough of his own. . . . Duncan too fed on those he admired, but like a true cannibal he digested their virtues to make them his, and they rose in him with a fresh life, both recognizable and altered.[470]

It is not difficult to imagine Gunn saying that the mockingbird is like Duncan: it is "derivative," cannibalizing the "virtues" of other bird-artists, but when it does, those virtues "[rise] . . . with a fresh life, both recognizable and altered." For Steele, the mockingbird-poet is an attention-hungry imitator who mindlessly steals from others and who deserves to be criticized or at least gently ridiculed. For Gunn, it has nothing to be ashamed of. It is an artist in its own right, and its "headlong song" is as legitimate as anyone's.

Gunn has been an inspiration to Steele (and to many other young American poets). Gunn and Steele were friends, and they worked together as poets.[471] They also, at times, found themselves on opposite sides in poetic and critical arguments. If Gunn's poem is a reply to Steele's—and a strong case can be made that it is—this strikes me as a cantankerous but charming twist on the usual relationship between an older poet and a younger one.[472] Ironically, in their younger days, both the Movement writers and the New Formalists depicted themselves as more *sensible* than many of their elders. Here, Gunn irreverently presents ideas that may be intended to challenge the more traditional and supposedly "sensible" ideas of the younger Steele.

In many cases, the poems of the New Formalists act very much like moments in an amiable conversation with their Movement forebears. Gioia's "View from the Second Story" echoes the setting, situation, and mood of Larkin's "Waiting for breakfast, while she brushed her hair." While there are differences, Gioia does not appear to be contending with the ideas in Larkin's poem. Instead, he seems to explore the same topic as Larkin while creating a poem that is by no means a mere "imitation" of the original. Although Gioia's "In Cheever Country" is far from identical to Larkin's "The Whitsun Weddings" or Davie's "In the Stopping Train," the differences do not suggest that Gioia is arguing with either. In its violence and theological focus, Gioia's "The Homecoming" is radically different from the poems that may have inspired it, but it does not appear to be intended as a quarrel with them. Mark Jarman's "The Home" faithfully echoes Larkin's "The Old Fools" and "The Building," and his "My Parents Have Come Home Laughing" almost reverently reiterates the theme of Larkin's "Coming." Jarman's "Greensleeves" and "Between Flights" serve almost as affirmations of the poems by Larkin and Davie that could have inspired them. Similarly, several of Steele's poems, including "Coming Now," "Old Letters," "Sapphics Against Anger," "Vermont Spring," "Small Lives," "From a Rooftop," "Near Olympic," and "The Wartburg," could be described as friendly replies to poems by Larkin or by Gunn.

A number of poems by these New Formalists, in contrast, seem intended to *counter* poems by the Movement writers, perhaps because of ideological, historical, or cultural differences. Gioia seems attracted to the Movement idea that being good at failing is an oxymoronic type of success, but not to the Movement implication that ambition is so dangerous that it must be resisted at all costs. His "The Room Upstairs" is such a compassionate poem that it may well be a deliberate counterpoint to "Mr Bleaney." Also, the religious and philosophical thinking suggested by Gioia's "The Burning Ladder" is quite different from that implied by Gunn's "Lazarus Not Raised" and Davie's "Jacob's Ladder." The same is true of Jarman's "Comparisons of Wonder," which shares the religious and philosophical doubt of Davie's "The Evangelist" and Larkin's "Faith Healing," but not the utter skepticism and near-contempt found in those poems, especially Larkin's. Steele, too, seems attracted to the Movement notion of a restrained, quiet life, but he sees it as one of acceptance and gentleness rather than Movement-like surrender and failure. Despite such variations—and *because* of them—these poems show that Gioia, Jarman, and Steele have significant long-term ties with these three Movement writers.

Surprisingly, Steele seldom disagrees with Gunn or Larkin in any substantive ways. In "Patch Work," however, *Gunn* may be sternly telling off his younger counterpart, whose "Mockingbird" chides "derivative" poets and implies that imitation can never result in originality.

It is ironic that Steele, who has repeatedly said that he has found inspiration in the poetry of many members of the "older generation," would criticize the mockingbird for finding inspiration in the songs of many other birds—except that, in his view, the mockingbird is merely *imitating* the other songs. In the explanation below, he clarifies the distinctions between imitation and inspiration:

> To imitate is to copy or impersonate. In art, it is a student exercise involving the direct mimicking of another artist's manner, in order to understand how he or she arranges and treats material. To be inspired, in contrast, is to have one's soul animated or exalted and moved to independent activity. Inspiration entails a much deeper, more indirect, more diffusive, and more productive influence.[473]

His point is well taken. Nevertheless, I think the juxtapositions and ever-changing variations of the mockingbird's songs make them creative in the sense that Gunn defines the term.[474]

The poems I have discussed in this chapter demonstrate that the New Formalists have often been inspired by the Movement writers in precisely the sense that Steele describes. To continue the mockingbird metaphor, Gioia, Jarman, and Steele have learned their own poetic sequences by engaging with the repertoire of songs written by Davie, Gunn, and Larkin. They have imitated these songs, found inspiration in them, paid homage to them, replied to them, varied them, questioned them, quarreled with them, even added "American" melodies here and there. In this process of learning and borrowing and improvising—and being inspired—they have created songs that are entirely their own.

CHAPTER 6

Concluding Remarks

> *We love Larkin for the moments in which the gloom lifts, but we love him even more for the gloom itself. It is not by proposing an alternative vision in the manner of Yeats or Eliot that Larkin transcends the darkness—whether of modern squalor, or death, or simply the banal disappointments of ordinary late-twentieth-century lives—but by crystallizing it in verse so sharp and exact and surprising that, once read, it is never forgotten.*[475]
>
> —*Katha Pollitt*

As shown in the preceding chapters—and even in the above poems—many New Formalists have strong ties with the work of the Movement writers, especially Davie, Gunn, and Larkin. They have long admired these elders, and they appear to have actively responded to their poetry and, in some cases, their criticism. While the New Formalist responses have usually been respectful, if not downright affectionate, it is important to reiterate that even those "conversations" that are contentious serve as evidence of such a relationship.

Why is this important? Because the examination of the personal and textual connections between and among the New Formalists and Movement writers enriches our understanding of both groups.

First, it adds a new and unanticipated chapter to the history of the Movement, something that becomes particularly meaningful when one remembers that both the Movement writers and the New Formalists have argued for the need to pay attention to poets who are underappreciated, especially those who tend to be shunned by the mainstream. The Movement writers have not been forgotten in the United States, but many American poets and critics see them as decidedly unfashionable. I suspect that these same dissenters are familiar with a handful of Larkin's poems, including "Home is So Sad," "This Be the Verse," "Church Going," "High Windows," and "The Whitsun Weddings." They probably know Gunn's early poems about alienated bikers and other outsiders and may know his later poems depicting the tragedy of AIDS. They may be familiar with his interest in both free verse and formal verse. They may respect Davie as a critic while knowing very little about his poetry. Amis is known only as a novelist. Conquest may be known as a specialist in Soviet history, especially that of the Stalinist period, but he is not well known as a poet. Enright, Jennings, Holloway, and Wain are almost totally unknown. In such an atmosphere, it is fortunate that the New Formalists found the Movement writers and turned to them for inspiration.

I hope that the examination in the preceding chapters has also resulted in a deeper and broader understanding of the writings of the Movement writers and the New Formalists. The poems that I have discussed (and some that I have not) strongly suggest that the younger generation of writers have absorbed ideas, themes, images, metaphors, techniques, and even language from Davie, Gunn, and Larkin, and that they have refracted these through lenses that are distinctively American or trans-Atlantic. The resultant poems are different from the originals, modified by the New Formalists to suit their own strengths, interests, experiences, beliefs, ideas, and occasionally, perhaps, their Americanness. These poems support Gunn's argument that "derivative" poets have nothing to be ashamed of, for the New Formalists appear to have done exactly as Robert Duncan did (in Gunn's estimation): "Duncan too fed on those he admired, but like a true cannibal he digested their virtues to make them his, and they rose in him with a fresh life, both recognizable and altered."[476]

The New Formalists have likewise taken in the work of their predecessors, resulting in poems that contain—"both recognizable and altered"—a number of the virtues and, perhaps, limitations of the Movement. Many New Formalists, like the mockingbird in Gunn's poem "Patch Work," have not only heard and admired the "repertoire of songs" written by Davie, Gunn, and Larkin but have also borrowed freely from that repertoire. The New Formalists have appropriated the "plangent notes" and "trills" of these Movement writers, creating "headlong song[s]" of their own. The resulting poems are much more than mere imitations or echoes, consisting of much more than "virtuosity of tone," a phrase Steele uses in his negative assessment of mockingbird-poets. Indeed, a substantial number of the New Formalist poems are equal in quality to the English poems that have evidently inspired them.

An examination of the connections that the New Formalists have with the Movement writers adds to our understanding of the younger poets themselves, providing at least partial answers to questions such as these: Where and how did the New Formalists first become acquainted with the Movement writers? To which Movement writers have the New Formalists been attracted and why? What obstacles have stood between the thoroughly American New Formalists and their acquaintance with these thoroughly English poets? What are the particular characteristics, themes, and ideas of the Movement that have interested the New Formalists? And which characteristics, themes, and ideas have the New Formalists either disregarded or failed to notice? For instance, is it significant that the Movement writers often argued against ambition, but that the New Formalists don't seem to have adopted that viewpoint? What about the Movement's (very British, it seems to me) skepticism towards shamanism and religious faith? And the Movement's occasional emphasis on social class? What impact has the relationship between the two groups had on the ideas, the poetry, and the criticism of the younger poets? Has the relationship *benefitted* them? Has it made their poetry or their criticism *different* from that written by other Americans?[477]

In the preceding chapters, I have dealt with most of these questions. Here, I shall venture some additional answers, which will, of necessity, be brief and speculative. Several emphases of the New Formalists that distinguish them from many other American poets and critics can be traced, in part, to the Movement: their self-depiction as sensible "clerks" rather than irrational "bards"; their insistence that suburban and white-collar lives are worthy subjects for poetry; their determination to reappraise underappreciated writers; and their efforts to write intelligent poetry and criticism capable of reaching audiences inside and outside academia. I find these emphases appealing, for they strike me as democratic and unpretentious. A number of American poets helped to inspire the New Formalists' interest in poetic traditions that have often been condemned as obsolete or worse, but the Movement writers have also been important in this respect. Although I enjoy both formal and free verse, I believe that the poetry written by the New Formalists often benefits from these lessons in form taught by various peers and predecessors, some hailing from this side of the Atlantic, some from the other.[478]

Have the New Formalists moved beyond the homogeneity that characterized the Movement? To a large degree, they have. Although New Formalism began as a loosely organized group of men, women quickly became both active and prominent in its ranks. Although the movement includes award-winning African American, Asian-American, and Hispanic poets, it is still largely homogeneous in terms of race. In recent years, at least six New Formalists have lived outside the United States, from Canada to France to Australia.[479] New Formalists seem to reject the uglier tendencies of the Movement itself (just as most of the *Movement* writers soon did). Off-putting Movement traits such as passivity, sexism, nihilism, political apathy, and philistinism rarely appear in the New Formalist poetry or criticism with which I am familiar. Many New Formalists have been admirably open, demonstrating a willingness to consider modernist and postmodernist ideas and approaches; reaching far beyond Western literature in their search for viable poetic models; redefining the very concept of "form" in fairly broad ways; and insisting that both free verse and formal poetry are equally legitimate options for poets. In these ways, Davie and Gunn have served as models of poetic and critical openness and flexibility.

Several goals of the Movement poets strike me as especially worthy of emulation. First, they wanted to write poetry that would appeal to a variety of readers, which they hoped to accomplish by using accessible language, by taking advantage of traditional poetic resources such as rhyme and meter, by broadening the scope of permissible subjects for poetry, and by avoiding what they saw as overly ornate metaphors and allusions. To be sure, not all of the Movement writers were interested in appealing to so-called ordinary readers. Indeed, they were sometimes unbearably snobbish. Even the very notion of reaching out to ordinary readers is laden with contradictions, but I still find much to respect in it (perhaps because, coming from a working-class background, I count myself among those readers).[480]

In addition, I appreciate the Movement's argument that poets share crucial responsibilities with other citizens. Poets, they maintained, should be contributing members of society, neither self-indulgent *artistes* who shut themselves away from the realities of daily life nor exhibitionists who surrender to voyeuristic pressures "to let down their hair in public, to undress in public, to let the reader into affairs which older generations would have regarded as private or intimate."[481] To avoid writing poetry that seems bland, hesitant, timid, or even cowardly, the Movement writers argued that poets must take care not to go to extremes in their efforts to be fair, to be judicious, to be precise. No doubt, they often failed to live up to their goals, but they were worthy goals nonetheless.

As critic Stephen Regan has suggested, it is long past time for a reassessment: "Movement poetry probably displays far more diversity and daring than subsequent critical accounts have given it credit for. Literary history has too readily equated the work of the Movement with parochialism and provincialism. Looking back on Conquest's anthology is to be reminded of the cosmopolitan, international interests of several contributors."[482] Regan makes a good point. Much of Davie's poetry, for instance, is cosmopolitan and international in its settings, its subjects, and even its origins (as illustrated by his numerous translations from the Russian). Much the same could be said of Gunn's poetry, and Enright's is decidedly international. And even when Larkin is guilty of "parochialism and provincialism," his best poems transcend such limitations. I readily concede that Movement ideology itself was flawed, tending to be smug, emotionally stunted, ethnocentric, xenophobic, and reactionary; however, the individual members of the group often transcend these weaknesses.

The New Formalists have, at times, exhibited their own array of unattractive traits, have occasionally made intemperate and inaccurate statements, and have written their share of mediocre poetry and ill-advised criticism. Nevertheless, they have had admirable goals and accomplishments of their own, some of which I see as especially important. For one thing, before the New Formalists came along, American poets and critics seemed largely to have washed their hands of poetic traditions predating the modernist era. In the United States, the insistence that formal verse is outdated and repressive, while free verse is democratic and modern, was, for many decades, largely unquestioned. Schoolchildren are often still taught that rhyming poems are old-fashioned and immature. Such teachings are absurd oversimplifications of modernist ideas, but they are widespread. Critical articles, manifestos, and poetry written by New Formalists, as well as conferences organized by them, have encouraged poets, critics, academics, and schoolteachers to rethink these attitudes. Perhaps the New Formalists have succeeded in their efforts to demonstrate that renewing what is old is a legitimate enterprise for poets (and other artists) and that rhyme, meter, and traditional forms can be the opposite of elitist or anti-democratic.[483]

Their mutual insistence that rhyme, meter, form, imagery, language, and other aspects of poetry are far more than surface concerns is one of the most significant parallels between the two groups—and it may be among their most significant legacies. Other writers have focused attention on such matters, but the New Formalists and the Movement writers have done so more extensively than most. I understand them to be saying that poetry is *worth* the effort. The Movement insistence on the responsibility of the writer has much the same impact. Of course, poetry that merely entertains also has a vital place in literature and in culture. The Movement writers and the New Formalists, who have written their share of light verse, comic verse, and largely plot-driven narrative verse, would undoubtedly agree. However, as Davie has said, poetry should do more than serve as a "curious entrancing murmur in the background."[484]

Given the Movement writers' perpetual tendency to dismiss their own group association as minor, short-lived, "loose," "foolish," "false"—and, finally, "dead"—it is satisfyingly ironic that their ideas and their poetry live on in these younger writers.[485] Regardless of how "loose" or "foolish" their coalition allegedly was, there is no doubt that the Movement writers, and their poetry, criticism, and manifestos, have had a sustained, critical influence on the New Formalists.

WORKS CITED

Acheson, James, and Romana Huk, editors. *Contemporary British Poetry: Essays in Theory and Criticism*. Albany, NY: State Univ. of NY Press, 1996.

Allen, Dick. Email interviews. 26 March 2002; 6 January 2004.

—. Email to author. 1 Sept. 2017.

—. "The Gift to Be Simple." *Poetry* 124.2 (May 1974): 103–116.

—, guest ed. *Crosscurrents* 8.2 (January 1989). Special Issue: "Expansionist [sic] Poetry: The New Formalism and the New Narrative."

—. "Overcoming the Tic of Techniques: The Emergence of Expansive Poetry." *Expansive Poetry and Music Online*. 17 Jan. 2002. Online at https://www2.southeastern.edu/Academics/Faculty/jbedell/exp.html.

—. "The Poetry Village." *Poetry* CXIX.2 (Nov. 1971): 109–111.

Amis, Kingsley. *Memoirs*. New York: Summit Books, 1991.

Atkinson, Donald. "An Interesting American Poet." *Spokes* 20 (Winter 1991): 64–66.

Baer, William. "An Interview with Timothy Steele." *The Formalist* 14 (Winter/Spring 2003): 20–40.

—. "Robert Conquest." *Fourteen on Form: Conversations with Poets*. Jackson, MS: Univ. Press of Mississippi, 2004. 120–136.

Barron, Jonathan, and Bruce Meyer. Introduction. *Dictionary of Literary Biography, Vol. 282: New Formalist Poets*. A Bruccoli Clark Layman Book. Detroit: Thomson Gale, 2003. xvii–xxii.

Bartlett, Lee. "Thom Gunn: 'For a Sign of Other Than Love'." *Talking Poetry: Conversations in the Workshop with Contemporary Poets*. Albuquerque: Univ. of New Mexico Press, 1987. 87–106.

Bergonzi, Bernard. "Davie, Larkin, and the State of England." *Contemporary Literature* 18.3 (Summer 1977): 343–360.

Bezner, Kevin. "An Interview with Dana Gioia." *Main Street Rag* 5.4 (Winter 2000): 35–46.

Bloom, Harold. *The Anxiety of Influence: A Theory of Poetry*. 2nd Edition. New York/Oxford: Oxford University Press, 1973, 1997.

Bowers, Edgar, et al. *A Few Friends: Poems for Thom Gunn's 60th Birthday*. Walkerton, Ontario, Canada: Stonyground Press, 1989.

Bradley, Jerry. *The Movement: British Poets of the 1950s*. New York: Twayne Publishers, 1993.

Brainard, Dulcy. Review of *Questions for Ecclesiastes*. *Publishers Weekly* 243.52 (30 Dec. 1996): 62.

Brame, Gloria G. "An Interview with Poet and Critic Dana Gioia. Paradigms Lost: Parts One & Two." *ELF: Eclectic Literary Forum*. Spring 1995. Online at http://danagioia.com/interviews/paradigms-lost-interview-with-gloria-brame/.

Breslin, Paul. "Two Cheers for the New Formalism." *Kenyon Review* 13.2 (Spring 1991): 143–148.

Brownjohn, Alan. "Elizabeth Jennings." *The Oxford Companion to Twentieth-Century Poetry in English*. Ed. Ian Hamilton. Oxford: Oxford Univ. Press, 1994. 254–255. (The author of this entry is identified only by the initials *AB*, but the list of contributors names the author as Alan Brownjohn.)

—. "A View of English Poetry in the Seventies." *British Poetry Since 1960*. Ed. Michael Schmidt and Grevel Lindop. Manchester: Carcanet Press, 1972. 240–249.

Byers, Thomas B. "The Closing of the American Line: Expansive Poetry and Ideology." *Contemporary Literature* 33.2 (1992): 396–415.

Cable, Thomas. "Connoisseurs of Sound and the New Formalism." *Revue Française d'Etudes Americaines* 84 (March 2000): 48–60.

Cambridge, Gerry. "Editorial." *The Dark Horse* 9/10 (Summer 2000): 4–7.

—. "The New Formalism." *Oxford Encyclopedia of American Literature*. Ed. Jay Parini. Oxford: Oxford University Press, 2003. 251–258.

Carlisle, Henry. "Letter to the Editor." *Northwest Review* 27.2 (July 1989): 11–13.

Chapman, Con. "The Life and Death of Rachel Wetzsteon." *Easy Street: A Magazine of Words and Culture.* 25 May 2015. Online at http://www.easystreetmag.com/life-and-death-of-rachel-wetzsteon/.

Chappell, Fred. "Once Upon a Time: Narrative Poetry Returns?" Georgia Review 46.2 (Summer 1992): 366–379.

Conquest, Robert. "But What Good Came of It At Last? An Inquest on Modernism." *Essays by Divers Hands.* Ed. Michael Holroyd. Bury St. Edmunds, England: St. Edmundsbury Press, 1982. (First presented as the Giff Edmonds Memorial Lecture in 1979.)

—. Letter to the author. 15 Oct. 2001.

—. Letter to the editor of *The New Statesman.* 7 June 1971. (I have quoted from a photocopy of the letter given to me by Robert Conquest.)

—, editor. *New Lines: An Anthology.* London: MacMillan & Co. Ltd., 1956, 1962.

—, editor. *New Lines II: An Anthology.* London: Macmillan & Co. Ltd., 1963.

—. Personal interview. 28 Dec. 2001.

—. "The Poetics of Procrustes." *The Abomination of Moab.* London: Maurice Temple Smith Ltd, 1979. 2–13.

—. "Saturnine Daylight: Roy Fuller." *The Abomination of Moab.* London: Maurice Temple Smith Ltd, 1979. 25–29.

Conte, Joseph M. *Unending Design: The Forms of Postmodern Poetry.* Ithaca and London: Cornell Univ. Press, 1991.

Corcoran, Neil. *English Poetry Since 1940.* Longman Literature in English Series. General Editors David Carroll and Michael Wheeler. London/New York: Longman, 1993.

Corrie, Daniel. "Beyond Formalism: The New Traditionalism." *The William and Mary Review* 27 (1989): 40–47.

—. "New Formalism and New Traditionalism." *Hellas* 2.2 (Fall 1991): 295–300.

Crozier, Andrew. "Thrills and Frills: Poetry As Figures of Empirical Lyricism." *Society and Literature 1945–1970.* Ed. Alan Sinfield. The Context of

English Literature Series. New York: Holmes & Meier Publishers, Inc., 1983. 199–233.

Dacey, Philip. "Loving Limits: Teaching the Use of Traditional Poetic Forms in the Classroom." *Freedom and Form: Essays in Contemporary American Poetry*. Ed. Esther Giger and Agnieszka Salska. Łódź: Univwersytetu Łódzkiego: 1998. 136–143.

Dacey, Philip, and David Jauss, editors. *Strong Measures: Contemporary American Poetry in Traditional Forms*. Foreword by Richard Wilbur. New York: Harper and Row, 1986.

Davidson, Chad. "Lathework: An Interview with B. H. Fairchild." *The Writer's Chronicle* 37.4 (Feb. 2005): 4–10.

Davie, Donald. *Collected Poems*. Ed. Neil Powell. Manchester, UK: Carcanet, 2002.

—. "Letter from England." *Parnassus: Poetry in Review* 6.1 (Fall/Winter 1977): 129–137.

—. "Lucky Jim and the Hobbits." *Thomas Hardy and British Poetry*. New York: Oxford University Press, 1972. 83–104.

—. "Post-modernism, Craft, and the Market for Poetry." *PN Review* 17.1 (Sept./Oct. 1991): 17–19.

—. *Purity of Diction in English Verse*. New York: Schocken Books, 1967. (First published in 1952.)

—. "Remembering the Movement." *With the Grain: Essays on Thomas Hardy and Modern British Poetry*. Ed. Clive Wilmer. Manchester, UK: Carcanet, 1998. 199–203.

—. "See, and Believe." *With the Grain: Essays on Thomas Hardy and Modern British Poetry*. Ed. Clive Wilmer. Manchester, UK: Carcanet, 1998. 192–198.

—. "Some Notes on Rhythm in Verse." *Trying to Explain*. Poets on Poetry Series. Series Ed. Donald Hall. Ann Arbor: University of Michigan Press, 1979. 199–202.

—. "Talking with Millicent Dillon." *Trying to Explain*. Poets on Poetry Series. Series Ed. Donald Hall. Ann Arbor: University of Michigan Press, 1979. 27–48.

—. *Thomas Hardy and British Poetry*. New York: Oxford University Press, 1972.

Dawson, Ariel. "The Yuppie Poet." *AWP Newsletter* (May 1985): 5–6. (Now called *AWP Writer's Chronicle*.)

Dennis, Helen. "Is Wyatt to Petrarch as Ezra Pound to Arnaut Daniel?" *Ezra Pound and Europe*. Ed. Richard Taylor and Claus Melchior. Rodopi: Amsterdam/Atlanta, 1993. 33–49.

D'Evelyn, Thomas. "Poetry That Matters: A Plunge Into Shared Experience." *The Christian Science Monitor* (2 July 1991): 14.

Dirda, Michael. "The Movement." *Grand Street* 6 (Spring 1987): 203–208.

Doerr, Joe Francis. "New Formalism." *Encyclopedia of American Poetry: The Twentieth Century*. Ed. Eric L. Haralson. Chicago, London: Fitzroy Dearborn Publishers, 2001. 503–506.

Durkin, Kevin. "An Interview with Timothy Steele." *Able Muse* 2000. 25 Sept. 2002. Online at http://www.ablemuse.com/2k/kdurkin-steele.htm.

Easthope, Anthony. "Donald Davie and the Failure of Englishness." *Contemporary British Poetry: Essays in Theory and Criticism*. Ed. James Acheson and Romana Huk. Albany, NY: State Univ. of NY Press, 1996. 17–33.

Enright, D. J. Letter to the author. 30 May 2001.

Feirstein, Frederick, ed. *Expansive Poetry: Essays on the New Narrative and the New Formalism*. Introduction with Frederick Turner. Santa Cruz, CA: Story Line Press, 1989.

Feirstein, Frederick, and Frederick Turner. Introduction. *Expansive Poetry: Essays on the New Narrative and the New Formalism*. Santa Cruz, CA: Story Line Press, 1989. vii–xv.

Finch, Annie, ed. *After New Formalism: Poets on Form, Narrative, and Tradition*. Ashland, OR: Story Line Press, 1999.

—. "Confessions of a Postmodern Poetess." *By Herself: Women Reclaim Poetry*. Ed. Molly McQuade. Saint Paul, MN: Graywolf Press, 2000. 213–225.

—. Email interviews. 17 Dec. 2001; 30 June 2004.

—. Email to the author. 25 Aug. 2000.

—, editor. *A Formal Feeling Comes: Poems in Form by Contemporary Women.* Ed. Annie Finch. Ashland, OR: Storyline Press, 1994.

—. *The Ghost of Meter: Culture and Prosody in American Free Verse.* Ann Arbor: Univ. of Michigan Press, 2000. (First published 1993.)

—. "In Defense of Meter." *The Body of Poetry: Essays on Women, Form, and the Poetic Self.* Ann Arbor: The Univ. of Michigan Press, 2005. 153–156. (Originally published in *Hellas*, Spring 1990.)

Finch, Annie, and Kathrine Varnes. "Omniformalism: A Manifesto." *The Body of Poetry: Essays on Women, Form, and the Poetic Self.* Ann Arbor: The Univ. of Michigan Press, 2005. 22–23.

—, eds. *An Exaltation of Forms: Contemporary Poets Celebrate the Diversity of Their Art.* Ann Arbor: The University of Michigan Press, 2002.

Flamm, Matthew. "Yearning Disabled." *The Village Voice* (August 19, 1986): 45. (Review of Dana Gioia's *Daily Horoscope.*)

Flinn, Mary. "An Interview with Mark Jarman." *Blackbird: An Online Journal of Literature and the Arts.* Fall 2002. Online at http://www.blackbird.vcu.edu/v1n2/features/jarman_m_120202/jarman_m_text.htm.

Foley, Jack. Emails to the author. 12 October 2004.

—. "*Interrogations at Noon*: Reviewed by Jack Foley." *Alsop Review.* 12 Oct. 2004. (Originally published online, but no longer available in this format.)

Fowler, Alastair. "Poetry Since 1950." *The Twentieth Century.* Penguin History of Literature. Vol. 7. Ed. Martin Dodsworth. London: Penguin Books Ltd., 345–374.

Frost, Robert. *The Poetry of Robert Frost.* Ed. Edward Connery Lathem. New York: Holt, Rinehart and Winston, 1969.

Gery, John. Emails to the author. 19 May 2005; 22 May 2005.

—. "The Paradox of Form." *Verse.* Special Edition: The New Formalism in American Poetry. Guest Editor Robert McPhillips. 7.3 (Winter 1990): 40–41.

Giles, Paul. "From Myth Into History: The Later Poetry of Thom Gunn and Ted Hughes." *Contemporary British Poetry: Essays in Theory and Criticism.* Ed. James Acheson and Romana Huk. Albany, NY: State Univ. of NY Press, 1996. 143–173.

Gioia, Dana. "The Barrier of a Common Language: New British Poetry in the Eighties." *Barrier of a Common Language: An American Looks at British Poetry*. Ann Arbor: The Univ. of Michigan Press, 2003. 1–19. (First published in 1984, in *The Hudson Review* 37.1, pages 6–20. Reviews *Contemporary British Poetry*, ed. by Blake Morrison and Andrew Motion; *Some Contemporary Poets of Britain and Ireland: An Anthology*, ed. by Michael Schmidt; and collections by Tom Paulin, Craig Raine, Christopher Reid, Douglas Dunn, and James Fenton.)

—. *Can Poetry Matter? Essays on Poetry and American Culture*. St. Paul, MN: Graywolf Press, 1992.

—. "Connect the Prose and the Passion." *Dark Horse* 1 (Spring 1995): 18–21.

—. *Daily Horoscope*. St. Paul, MN: Graywolf Press, 1986, 2002.

—. "The Dilemma of the Long Poem." *Can Poetry Matter? Essays on Poetry and American Culture*. St. Paul, MN: Graywolf Press, 1992. 25–30.

—. "Donald Davie." *Sequoia* 22.2 (Winter 1977/8): 16–19.

—. Emails to the author. 20 May 2004; 25 June 2004; 16 May 2005.

—. "Fallen Western Star: The Decline of San Francisco as a Literary Region." *The "Fallen Western Star" Wars: A Debate About Literary California*. Ed. Jack Foley. Oakland, CA: Scarlet Tanager Books: 2001. 7–26. (First published in the Winter 1999–2000 issue of *Hungry Mind Review*.)

—, ed. *Formal Introductions: An Investigative Anthology*. West Chester, PA: Aralia Press, 1994.

—. *The Gods of Winter*. Saint Paul, MN: Graywolf Press, 1991.

—. *Interrogations at Noon*. Saint Paul, MN: Graywolf Press, 2001.

—. Interview conducted by post. May 2001.

—. "An Interview with Donald Davie." *Sequoia* 22.2 (Winter 1977/8): 21–27. (Later published as "Talking with Dana Gioia" in *Trying to Explain*, 203–213.)

—. Introduction. *The Diviners*. Robert McDowell. Cornwall, UK: Peterloo Poets, 1995. ix–xiii.

—. Letters to the author. 2 January 2001; 12 April 2004.

—. "A Map of *The Shires*." *Donald Davie and the Responsibilities of Literature*. Ed. George Dekker. Manchester, UK: Carcanet Press / Orono, ME: The National Poetry Foundation, 1983. 103–111.

—. "Notes on the New Formalism." *Expansive Poetry: Essays on the New Narrative and the New Formalism*. Ed. Frederick Feirstein. Santa Cruz, CA: Story Line Press, 1989. 158–175. (Also published in *Can Poetry Matter?* 31–45.)

—. Personal interview. 20 Dec. 2001.

—. "A Personal Tour of Donald Davie's Imaginary Museum." *The Southern Review* 15:3 (Summer 1979): 724–729.

—. "Picketing the Zeitgeist Picket." Replies to Diane Wakoski, from Robert Mezey, Lewis Turco, David Radavich, Brian Richards and Dana Gioia. *American Book Review* 8.6 (Nov./Dec. 1986): 3, 23.

—. "The Poet in an Age of Prose." *Can Poetry Matter? Essays on Poetry and American Culture*. St. Paul, MN: Graywolf Press, 1992. 245–257.

—. "Poetry and the Fine Presses." *Hudson Review* 35.3 (Autumn 1982): 483–498. (Reviews poetry by John Quinn, Thom Gunn, W. D. Snodgrass, Galway Kinnell, William Stafford, Edgar Bowers, Turner Cassity, and Charles Gullans.)

—. "Poetry Chronicle." *Hudson Review* 33.4 (Winter 1980–1981): 611–627. (Reviews poetry by Kingsley Amis, Ted Hughes, Joseph Brodsky, Dick Davis, Ted Kooser, Vickie Hearne, and Alfred Corn.)

—. "Poetry Chronicle." *Ontario Review* 19 (Fall/Winter 1983–1984): 99–107. (Reviews poetry by Tom Disch, Timothy Steele, Charles Martin, and Mary Kinzie, as well as translations of poetry by Tadeusz Rozewicz and Sandro Penna.)

—. "The Still, Sad Music of Philip Larkin." *The Washington Post Book World* XXIII: 33 (15 Aug. 1993): 1, 9.

—. "Three Poets in Mid-Career." *Southern Review* 17.3 (July 1981): 667–674. (Reviews poetry by Donald Justice, Anthony Hecht, and Frederick Morgan. Compares Justice to Larkin.)

—. "Top Gunn." *San Francisco Magazine* 46.12 (Dec. 1999): 63.

Gioia, Dana, and Michael J. Smith. Introduction. *Sequoia Twentieth Anniversary Issue: Poetry 1956–1976:* iii–vi.

Gray, Jason. "An Interview with Mark Jarman." *AWP Writer's Chronicle* 39.4 (February 2007): 46–51.

Gray, Richard J. *American Poetry of the Twentieth Century*. Longman Literature in English Series. David Carroll and Michael Wheeler, Gen. Eds. London/New York: Longman Group UK Limited, 1990.

—. Emails to the author. 22 Dec. 2002; 31 March 2003; 16 May 2003; 18 Sept. 2003.

—. Notes to the author. Feb. 2003, Oct. 2003, March 2005 (exact dates not specified).

Gross, Harvey, and Robert McDowell. *Sound and Form in Modern Poetry*. 2nd edition. Ann Arbor: Univ. of Michigan Press, 1996.

Gunn, Thom. "Adventurous Song: Robert Duncan as Romantic Modernist." Shelf Life: Essays, Memoirs, and an Interview. Poets on Poetry Series. Ann Arbor: The University of Michigan Press, 1993. 143–170.

—. "An Anglo-American Poet: Interview with Jim Powell." *Shelf Life: Essays, Memoirs, and an Interview*. Poets on Poetry Series. Ann Arbor: The University of Michigan Press, 1993. 218–230.

—. "Ben Jonson." *The Occasions of Poetry: Essays in Criticism and Autobiography*. Ed. Clive Wilmer. Poets on Poetry Series. Ann Arbor: Univ. of Michigan Press, 1999. 106–117.

—. *Collected Poems*. London: Faber and Faber, 1993.

—. "Enmeshed with Time: The Sixteenth Century." *Shelf Life: Essays, Memoirs, and an Interview*. Poets on Poetry Series. Ann Arbor: The University of Michigan Press, 1993. 3–14.

—. "Fever in the Morning: Jim Powell." *Shelf Life: Essays, Memoirs, and an Interview*. Poets on Poetry Series. Ann Arbor: The University of Michigan Press, 1993. 121–125.

—. "Forays Against the Republic: Whitman." *Shelf Life: Essays, Memoirs, and an Interview*. Poets on Poetry Series. Ann Arbor: The University of Michigan Press, 1993. 15–21.

—. "Immersions." *The Occasions of Poetry: Essays in Criticism and Autobiography*. Ed. Clive Wilmer. Poets on Poetry Series. Ann Arbor: Univ. of Michigan Press, 1999. 138–141. (Reviews Dick Davis's first book, *In The Distance*.)

—. Letter to the author. 27 June 2001.

—. "My Life Up to Now." *The Occasions of Poetry: Essays in Criticism and Autobiography*. Poets on Poetry Series. Ed. Clive Wilmer. Ann Arbor: Univ. of Michigan Press, 1999. 169–186.

—. "On a Drying Hill: Yvor Winters." *Shelf Life: Essays, Memoirs, and an Interview*. Poets on Poetry Series. Ann Arbor: The University of Michigan Press, 1993. 197–212.

—. "Out of the Box: Elizabeth Bishop." *Shelf Life: Essays, Memoirs, and an Interview*. Poets on Poetry Series. Ann Arbor: The University of Michigan Press, 1993. 77–86.

—. Personal interview. 27 Dec. 2001.

—. "Playing Politics with Poetry." *The Threepenny Review* (Summer 1981): 4–5.

—. "A Record: Allen Ginsberg's Poetry." *Shelf Life: Essays, Memoirs, and an Interview*. Poets on Poetry Series. Ann Arbor: The University of Michigan Press, 1993. 102–115.

—. "Responsibilities: Contemporary Poetry and August Kleinzahler." *Shelf Life: Essays, Memoirs, and an Interview*. Poets on Poetry Series. Ann Arbor: The University of Michigan Press, 1993. 22–32.

—. "Three Hard Women: H. D., Marianne Moore, and Mina Loy." *Shelf Life: Essays, Memoirs, and an Interview*. Poets on Poetry Series. Ann Arbor: The University of Michigan Press, 1993. 33–52.

Gunn, Thom, and Ted Hughes. *Selected Poems by Thom Gunn and Ted Hughes*. London: Faber and Faber, 1962.

Gwynn, R. S. Email interviews. 13 March 2003; 13 July 2004.

—, ed. "An Expansive Moment: Introduction to the Revised Edition." *New Expansive Poetry: Theory, Criticism, History*. Ashland, OR: Story Line Press, 1999. 9–14.

—. "*New Poets of England and America*." *The Oxford Companion to Twentieth-Century Poetry in English*. Ed. Ian Hamilton. Oxford: Oxford Univ. Press, 1994. 383–384. (The author of this entry is identified only by the initials *RSG*, but the list of contributors names R. S. Gwynn as the author.)

Hacker, Marilyn. Email interview. 17 April 2003.

Hadas, Rachel. "On Bonnefoy." *Conversant Essays: Contemporary Poets on Poetry*. Ed. James McCorkle. Detroit, MI: Wayne State Univ. Press, 1990. 253–262.

Haines, John. "Formal Objections." *Hudson Review* 43.2 (Summer 1990): 345–351.

—. "Rebels Not Yet Angels." *Sewanee Review* 106.1 (Winter 1998): ii–vi.

Hamburger, Michael. *The Truth of Poetry: Tensions in Modern Poetry from Baudelaire to the 1960s*. New York: Harcourt Brace Jovanovich, 1969.

Hamilton, Ian. "The Making of the Movement." *British Poetry Since 1960: A Critical Survey*. Ed. Michael Schmidt and Grevel Lindop. Oxford: Carcanet Press, 1972. 70–73. (Originally published in *New Statesman* in 1971.)

Hardy, Thomas. *The Selected Poems of Thomas Hardy*. Edited and with an introduction by John Crowe Ransom. London: Macmillan Co., 1960, 1961. Rpt. Collier Books, 1969.

Harvey, Gordon. "Illusions Not Illusions Any Longer." *Sequoia* 28 (Spring 1984): 91–98. (Reviews poetry by Timothy Steele.)

Hatch, James. "Rebels Without a Case." *American Book Review* 19.4 (May-June 1998): 16, 30, 31.

Haven, Cynthia. "The Bards of the 'Burbs." *Philadelphia* 91.11 (Nov. 2000): 65–75.

—. "Interview with Timothy Steele." *The Cortland Review* June 2000. 29 Jan. 2002. Online at http://www.cortlandreview.com/features/00/06/index.html.

—. "Poetic License." *Stanford Magazine* May/June 1999: 64–68.

Hix, H. L. "New Formalism Among the Postmoderns." *Paintbrush* 26 (1999/2000): 146–153.

—. "New Formalism at a Crossroads." *Sparrow* 65 (Sept. 2000): 44–52.

Honicker, Nancy. "Marilyn Hacker's *Love, Death and the Changing of the Seasons*: Writing/Living within Formal Constraints." *Freedom and Form: Essays in Contemporary American Poetry*. Ed. Esther Giger and Agnieszka Salska. Łódź: Univwersytetu Łódzkiego: 1998. 94–103.

Hudgins, Andrew. Email interview. 28 April 2005.

—. "Poetry Chronicle." *Hudson Review* 42.4 (Winter 1990): 675–684. (Reviews poetry by Brooks Haxton, Edward Hirsch, Norman Dubie, Adrienne Rich, and Philip Larkin.)

Huk, Romana. Introduction. *Contemporary British Poetry: Essays in Theory and Criticism*. Ed. James Acheson and Romana Huk. Albany, NY: State Univ. of NY Press, 1996. 1–15.

—. "Poetry of the Committed Individual: Jon Silkin, Tony Harrison, Geoffrey Hill, and the Poets of Postwar Leeds." *Contemporary British Poetry: Essays in Theory and Criticism*. Ed. James Acheson and Romana Huk. Albany, NY: State Univ. of NY Press, 1996. 175–219.

Jarman, Mark. *The Black Riviera*. Middletown, CT: Wesleyan Univ. Press, 1990.

—. "Br'er Rabbit and Br'er Possum: The Americanness of Ezra Pound and T. S. Eliot." *The Secret of Poetry*. Ashland, OR: Story Line Press, 2001. 46–65. (First published in 1994, in *Forked Tongues?: Comparing Twentieth Century British and American Literature*, ed. Ann Massa and Alistair Stead.)

—. Email interviews. 28 May 2001; 13 July 2001; 31 Dec. 2001.

—. Email to the author. 14 Dec. 2001.

—. *Far and Away*. Carnegie-Mellon Univ. Press, 1985.

—. *Iris*. Brownsville, OR: Story Line Press, 1992.

—. *North Sea*. Cleveland, OH: Cleveland State Univ. Poetry Center, 1978.

—. *Questions for Ecclesiastes*. Ashland, OR: Story Line Press, 1997.

—. *The Rote Walker*. Pittsburgh: Carnegie-Mellon Univ. Press, 1981.

—. "A Shared Humanity: 'In the Stopping Train' and 'The Whitsun Weddings'." *On Modern Poetry: Essays Presented to Donald Davie*. Ed. Vereen Bell and Laurence Lerner. Nashville, TN: Vanderbilt Univ. Press, 1988. 89–101.

—. *Unholy Sonnets*. Ashland, OR: Story Line Press, 2000.

Jarman, Mark, and David Mason, eds. *Rebel Angels: 25 Poets of the New Formalism*. Brownsville, OR: Story Line Press, 1996.

Jarman, Mark, and Robert McDowell. "Navigating the Flood." *The Reaper Essays*. Brownsville, OR: Story Line Press, 1996. 3–16.

—. "*The Reaper*'s Non-Negotiable Demands." *The Reaper Essays*. Brownsville, OR: Story Line Press, 1996. 34–44.

Jones, Peter, and Michael Schmidt, eds. Introduction. *British Poetry Since 1970: A Critical Survey*. Manchester, UK: 1980.

Kinzie, Mary. "The Overdefinition of the Now." *American Poetry Review* 11.2 (March-April 1982): 13–17.

Kirby, David. "Free Verse, New Formalism, and the Next Big Thing." *Literary Magazine Review* 11 (1992): 38–42.

Kirby-Smith, H. T. "Behind the Lines." *Southern Review* 35.3 (Summer 1999): 635–650.

Kirsch, Adam. "In Memory, and Admiration, of Rachel Wetzsteon." *The New Republic*. 30 Dec. 2009. Online at https://newrepublic.com/article/72213/rachel-wetzsteon.

Knoll, Robert E. Untitled review. *Prairie Schooner* 60.3 (Fall 1986): 122–125.

Kuzma, Greg. "Dana Gioia and the Poetry of Money." *Northwest Review* 26.3 (Nov. 1988): 111–121.

Lake, Paul. "Disorderly Orders: Free Verse, Chaos, and the Tradition." *The Southern Review* 34.4 (Fall 1998): 780–803.

—. Email interview. 24 May 2004.

—. Email to the author. 21 May 2004.

—. "Old Adam in the New World Garden: Three English Poets." *Threepenny Review* 1.4 (Winter 1981): 9–10.

"Larkin Is Nation's Top Poet." BBC News Online. 15 Oct. 2003. Online at http://news.bbc.co.uk/1/hi/entertainment/arts/3193692.stm.

Larkin, Philip. *Collected Poems*. Ed. Anthony Thwaite. London: Farrar Straus Giroux and The Marvell Press, 1988.

—. "An Interview with *Paris Review*." Interviewed by Robert Phillips. *Required Writing: Miscellaneous Pieces 1955–1982*. Poets on Poetry Series. Series Editor David Lehman. Ann Arbor: Univ. of Michigan Press, 1999. 57–76.

—. "An Interview with *The Observer*." Interviewed by Miriam Gross. *Required Writing: Miscellaneous Pieces 1955–1982*. Poets on Poetry Series. Series

Editor David Lehman. Ann Arbor: Univ. of Michigan Press, 1999. 47–56.

—. "Introduction to *All What Jazz*." *Required Writing: Miscellaneous Pieces 1955–1982*. Poets on Poetry Series. Series Editor David Lehman. Ann Arbor: Univ. of Michigan Press, 1999. 285–298.

—. *Selected Letters of Philip Larkin: 1940–1985*. Ed. Anthony Thwaite. London: Faber & Faber, 1992.

Leary, Paris. "The Movement in England." *Beloit Poetry Journal* 8.2 (Winter 1957–58): 20–22.

Lehman, David. "The Not-So-New Formalism." *Michigan Quarterly Review* 29.1 (Winter 1990): 140–144.

Leithauser, Brad. "The Confinement of Free Verse." *The New Criterion* May 1987: 4–14.

—. "Metrical Illiteracy." *New Expansive Poetry: Theory, Criticism, History*. Ed. R. S. Gwynn. Ashland, OR: Story Line Press, 1999. 148–156.

Lindner, April. "Michael Dana Gioia: A Chronology." *Dana Gioia: A Descriptive Bibliography with Critical Essays*. Ed. Jack W. C. Hagstrom & Bill Morgan. Jackson, MS: Parrish House Books, 2002. ix–xiii.

Link, Franz. "Dana Gioia: Critic and Poet of the New Formalism." *Symbolism: A New International Journal of Critical Aesthetics* 2 (2002): 207–228.

—. "The New Formalism." *Anglistik: Organ des Verbandes Deutscher Anglisten* 8.2 (1997): 81–94.

Locke, Duane. "Trivial or Mechanistic Sound versus Cosmic or Superior Sound." *Mississippi Review* 6.1 (Summer 1977): 10–11.

Lucas, John. "The Tame and the Just?" *Dark Horse* 5 (Summer 1997): 60–64.

Maillard, Keith. "The New Formalism and the Return of Prosody." *New Expansive Poetry: Theory, Criticism, History*. Ed. R. S. Gwynn. Ashland, OR: Story Line Press, 1999. 52–71.

Maio, Samuel. "A Sound and Fruitful Attitude: The Poetry of Robert Conquest, Elizabeth Jennings, and Charles Causley." *The Formalist* 2.2 (1991): 16–31.

"Mark (F.) Jarman." *Contemporary Authors Online*. Gale Group, 2002. 3 July 2003. Online at Gale Literary Databases.

Martin, Bruce. *Philip Larkin*. Twayne's English Authors Series. Boston: G. K. Hall & Co., 1978.

Martin, Charles. Email interview. 16 May 2005.

—. Emails to the author. 16 May 2005.

—. "Just a Smack at Larkin." *Hudson Review* 52.3 (Autumn 1999): 400–401.

—. *Starting from Sleep: New and Selected Poems*. The Sewanee Writers' Series. Woodstock, NY: The Overlook Press, 2002.

Mason, David. "Dana Gioia." *Encyclopedia of American Poetry: The Twentieth Century*. Ed. Eric L. Haralson. Chicago, London: Fitzroy Dearborn Publishers, 2001. 247–248.

—. "Dana Gioia's Case for Poetry." *The Poetry of Life and The Life of Poetry: Essays and Reviews*. Ashland, OR: Story Line Press, 2000. 170–179.

—. Email interviews. 27 May 2001; 19 December 2001; 21 December 2001.

—. Emails to the author: 16 February 2001; 14 December 2001; 20 April 2004; 28 April 2005; 29 April 2005; 2 May 2005; 30 August 2017.

—. "Larking with Larkin." *Sewanee Review* 14.4 (Fall 2006): 528.

—. "Louis Simpson's Singular Charm." *The Poetry of Life and The Life of Poetry: Essays and Reviews*. Ashland, OR: Story Line Press, 2000. 123–133.

—. "The Passionate Pursuit of the Real." *The Hudson Review* 58.2 (June 2005): 319–328.

—. Review of *Expansive Poetry: Essays on the New Narrative and the New Formalism*, edited by Frederick Feirstein. *The Georgia Review* 44.4 (Winter 1990): 730–733.

McClatchy, J. D. "Mortal Listeners." *Poetry* 149.1 (October 1986): 31–47. (Reviews poetry by Stephen Spender, James Schuyler, Norman Williams, George Bradley, Dana Gioia, Anne Winters, Debora Greger, Alice Fulton, and Allen Grossman.)

—. "Summaries and Evidence." *Partisan Review* 47.4 (1980): 639–644. (Reviews poetry by Irving Feldman, Donald Justice, Thom Gunn, Timothy Steele, and Anthony Hecht.)

McDowell, Robert. Email interview. 18 Feb. 2002.

—. "New Schools and Late Discoveries." *Hudson Review* 34.4 (Winter 1987): 673–689.

—, ed. *Poetry After Modernism*. Brownsville, OR: Story Line Press, 1998.

McDowell, Robert, Frederick Feirstein, Frederick Turner, and Thomas B. Byers. "An Exchange on Thomas B. Byers's 'The Closing of the American Line: Expansive Poetry and Ideology." *Contemporary Literature* 34.4 (1993): 803–828.

McPhillips, Robert. "Dana Gioia Interviewed by Robert McPhillips." *Verse* 9.2 (Summer 1992): 9–27.

—. "*The Gods of Winter* by Dana Gioia." *Verse* 9.2 (Summer 1992): 111–114.

—. *The New Formalism: A Critical Introduction*. Charlotte, NC: Volcanic Ash Books, 2003.

—. "Reading the New Formalists." *Poetry After Modernism*. Ed. Robert McDowell. Brownsville, OR: Story Line Press, 1991. 300–328. (Not included in the 1998 edition.)

—. "Timothy Steele." *The Oxford Companion to Twentieth-Century Poetry in English*. Ed. Ian Hamilton. Oxford/New York: Oxford University Press, 1994. 288–289. (The author of this entry is identified only by the initials *RMcP*, but the list of contributors names Robert McPhillips as the author.)

—, editor. *Verse* 9.2 (Summer 1992). (Special issue dedicated to New Formalism.)

—. "What's New About the New Formalism." *New Expansive Poetry: Essays on the New Narrative and the New Formalism*. Ed. Frederick Feirstein. Santa Cruz, CA: Story Line Press, 1989. 195–208. (First published in a 1989 issue of *Crosscurrents*, guest-edited by Dick Allen, with a focus on Expansive Poetry.)

Melton, Christine. Interview with Molly Peacock. Originally published online, at <http://www.mipoesias.com/2003/ELEVEN.jpg>. No longer available online.

"Michael Donaghy." *Telegraph* 1 Oct. 2004. 8 March 2005. Online at http://www.telegraph.co.uk/news/main.jhtml?xml=/news/2004/10/01/db0102.xml&sSheet=/portal/2004/10/01/ixportal.html.

Miller, John N. "A Renewable Disguise." *The Chowder Review* 14 (Spring/Summer 1980): 60–62. (Reviews *Uncertainties and Rest*, by Timothy Steele.)

Mole, John. "Daily Horoscope: Review by John Mole." *Poetry Matters* 8 (Winter 1990): 25–28. (Mole is reviewing an edition of *Daily Horoscope* that was published in the UK by Peterloo Poets.)

Morrison, Blake. "In and Out of the Movement." *Life by Other Means: Essays on D. J. Enright*. Ed. Jacqueline Simms. Oxford, UK; New York: Oxford Univ. Press, 1990. 69–73.

—. *The Movement: English Poetry and Fiction of the 1950s*. Oxford: Oxford Univ. Press, 1980.

—. "Philip Larkin." *The Oxford Companion to Twentieth-Century Poetry in English*. Ed. Ian Hamilton. Oxford/New York: Oxford University Press, 1994. 288–289. (The author of this entry is identified only by the initials *PBM*, but the list of contributors names Blake Morrison as the author.)

—. "Young Poets in the 1970s." *British Poetry Since 1970: A Critical Survey*. Ed. Peter Jones and Michael Schmidt. Manchester, UK: Carcanet Press, 1980. 141–156.

Murphy, Jim. "A Conversation with Mark Jarman." *Image: A Journal of the Arts and Religion* 33 (Winter 2001–2002): 63–78.

Nelson, Marilyn. Facebook message to author. 6 Sept. 2009.

—. "Owning the Masters." *After New Formalism: Poets on Form, Narrative, and Tradition*. Ed. Annie Finch. Ashland, OR: Story Line Press, 1999. 8–17.

O'Brien, Sean. "Contemporary British Poetry." *A Companion to Twentieth-Century Poetry*. Ed. Neil Roberts. Oxford, UK; Malden, MA: Blackwell Publishers, 2001. 571–584.

Ostriker, Alicia Suskin. *Stealing the Language: The Emergence of Women's Poetry in America*. Boston: Beacon Press, 1986.

Oxenhorn, Harvey. "Donald Davie and the American Poetry Workshop." *Donald Davie and the Responsibilities of Literature*. Ed. George Dekker.

Manchester, UK: Carcanet Press; Orono, ME: The National Poetry Foundation, 1983. 64–73.

Oxley, William. "The First Shall Be Last." *Acumen* (September 2001): 101–104.

Peacock, Molly. Email interview. 21 March 2003.

—. Email to the author. 23 April 2005.

—. *Original Love.* New York/London: W. W. Norton and Company, 1995.

—. *Raw Heaven.* New York: Random House, 1980.

—. *Take Heart.* New York: Random House, 1984.

Pepple, Alex. "A Conversation with Leslie Monsour, Featured Poet." *Able Muse.* Millennial Issue Spring 2000. Online at http://www.ablemuse.com/2k/lmonsour.htm.

Perkins, David. *A History of Modern Poetry: Modernism and After.* Vol. 2. Cambridge, MA: The Belknap Press of Harvard Univ. Press, 1987.

Peschiera, Raúl. "America and the Culture of Poetry." *The Review: An International Literary Magazine* 3 (Summer 1997): 87–99. (An interview with Dana Gioia.)

Peters, Robert. "Commuter Poetry: Dana Gioia's *Daily Horoscope.*" *Paintbrush* 14.28 (Autumn 1987): 50–54.

Phillips, Robert. "Assessing the New Formalism (So-Called)." *Hudson Review* 50.1 (Spring 1997): 147–153.

Pollitt, Katha. Email interview. 23 Sept. 2005.

—. "Philip Larkin." *Grand Street* 9.3 (Spring 1990): 250–260.

—. "Playground." *Ecstatic Occasions, Expedient Forms: 85 Leading Contemporary Poets Select and Comment on Their Poems.* Ed. David Lehman. Ann Arbor: The Univ. of Michigan Press, 1996. 177–179.

Powell, James, and Paul Lake. "An Interview with Donald Davie." *Occident* 101.1 (Winter 1981): 19–26.

Powell, Neil. *Carpenters of Light: Some Contemporary English Poets.* Harper & Row, 1979, 1980.

Press, John. *Rule and Energy: Trends in British Poetry Since the Second World War.* The George Elliston Poetry Foundation Lectures, University of Cincinnati, 1962. London: Oxford Univ. Press, 1963.

Prunty, Wyatt. "Reciprocals." *Southern Review* 17.3 (July 1981): 634–641.

Raban, Jonathan. *The Society of the Poem.* London: George G. Harrap & Co. Ltd., 1971.

Regan, Stephen. "The Movement." *A Companion to Twentieth-Century Poetry.* Ed. Neil Roberts. Oxford, UK; Malden, MA: Blackwell Publishers, 2001. 209–219.

Richman, Robert, ed. Introduction. *The Direction of Poetry: An Anthology of Rhymed and Metered Verse Written in the English Language Since 1975.* Boston: Houghton Mifflin, 1988. xiii–xxi.

Rothman, David J. "A Literary Conference for the 1990's." *Sparrow* 62 (Oct. 1996): 96–99.

Russell, Peter. "Dana Gioia and the New Formalism." *Edge City Review* 1.2 (1994): 13–19. (A review of *Daily Horoscope* and *The Gods of Winter.*)

Sadoff, Ira. "Neo-Formalism: A Dangerous Nostalgia." *The American Poetry Review* 19.1 (January/February 1990): 7–13.

Schoerke, Meg. "A Controversy Reignited: The Early Twentieth-Century Vers Libre Debate as an Antecedent of New Formalist Criticism." *New Expansive Poetry: Theory, Criticism, History.* Ed. R. S. Gwynn. Ashland, OR: Story Line Press, 1999. 72–85.

—. Introduction. *The Reaper Essays.* Ed. Mark Jarman and Robert McDowell. Brownsville, OR: Story Line Press, 1996. vii–xiv.

Scott, A. O. "This Be the Prose." *New York Times Book Review* (21 Nov. 2004): 16.

Shaw, Robert B. "Philip Larkin: A Stateside View." *Poetry Nation* 6 (1976): 100–109.

Sheehy, Donald G. "Measure for Measure: The Frostian Classicism of Timothy Steele." *The Robert Frost Review* (1995): 73–97.

Simic, Charles. "1998 Lenore Marshall Poetry Prize." *The Nation* 267.14 (2 Nov. 1998): 29–30. (About Mark Jarman's *Questions for Ecclesiastes.*)

"Smokin' Gunn." *Goblin* 8. 11 Dec. 2001. No longer available online.

Solway, David. "Illuminating Ardor." *Sewanee Review* 108.1 (January-March 2000): xi–xv.

Spalding, J. M. "Interview with Mark Jarman." *Cortland Review*. Jan. 1999. Online at http://www.cortlandreview.com/features/99/01/.

Stanford, Donald. "American Formalism." *The Southern Review* 31.2 (April 1995): 381–387.

Steele, Timothy. *All the Fun's in How You Say a Thing: An Explanation of Meter and Versification*. Athens: Ohio University Press, 1999.

—. *The Color Wheel*. Baltimore and London: The Johns Hopkins Univ. Press, 1994.

—. Email interview. 25 May 2004.

—. "The Forms of Poetry." *Brandeis Review* 12 (Summer 1992): 28–33.

—, ed. Introduction. *The Poetry of J. V. Cunningham*. Athens, OH: Swallow Press / Ohio University Press, 1997. xiii–xxxviii.

—. "Keeping Angels in Line." *Counter/Measures* 3 (1974): 191–193.

—. *Missing Measures: Modern Poetry and the Revolt Against Meter*. Fayetteville, London: The Univ. of Arkansas Press, 1990.

—. *Nine Poems*. Florence, KY: Robert L. Barth, 1984.

—. *On Harmony*. Abbatoir Editions. Omaha: The University of Nebraska at Omaha, 1984.

—. *The Prudent Heart*. Los Angeles: The Symposium Press, 1983.

—. *Sapphics Against Anger and Other Poems*. New York: Random House, 1986.

—. *Sapphics and Uncertainties: Poems 1970–1986*. Fayetteville: The Univ. of Arkansas Press, 1995.

—. "Symposium." *Crosscurrents* 8.2 (January 1989): 101–104. (Special issue titled "Expansionist Poetry: The New Formalism and the New Narrative." Guest Editor Dick Allen.)

—. "Thom Gunn." *The Oxford Companion to Twentieth-Century Poetry in English*. Ed. Ian Hamilton. Oxford/New York: Oxford University Press, 1994. 201–203. (The author of this entry is identified only by the initials *TS*, but the list of contributors names Timothy Steele as the author.)

—. *Uncertainties and Rest.* Baton Rouge and London: Louisiana State Univ. Press, 1979.

Stefanile, Felix. "Poets of Emulation: Dana Gioia and Jay Parini." *Voices in Italian Americana* 1.1 (Spring 1990): 35–50.

Swarbrick, Andrew. "No Shocks Left from the Rude Poet." *The Oxford Times* (18 October, 1991): 13. (Reviews Fiona Pitt-Keithley, Dana Gioia, Christopher Reid, and E. J. Scovell. Swarbrick classifies Pitt-Keithley as a "rude poet.")

Swiss, Thomas. "Six Poets." *Sewanee Review* 94 (Spring 1986): 302–311.

Thiel, Diane. *Echolocations.* Ashland, OR: Story Line Press, 2000.

—. Email interview. 23 Oct. 2004.

Thwaite, Anthony. Introduction. *Selected Letters of Philip Larkin 1940–1985.* Ed. Thwaite. London: Faber and Faber, 1992. xi–xv.

Tillinghast, Richard. "Bookshelf: The Pleasures of Disciplined Verse." *Wall Street Journal* Eastern Edition 229.3 (6 Jan. 1997): A10.

Timms, David. *Philip Larkin.* The 'Modern Writers' Series. Edinburgh: Oliver & Boyd, 1973.

Tuma, Keith. Email to the author. 16 July 2003.

—. *Fishing by Obstinate Isles: Modern and Postmodern British Poetry and American Readers.* Avant-Garde and Modernism Studies. Evanston, IL: Northwestern Univ. Press, 1998.

Turco, Lewis. "The Year in Poetry." *Dictionary of Literary Biography Yearbook: 1983.* Ed. Mary Bruccoli and Jean W. Ross. Assoc. Ed. Richard Ziegfield. A Bruccoli Clark Book. Detroit, MI: Gale Research Co., 1984. 77–91.

—. "The Year in Poetry." *Dictionary of Literary Biography Yearbook: 1986.* A Bruccoli Clark Layman Book. Ed. J. M. Brook. Detroit, MI: Gale Research Co., 1987. 168–179.

Turner, Frederick. "'Mighty Poets in Their Misery Dead': a Polemic on the Contemporary Poetic Scene." *The Missouri Review* 4.1 (Fall 1980): 77–96.

Turner, Frederick, and Ernst Pöppel. "The Neural Lyre: Poetic Meter, the Brain, and Time." *Expansive Poetry: Essays on the New Narrative and the New Formalism*. Ed. Frederick Feirstein. Santa Cruz, CA: Story Line Press, 1989. 209–254.

Varnes, Kathrine. "Feminist Formalist: A Critical Oxymoron?" *After New Formalism: Poets on Form, Narrative, and Tradition*. Ed. Annie Finch. Ashland, OR: Story Line Press, 1999. 158–165.

—. "'Practicing for the Real Me': Form and Authenticity in the Poetry of Julia Alvarez." *Antípodas* 10 (1998): 67–77.

Wakoski, Diane. "The New Conservatism in American Poetry." *American Book Review* (May/June 1986): 3.

Walzer, Kevin. "Dana Gioia and Expansive Poetry." *Italian Americana* 16.1 (Winter 1998): 24–40.

—. *The Ghost of Tradition: Expansive Poetry and Postmodernism*. Ashland, OR: Story Line Press, 1998.

—. "An Interview with Timothy Steele." 13 Feb. 2001. Online at http://www.modernamericanpoetry.org/content/kevin-walzer-interview-timothy-steele.

—. "The Poetry of Timothy Steele." *The Tennessee Quarterly* 2.3 (Winter 1996): 16–30.

Weinberger, Eliot. "What Was Formalism?" *Jacket* #6. 1998. Online at http://jacketmagazine.com/06/wein-form.html.

Wetzsteon, Rachel. Email interview. 12 March 2005.

—. Email to the author. 1 April 2005.

—. "Philip Larkin and Happiness." *Contemporary Poetry Review*. 2010. http://www.cprw.com/Misc/larkin1.htm.

Wilbur, Richard. "For Better or For Worse." *Mississippi Review* 6.1 (Summer 1977): 157.

—. "Foreword." *Strong Measures: Contemporary Poetry in Traditional Forms*. Ed. Philip Dacey and David Jauss. New York: Harper & Row, 1986.

Wilmer, Clive. "On Freedom." *PN Review* 26.6 (July-August 2000): 40–44.

Wiman, Christian. "An Idea of Order." *After New Formalism: Poets on Form, Narrative, and Tradition*. Ed. Annie Finch. Story Line Press, 1999. 204–216.

Wojahn, David. "'Yes, But...': Some Thoughts on the New Formalism." *Crazyhorse* 32 (Spring 1987): 64–81.

OTHER WORKS CONSULTED OR NAMED

Allen, Dick. "After the Avant-Garde." *Counter/Measures* 3.3 (1974): 201–203.

—. "The Donner Party." *Poetry* CXXII.3 (June 1973): 173–176.

—. "Shifts." *Poetry* CXX.4 (July 1972): 235–245.

—. "To the Wall." *Poetry* CXXX.6 (Sept. 1977): 342–352.

—. "What Rough Beast: SF-Oriented Poetry." *Extrapolation* 17 (1975): 8–17.

Allen, Donald, editor. *The New American Poetry*. New York: Grove, 1960.

Bakhtin, Mikhail. *The Dialogic Imagination: Four Essays*. Ed. Michael Holquist. Trans. Caryl Emerson and Michael Holquist. University of Texas Press Slavic Series 1. 1975 (Russian). Austin: University of Texas Press, 1981.

—. *Problems of Dostoevsky's Poetics*. Ed. and trans. Caryl Emerson. Theory and History of Literature 8. 1963 (Russian). Minneapolis: Univ. of Minnesota Press, 1984.

Enright, D. J., ed. *Poetry of the 1950s: An Anthology of New English Verse*. Tokyo: Kenkyusha Ltd., 1955.

Feirstein, Frederick. *Manhattan Carnival: A Dramatic Dialogue*. Preface by X. J. Kennedy. Woodstock, VT: Countryman Press, 1981.

Gates, Henry Louis. *The Signifying Monkey: A Theory of Afro-American Literary Criticism*. New York: Oxford Univ. Press, 1988.

Gery, John. *Nuclear Annihilation and Contemporary American Poetry: Ways of Nothingness*. Gainesville: University Press of Florida, 1996.

Golding, Alan. *From Outlaw to Classic: Canons in American Poetry*. Madison: Univ. of Wisconsin Press, 1995.

Hacker, Marilyn. *Presentation Piece*. New York: Viking Press, 1974.

Hall, Donald, Robert Pack, and Louis Simpson, editors. *New Poets of England and America*. Introduction by Robert Frost. Cleveland / New York: Meridian Books, 1957.

Leithauser, Brad. *Hundreds of Fireflies*. New York: Knopf, 1982.

Martin, Charles. *Room for Error*. Athens: Univ. of Georgia Press, 1977.

Moore, Richard. *Empires: Poems*. Princeton, NJ: Ontario Review Press, 1981.

Schnackenberg, Gjertrud. *The Lamplit Answer*. New York: Farrar, Straus & Giroux, 1985.

—. *Portraits and Elegies*. Boston: D. R. Godine, Inc., 1982.

Seth, Vikram. *The Golden Gate*. New York: Vintage International, 1986.

ENDNOTES

1 Leslie Monsour made these remarks in an online interview conducted in 2000 by Alex Pepple and published by Able Muse:<http://www.ablemuse.com/2k/lmonsour.htm>.

2 Blake Morrison, The Movement, page 6.

3 William Baer's interview with Robert Conquest appears on pages 120–136 in Fourteen on Form: Conversations with Poets. Jackson, MS: Univ. Press of Mississippi, 2004. The quoted phrase is from pages 122–123.

4 All of Tuma's comments in this paragraph are from an email message to the author (16 July 2003).

5 Kirby-Smith, "Behind the Lines," page 641.

6 Harvey, "Illusions Not Illusions Any Longer," page 91.

7 Joe Francis Doerr, "New Formalism," Encyclopedia of American Poetry: The Twentieth Century, page 503.

8 New Poets of England and America was edited by Donald Hall, Robert Pack, and Louis Simpson.

9 Unless otherwise noted, all of Dick Allen's comments in this section are from email interviews that I conducted with him (26 March 2002 and 6 Jan. 2004).

10 All of Martin's comments in this paragraph are from an email interview that I conducted with him in 2005 (May 15 and 16). Martin also mentioned that he has used Larkin's poem "Aubade" as an example in lectures he has given on poetic voice. Martin did note, though, that when he first encountered Davie, Gunn, and Larkin, he did not know that they were "members of something called The Movement."

11 Timothy Steele, A Few Friends, page 44.

12 Steele's remarks about Larkin appear in "An Interview with Timothy Steele," conducted by William Baer, The Formalist 14 (Winter/Spring 2003): 20–40.

13 Mark Jarman, email interview, 28 May 2001.

14 Mary Flinn's interview with Jarman appears in Blackbird: An Online Journal of Literature and the Arts.

15 Mark Jarman, email interview, 28 May 2001. In this interview, Jarman stated that these poets have had an influence on his own poetry: W. H. Auden, Kate Daniels, Emily Dickinson, T. S. Eliot, Robert Frost, Garrett Hongo, Andrew Hudgins, Robinson Jeffers, Philip Larkin, Philip Levine, Robert McDowell, Edwin Arlington Robinson, Wallace Stevens, Walt Whitman, and Charles Wright.

16 Mark Jarman, email interview, 28 May 2001.

17 Gioia's comments can be found in a 1995 interview called "An Interview with Poet and Critic Dana Gioia," subtitled "Paradigms Lost: Part Two." In this same interview, as he describes his feelings when he encounters a "really splendid new poem," Gioia invokes Larkin to support what he is saying: "This electrifying feeling of discovery and kinship reminds me of Larkin's description of his passion for New Orleans jazz, 'On me your voice falls as they say love should, / Like an enormous yes'."

18 Dana Gioia, personal interview, 20 Dec. 2001.

19 John Gery, "Paradox of Form," page 40.

20 Alastair Fowler alleges that the Movement has caused enormous harm: "The Movement poems . . . contributed to the greatest rupture in cultural tradition since the eighteenth century. They rejected old literature; Romanticism; tradition; ideas; psychoanalysis; the common 'myth-kitty' (Larkin's phrase, in Poets of the 1950s); even literary allusions and diction—what Amis calls 'bookish cries' ('Against Romanticism'). Simplifications so radical were easily taken as a prescription for philistinism" ("Poetry Since 1950," 346). In another assessment, Andrew Crozier states, "It need not concern us much that Conquest's arguments in 1956 were incoherent and question-begging; what matters is that he codified a successfully assertive group position based on exclusion and prejudice" ("Thrills and Frills," 212). In Poets of the 1950s, a young—and seemingly smug—Larkin notoriously

announced that poets should steer clear of "'tradition' or a common myth-kitty" and should avoid "casual allusions in poems to other poems or poets . . . " (qtd. in Morrison, 192). For an argument that Larkin's views have been misunderstood, see David Timms' 1973 book Philip Larkin (60–61). Alan Brownjohn, writing for The Oxford Companion to Twentieth-Century Poetry in English, says, "Thom Gunn, Elizabeth Jennings, and Philip Larkin are among the most important English poets of the late twentieth century, whose diversity clearly rebuts the accusations of uniformity levelled at New Lines" (382).

21 Morrison, The Movement, page 6.

22 Morrison, The Movement, page 9.

23 Morrison, The Movement, pages 6 and 7.

24 Morrison, The Movement, page 8.

25 Morrison, The Movement, page 9.

26 Morrison, The Movement, page 9.

27 Larkin, "Modesties," Collected Poems, page 26.

28 Davie, Purity of Diction in English Verse, 26–27.

29 Davie's statement appears on page 24 of a 1977/1978 interview conducted by Dana Gioia and published in a journal called Sequoia. (Later published as "Talking with Dana Gioia" in Trying to Explain, 203–213.)

30 Morrison, The Movement, pages 20, 21, 34.

31 Mandrake editors quoted in Morrison, page 19.

32 Jennings, "Modern Poet," quoted in Morrison, pages 21–22.

33 Richard J. Gray, email to author, 22 Dec. 2002.

34 Jennings, "Modern Poet," quoted in Morrison, pages 21–22.

35 Morrison, The Movement, page 25.

36 Kingsley Amis, Memoirs, page 133.

37 Amis, Memoirs, page 136.

38 Morrison, The Movement, page 25.

39 Morrison, The Movement, page 146.

40 Gunn, "My Life Up to Now," page 174.

41 Gunn, letter to the author, June 2001.

42 In a 1989 interview, Gunn once again insisted that "the Movement didn't really exist: what we had in common was a period style. I'm pretty sure I'm right because people not included in the Movement wrote in the same style" ("Anglo-American Poet," 219). Gunn makes a good point. Nevertheless, his critical writings reveal that he continued to embrace many ideas that were also formerly held by the Movement. It would not be accurate to say that such ideas dominate the following articles in Shelf Life, but it would certainly be accurate to say that they are there: "Responsibilities: Contemporary Poetry and August Kleinzhaler"; "Forays against the Republic: Whitman"; "Three Hard Women: H.D., Marianne Moore, and Mina Loy"; "Enmeshed with Time: The Sixteenth Century"; "On a Drying Hill: Yvor Winters"; and "Out of the Box: Elizabeth Bishop."

43 Davie, "Remembering the Movement," page 199.

44 Steele's description appears in a 1995 interview conducted by Kevin Walzer (originally published by Edge City Review, online).

45 This description appears in Steele's article "The Forms of Poetry," page 3. In an email interview, Steele explained that the way both groups were "announced" was an "interesting," albeit small, parallel between the two groups: "It is interesting that the Movement was announced not by anybody subsequently associated with it, but by the editor J. D. Scott. In similar fashion, 'New Formalism' was first discussed . . . by critics inimical to it and not by poets who have eventually come to be identified as New Formalists" (25 May 2004).

46 Bergonzi, "Davie, Larkin, and the State of England," page 359.

47 Bergonzi, "Davie, Larkin, and the State of England," pages 359–360.

48 Larkin, "Interview with Paris Review," page 69.

49 Bergonzi, "Davie, Larkin, and the State of England," page 360.

50 Unless otherwise noted, all of Bruce Martin's comments are from page 144 in his book Philip Larkin.

51 Samuel Maio, "A Sound and Fruitful Attitude: The Poetry of Robert Conquest, Elizabeth Jennings, and Charles Causley," page 17.

52 All of Gioia's comments in this paragraph are from "A Personal Tour of Donald Davie's Imaginary Museum," pages 724–729. First published in Southern Review.

53 Davie's comments appear on page 23 of "Interview with Donald Davie," which was conducted by Dana Gioia in 1977/1978. (Later published as "Talking with Dana Gioia" in Trying to Explain, 203–213.)

54 Gioia, "Interview with Donald Davie," page 24.

55 Gioia, "Interview with Donald Davie," page 23.

56 Richard J. Gray, note to author, Feb. 2003. See also Harvey Oxenhorn's "Donald Davie and the American Poetry Workshop" for clues that Davie retained some Movement ideas: an emphasis on "control," "prudence," "judiciousness," "fair-mindedness," and "responsibility." Oxenhorn's article is discussed in detail in Chapter Two. Gunn's critical writing shows that he too held onto some Movement ideas.

57 All of the statements in this paragraph are from page 23 of "Interview with Donald Davie," conducted by Dana Gioia.

58 Gioia, "Interview with Donald Davie," page 21.

59 Gioia, "Interview with Donald Davie," page 21.

60 All of the descriptions in this paragraph appear in the introduction to Expansive Poetry, pages vii–xv. (Frederick Feirstein edited this essay collection; he and Frederick Turner co-authored the introduction.)

61 David Mason, email to author, 21 April 2004.

62 David Mason, untitled review of Expansive Poetry, page 730.

63 A discussion of what makes a person a "New Formalist" seems appropriate at this point. Defining such a large group is difficult, but some shared characteristics can be identified. Although the name is disliked by many in the group, "New Formalism" is apt, for their poetry generally is "formal" in the sense that it involves meter, rhyme, and traditional poetic forms, and they themselves are "new" in the sense that they are a generation (or two) younger than formalist poets including Richard Wilbur and Anthony Hecht. They (and their allies) also argue that, compared to these earlier formalists, they are "new" in other ways, including their emphasis on "non-elite" language and subjects, as well as their interest in appealing to non-academic readers. The New Formalists advocate formal poetry, typically using rhetoric

that, whether implicitly or explicitly, criticizes free verse and the poets who write it, teach it, and endorse it. Especially in the early years, poetry written by the New Formalists typically appeared in journals including Hudson Review, Kenyon Review, New Criterion, and Counter/Measures. Most, if not all, of the founding members of New Formalism, as well as several "second-generation" members, have also published essays in collections that can be characterized as "manifestos." When those who would become the New Formalists first began to gravitate toward each other in the 1970s and 1980s, most were in their twenties or early thirties and were united by a desire to rebel against the "ruling orthodoxy," "tenured radicalism," and "eternal avant-garde" of the older generation—the older generation who wrote free verse, that is. The founding members of New Formalism embraced the formalism of their own teachers, including Elizabeth Bishop, J. V. Cunningham, Robert Fitzgerald, Anthony Hecht, John Hollander, Donald Justice, Penelope Laurans, Miller Williams, and Richard Wilbur. These youthful connections with the older generation of American formalists have undoubtedly had a major impact on the New Formalists. As it turns out, the poetic and critical ideas of many founding members of New Formalism has also been shaped by their youthful connections with Davie, Gunn, and Larkin. (They also have indirect connections with Yvor Winters, who was himself a major influence on the Movement.)

Other poets who are not necessarily considered "members" of any "official" movement but who could nevertheless be called "new formalists"—meaning that they often write in form, they advocate formal poetry, and they are at least somewhat younger than the "older formalists"—are Thomas Carper, Jared Carter, Kelly Cherry, Christopher Clausen, Alfred Corn, Brooks Haxton, H. L. Hix, Mary Kinzie, Phillis Levin, William Logan, J. D. McClatchy, Timothy Murphy, Bruce Meyer, Suzanne Noguere, Meg Schoerke, and Carolyn Beard Whitlow. In "Connoisseurs of Sound and the New Formalism," critic Thomas Cable classifies Annie Finch, Rachel Wetzsteon, and Greg Williamson as "second-generation" New Formalists (Revue Française d'Etudes Américaines, March 2000, 50). Since Finch has been involved in New Formalism from nearly the beginning, Cable's classification of her is questionable, but his classification of Wetzsteon and Williamson seems accurate. Gerry Cambridge lists "younger poets associated with New Formalism," including Kate Light, Wilmer Mills, Len Krisak, A. E. Stallings, Leslie Monsour, Catherine Tufariello, and Chryss Yost ("The New Formalism," 256). Elizabeth Alexander, Aga Shahid

Ali, Julia Alvarez, Rhina Espaillat, Allison Joseph, Diane Thiel, and Kathrine Varnes are also among those who may accurately be termed second-generation New Formalists. For a variety of reasons, probably including a reluctance to be included within a movement that is often seen as neo-conservative, not to mention male-dominated, some poets who write in form describe themselves by saying, "I'm not a formalist, but . . . " (a disclaimer bearing an obvious resemblance to "I'm not a feminist, but . . . "). There are also some, such as Rita Dove, Gjertrud Schnackenberg, and Marilyn Hacker, who typically write formal poetry but do not wish to be counted among the New Formalists. Adding to the confusion is that some of the second-generation New Formalists are the same age as the original members, and some are actually older. Given all these factors, it is not surprising that the "membership" lists for this movement tend to be inconsistent.

64 Mark Jarman, email interview, 31 December 2001.

65 All of Dirda's comments in this paragraph are from "The Movement," pages 203–208 (published in Grand Street). Seemingly disapproving of the contemporary poetry scene, Dirda says, "Poets have settled comfortably into academic respectability" (207). Certainly, this criticism does not fit all American poets, but prominent American poets at that time were firmly established in academic settings (and continue to be), and this criticism has been made repeatedly by many New Formalists—even those who are academics. The Movement writers had similarly conflicting views towards academia.

66 Gioia, "Notes on the New Formalism," page 158.

67 David Mason has said that Wilbur and Hecht "have made some of the finest postwar poems in English" and that they are "now American poetry's elder statesmen" ("Louis Simpson's Singular Charm," 123).

68 Morrison quoted in Huk, "Introduction," page 2.

69 Morrison quoted in Huk, "Introduction," page 2.

70 Morrison, "Young Poets," 142.

71 Morrison, "Young Poets," 143.

72 Morrison, "Young Poets," pages 143 and 144.

73 Morrison, "Young Poets," page 144.

74 Romana Huk, "Introduction," page 2.

75 Peter Jones and Michael Schmidt, British Poetry Since 1970: A Critical Survey, page ix.

76 Richard J. Gray asks, "Has any school of poets ever really been uninterested in audience? Aren't we talking about imaginative constructions of just what that audience is and needs?" (email to author, 18 Sept. 2003). Gray's point is valid. However, it seems to me that few groups of poets have devoted as much attention to audience—and "imaginative constructions" of that audience—as the Movement writers and the New Formalists. Furthermore, few groups have concentrated so intensely on "lost" readers and the importance of writing poetry that might attract them. Morrison, who devotes an entire chapter to the Movement poets and audience, emphasizes that their "desire to reach two seemingly different audiences—one a small intellectual circle, the other a large body of 'Common Readers'—is one of the most important features of the group" (109). For Mark Jarman, an "imaginative construction" of the ordinary reader requires an elimination of economic or class status, an approach that differs dramatically from the Movement's emphatic and overt (but, often, contradictory) approach to class. Jarman's desire to eliminate class as a factor seems especially interesting in light of the differing emphases on class in the U.S. and England.

77 Mark Jarman used the word "evergreen" in an email interview (28 May 2001).

78 For an article that sympathetically outlines the aims and characteristics of the Movement, see Paris Leary's 1957 article "The Movement in England." Although Leary obviously had no way of forecasting the development of the New Formalists, his article highlights many traits of the Movement that have also been adopted by the New Formalists.

79 Although the Movement writers insisted on depicting themselves as "outsiders," New Formalist Dick Allen believed that they were "mainly the insiders from the beginning," whereas the New Formalists—or Expansive poets, as he prefers to call them—"have been outsiders" (email interview, 26 March 2002). The New Formalists, who are themselves "insiders" in many ways, with ties to universities, publishing houses, and literary conferences, have similarly insisted on depicting themselves as outsiders. Both groups have also depicted themselves as insiders to "regular" society. For a description of why feminist formalist poets often "have a troubled, uncomfortable relationship with the

academy even if employed in higher education," see Kathrine Varnes's article "Feminist Formalist: A Critical Oxymoron?" (158–163 in After New Formalism). Jack Foley, a poet and critic who writes poetry unlike that of the New Formalists but sympathizes with some of their aims, has commented on the contradictory ways in which the New Formalists have depicted themselves.

80 The reference to the poet "as not seer but civil servant, a responsible citizen responsibly employed" comes from Blake Morrison, The Movement, page 178. See Morrison for a discussion of the Movement rebellion against Romanticism (145–191).

81 Morrison, The Movement, page 175.

82 Morrison, The Movement, page 175.

83 Jarman, email interview, 28 May 200). Jarman is often classified as a "New Narrative" poet rather than a "New Formalist," but his publications and activities link him with both groups, which are often grouped under the heading of "Expansive Poetry."

84 Mason, "Dana Gioia's Case," 177. Jack Foley's description of Gioia also links him to this Movement-like depiction of the poet: "To those who know him, Dana Gioia is, as he said of T. S. Eliot, the 'Bourgeois in Bohemia', the man 'determined to live a responsible life'" ("Interrogations at Noon, Reviewed by Jack Foley," 5 of 6).

85 Jarman, email interview, 28 May 2001.

86 Gunn, "Responsibilities," page 29.

87 Morrison's comment is from page 142 of his article "Young Poets in the 1970s."

88 When I refer to poetry as "non-formal" in this context, I intend no judgment. I am simply speaking of free-verse poetry, which does not employ regular form or meter.

89 On page 215 of his essay "An Idea of Order," Christian Wiman puts it this way: ". . . It requires no great talent to imitate chaos, or to illustrate the inability of the mind and language to make meaning. Those who do so, as Wallace Stevens suggested, are simply exacerbating our confusion . . . ." Wiman states further that he has "not intended this to be an argument in favor of a 'return to traditional forms'" and that "Much of

the self-satisfied metrical poetry that [he reads] makes [him] nostalgic for Dadaism."

90 Wain quoted in Morrison, The Movement, page 89.

91 Wain quoted in Morrison, The Movement, page 89.

92 Steele's comment on the value of poetic form as a constructive way to deal with "the obvious disorder and chaos of the world" appears in a 2002 interview conducted by William Baer, editor of The Formalist (28). Annie Finch stated in an email interview that she believes "there is something healthy and useful about poetic form for the survival of the human race" (17 Dec. 2001).

93 Conquest's description of the "Permanent Revolution" involved in Modernism appears on page 76 of his article "But What Good Came of It At Last? An Inquest on Modernism." Gioia has commented on the "eternal avant-garde" of Modernist and contemporary poetry in a number of settings, including a personal interview in December 2001.

94 Giles, "From Myth Into History: The Later Poetry of Thom Gunn and Ted Hughes," page 14. Note: Many writers do not capitalize "Modernism." When I use the term, I do capitalize it, but if it is not capitalized when I quote it, I shall leave it as it is. To avoid interruptions and implicit disapproval of what seems to have become a simple matter of choice, I shall not use the label [sic].

95 Davie quoted in Morrison, The Movement, page 133.

96 Morrison, The Movement, page 133.

97 Bruce Martin, page 31.

98 Morrison, The Movement, page 76.

99 Morrison, The Movement, page 76.

100 These comments about Larkin and Gunn are from an email interview that I conducted with Dick Allen in 2002. Allen first encountered the Movement writers in the late 1950s.

101 All of the statements by Feirstein and Turner in these three paragraphs are from the Introduction to Expansive Poetry (1989). Feirstein and Turner also allege that the "poseurs" of American poetry typically "express profound hostility to the intellectual imagination, especially in the forms of science and technology, and a sentimental preference

for nature over culture"; in other words, according to Feirstein and Turner, the "poseurs," though almost "invariably" academics, were anti-intellectuals, and were, in addition, sentimental about nature and reflexively opposed to science and technology.

102 All of Dawson's comments in this paragraph are from her editorial "The Yuppie Poet," pages 5–6, AWP Newsletter (now called AWP Writer's Chronicle).

103 All of Locke's comments in this paragraph are from his article "Trivial or Mechanistic Sound," which appears in the "Freedom and Form" issue of Mississippi Review (Summer 1977), pages 10–11.

104 In the same "Freedom and Form" issue of Mississippi Review that published Duane Locke's attack on formal poetry (Summer 1977), R. S. Gwynn says, "I'm not saying that we should all go back to heroic couplets and counting our words on our fingers, but a poet shouldn't have to apologize for offering up a sonnet" (page 12).

105 Gwynn, Introduction to New Expansive Poetry, page 11.

106 In an online article called "Overcoming the Tic of Techniques: The Emergence of Expansive Poetry," Dick Allen says that he prefers the term "expansive poetry" because, in his opinion, New Formalism, which is merely a "sub-genre" of Expansive Poetry, tends to attract poets who are overly concerned with technique, sometimes resulting in poetry that is no more than "trivial or polished light verse."

107 "Natural Classicism" is the "umbrella term" that Frederick Turner says he uses to describe one large movement which includes the Expansive Movement, New Formalism, and New Narrative (Crosscurrents, Jan. 1989, 105).

108 These are the creators of the following labels for the New Formalists: "piddling Pounds" (John Haines, "Formal Objections"); "commuter poets" and "prince[s] of the Blanc Mange Mode" (Robert Peters, "Commuter Poetry: Dana Gioia's Daily Horoscope"); "the radical right of poetry," "wimps," and "café Republicans" (Eliot Weinberger, "What Was Formalism?"); "cultural neoconservatives" (Joseph M. Conte, Unending Design: The Forms of Postmodern Poetry); "Yuppie Poets" (Ariel Dawson, article of the same title); "Rebels Without a Case" (James Hatch, article of the same title); "il-literati," "the Reaganites of poetry," and "anti-Americans" (Diane Wakoski, "Picketing the Zeitgeist: The New Conservatism in American Poetry"); and, finally,

"low proppers-up of state ideology" (Robert Hass, qtd. in Clive Wilmer, "On Freedom"). Henry Carlisle also uses the term "Reaganites" to indict some poets interested in "new formalism" ("Letter to the Editor," Northwest Review, July 1989). In satirical self-defense, R. S. Gwynn sometimes calls the group the "Few Normalists." Because New Formalism is the most widely recognized label, I use it when referring to the New Narrative movement or the New Formalist movement, although both are subcategories within the so-called Expansive movement.

109 Wakoski, "The New Conservatism in American Poetry," page 3.

110 Kathrine Varnes, "'Practicing for the Real Me': Form and Authenticity in the Poetry of Julia Alvarez," page 67.

111 Dick Allen, email interview, 26 March 2002.

112 Dick Davis, John Gery, Dana Gioia, R. S. Gwynn, Marilyn Hacker, Andrew Hudgins, Mark Jarman, Paul Lake, Brad Leithauser, Charles Martin, David Mason, Leslie Monsour, Molly Peacock, Katha Pollitt, Vikram Seth, Robert B. Shaw, Timothy Steele, Diane Thiel, and Rachel Wetzsteon have also said that the Movement writers—specifically Davie, Gunn, and/or Larkin—have been important to them.

113 Donald Davie quoted in John Press, Rule and Energy, page 25.

114 See also Robert Peters's "Commuter Poetry: Dana Gioia's Daily Horoscope."

115 Somerset Maugham quoted in Blake Morrison, The Movement, page 59.

116 These details about Stephen Spender appear in Bradley, page 88, and Morrison, page 58.

117 Sitwell quoted in Morrison, The Movement, page 58.

118 Waugh quoted in Morrison, The Movement, page 58. John Press, writing in 1963, did not stoop to class-based name-calling, but he did condemn the poetry of the 1940s and 1950s, including that of the Movement, as "puny" compared to that of "Yeats, Pound, Eliot, Lawrence, Stevens, Auden, and Dylan Thomas" (Rule and Energy, 28).

119 It seems likely that Edith Sitwell's emphasis was on the alleged "lifeless[ness]" of the "quatrains" written by the Movement writers.

Whatever her emphasis was intended to be, her class-based snobbishness is unquestionable.

120 Gerry Cambridge, Oxford Encyclopedia of American Literature, page 252.

121 In a 1990 review of Gioia's Daily Horoscope, British critic John Mole suggests that English readers may share the American suspicion of the "conspicuously well-crafted poem" (25). His description also calls to mind the depictions of the poet that are characteristic of the Movement and New Formalism, though Mole is saying that most readers see these characteristics as negative: "Both here and in the USA there still seems a residual mistrust of the conspicuously well-crafted poem. It is associated with buttoned-up restraint, campus men in grey-flannel suits, pale-face academicians, a timid propriety afraid of the confessional, and—most damning of all—an essentially unadventurous conservatism. Lowell's praise of Larkin is still seen by many as merely admiration of his content . . . and, overall, there appears a far greater sympathy with the attitudes expressed by Louis Simpson who, in the early seventies, declared that he was abandoning the rhyme and metre which had resulted in such memorable poems as 'My Father in the Night Commanding No' because 'I found that I no longer wished to please'." Although Mole does not make an explicit connection between Gioia and Larkin, the very fact that he chooses to bring up Larkin in this context suggests that he sees an implicit connection between the two. Incidentally, when Mole says that "several of Gioia's more extended poems . . . achieve the kind of numinous glow around a hard core of poetic intelligence which is reminiscent of certain passages from Rilke's 'Duino Elegies'" (27), he is clearly offering praise of the highest order.

122 Gunn, "Anglo-American Poet," page 218.

123 Gioia, "Notes on the New Formalism," page 16.

124 Steele told this story in an interview conducted by Cynthia Haven in June 2000. Available online at http://www.cortlandreview.com/features/00/06/index.html.

125 Lewis Turco, "Year in Poetry 1986," page 169.

126 Gioia, "Picketing the Zeitgeist Picket," page 23.

127 In mentioning the combination of the "elite" and the "vulgar" in New Formalist poetry, I mean "vulgar" in the same sense that Gioia

uses it in his article "Can Poetry Matter?" (1991). In this essay, he argues that "it is time to experiment, time to leave the well-ordered but stuffy classroom, time to restore a vulgar vitality to poetry and unleash the energy now trapped in the subculture" (24). When asked in an interview if he thought poetry needed to be coarse, he clarified that he was using the term "vulgar" to mean "of the people" (Brame, "Paradigms Lost: Part One," 5 of 9). Finch's argument that an interest in form is Postmodern appears, for example, in her essay "Confessions of a Postmodern Poetess," in her essay "In Defense of Meter," and in her introduction to An Exaltation of Forms (co-written with Kathrine Varnes). Interestingly, British critic Sean O'Brien implicitly suggests that Modernism's stance on form is often misunderstood or oversimplified: "For some readers, concern with verse-form, and with formality, suggests anti-modernist attitudes; but an interest in form, in the how as well as the what of poetry, is characteristic of modernism, and it is possible to see in contemporary practice both an understanding of modernist principles and a sense that tradition has been 'repaired' following the necessary disruptions caused by pioneering modernists such as Pound and Eliot (578)."

128 All of the statements from Gwynn appear in the Introduction to New Expansive Poetry (pages 9–14). Conquest's description of Modernism as a "Permanent Revolution" appears on page 76 of his article "But What Good Came of It At Last? An Inquest on Modernism." Because his term fits Gwynn's discussion of the New Formalist rationale for returning to traditions predating Modernism, I have interjected it here. Gwynn himself does not mention Conquest.

129 Gioia, personal interview, 20 Dec. 2001.

130 Larkin, "Introduction to All What Jazz," 296.

131 Morrison, The Movement, page 93.

132 In the introduction to New Expansive Poetry, Gwynn mentions several editors of literary journals who, throughout the 1980s, helped to ensure "a wider readership for expansive poetry": X. J. Kennedy at Counter/Measures, Frederick Morgan at Hudson Review, Donald Stanford at Southern Review, Frederick Turner and, later, Marilyn Hacker at Kenyon Review (14). Journals including Sparrow, The Formalist, Hellas, and Dark Horse—a journal published in Scotland and co-founded by Dana Gioia—have also specialized in formal poetry.

133 Gioia, "The Poet in an Age of Prose," page 251.

134 Annie Finch advocates "multiformalism" in the introduction to After New Formalism (xi). Finch and Kathrine Varnes advocate "omniformalism" in a manifesto that they co-wrote in 2002 (The Body of Poetry, 22–23).

135 Jarman, email interview, 31 December 2001.

136 Gioia, "Poet in an Age of Prose," page 25.

137 For an argument that the New Formalists are reactionary anti-Modernists and anti-Postmodernists, see Thomas Byers's 1992 article "The Closing of the American Line: Expansive Poetry and Ideology." Byers weakens his argument by claiming that journal editors Gerald Harnett and Thomas Fleming speak for the New Formalists, when in reality they have never been counted among the members of the group. However, in almost every other way, he makes a strong case. Annie Finch, Dana Gioia, Marilyn Hacker, and Kathrine Varnes—"insiders" to New Formalism—have made points similar to those made by Byers. See Kevin Walzer's The Ghost of Tradition: Expansive Poetry and Postmodernism (1998) for an argument that New Formalism is Postmodern. In "New Formalism and New Traditionalism," Daniel Corrie makes a similar point. Robert McPhillips, in The New Formalism: A Critical Introduction (2003), brings up an implicitly populist reason to dismiss the whole question of whether New Formalism is or is not Postmodern: "Unlike [Kevin] Walzer, however, I do not believe that the New Formalism needs to establish its identity to conform with theories currently in vogue in the academy but of little relevance to the general reader, inside or outside the academy" (xv).

138 Turco quoted in Doerr, page 504.

139 All of the remarks by Dick Allen appear in "Poetry Village," pages 109–111. The italics appear in the original version of this article.

140 Allen inadvertently contradicts himself: if the poetic scene in America is lively and varied, as his mention of racially diverse poets, "folk rock poetry," and "concrete poetry" seems to suggest, it would be more accurate for him to say that the American poetic mainstream, which is featured in this anthology, is plagued with "terrible sameness."

141 In 1984, Philip Dacey and David Jauss published Strong Measures: Contemporary American Poetry in Traditional Forms, described by

Joe Francis Doerr as "the first major anthology of formal poetry to be published since the so-called War of the Anthologies of the late 1950s and early 1960s" (504). Dacey and Jauss, it should be noted, are not New Formalists, and as Keith Maillard points out, they are "not championing formal verse over free" ("The New Formalism," 52). In a 1998 essay about teaching traditional poetic forms, Philip Dacey claims that the New Formalist movement "can arguably be dated from 1986, the year that saw the publication of Strong Measures: Contemporary Poetry in Traditional Forms" (137). Although he thus claims rather a surprising amount of credit for the origins of New Formalism (along with his coeditor, David Jauss), Dacey dissociates himself from it, saying that, "like most -isms, [it] is best understood as a bully stick, an instrument of ideological thinking whose practitioners are in love with the notion of one poetry rather than many poetries and tend to set themselves up as a council of Popes" (138).

142 The writers who are associated with New Formalism and who appear in The Direction of Poetry are Dick Davis, Dana Gioia, Marilyn Hacker, Andrew Hudgins, Brad Leithauser, Frederick Morgan, Mary Jo Salter, Gjertrud Schnackenberg, Timothy Steele, and Anne Stevenson. Davis is an English writer who has lived in the United States for many years, and Stevenson is an American writer who has lived in England for many years. Richman's anthology evoked a number of negative responses, including Ira Sadoff's "Neo-Formalism: A Dangerous Nostalgia."

143 Robert Richman, who is associated with The New Criterion, a self-proclaimed politically conservative formalist journal, condemns the "insidious assault on mind that was one of the most repulsive features of the radical movement of the Sixties" and the "orthodox leftist pieties" that, in his view, had ruined poetry and criticism (qtd. in Maillard, 55). Richman is not generally counted among the New Formalists, but because their work often appears in his journal, proclamations like his have contributed to the widespread perception that the New Formalists are political reactionaries, just as declarations made by Amis, Conquest, and Larkin contributed to the perception that the Movement poets were political reactionaries (or even fascists). While it is accurate to say that some New Formalists have expressed extremely conservative viewpoints, it is probably accurate to say that just as many are liberal or apolitical. The journals New Criterion and Hellas are well-known for their conservative stances, as is (was) the online journal Edge City Review. Kathrine Varnes has also argued that The Formalist is not only

anti-academic but also anti-female, an allegation that William Baer, the editor, has contested. Since New Formalist work has appeared in all of these venues, the assumption that the poets share the politics of the editors is not surprising. In some cases, the perception is undoubtedly correct; in others, it is less certain. Ultimately, though, the political leanings of the New Formalists—or the Movement writers—are no more, and no less, relevant than those of any other poets.

144 In the introduction to Rebel Angels (1996), Jarman and Mason include Davie among those professors who offered students training in meter and form in the 1960s and 1970s, when such training was rare in the United States (xvi). Incidentally, while Rebel Angels is invariably called the first "official" anthology of New Formalist poetry, Annie Finch's edited collection A Formal Feeling Comes: Poems in Form by Contemporary Women pre-dates Rebel Angels by two years. Finch's anthology, however, is not described as the first New Formalist anthology. As far as I know, the actual reasons have not been stated, but they may include these: one, Finch's anthology leaves out all male New Formalists; two, it includes many poets who occasionally write formal poetry but who aren't "officially" New Formalists; and, three, the definition of "form" put forth by Finch and by many of her contributors is much broader than those used by many New Formalists. A less attractive possibility correlating with the first theory above may be that the male poets and critics who have historically dominated New Formalism have actively resisted calling A Formal Feeling Comes the first New Formalist anthology because of its all-female constituency.

145 Gioia, letter to author, 2 January 2001. In this letter, Gioia noted that, in addition to being a former student of Donald Davie, he has "written on Davie, Larkin, Gunn, and Amis," and he has "anthologized Jennings, Larkin, Gunn, and others." He mentioned, too, that R. S. Gwynn, David Mason, Robert B. Shaw, Brad Leithauser, and others have written about the Movement writers.

146 In "'Mighty Poets in Their Misery Dead': a Polemic on the Contemporary Poetry Scene," Frederick Turner says that "no truly great poetry has been written in English since the Second World War." He finds "very little metrical virtuosity" and very little generic variety in contemporary poetry: "no major narrative poetry; no philosophical poetry; no major religious poetry; no poetry with invented human characters in it; no important satirical poetry," and so on (79–80).

Turner's "polemic" was answered by twenty-one pages of "Responses to Frederick Turner," appearing in a 1981–1982 issue of the same journal (The Missouri Review).

147 Maillard, "The New Formalism and the Return of Prosody," page 54.

148 Gioia, "The Dilemma of the Long Poem," page 26.

149 The "Expansive Poetry" movement was inadvertently called "Expansionist Poetry" on the title page of the special issue of Crosscurrents.

150 For a discussion of "canon formation" in American poetry, see Alan Golding's From Outlaw to Classic: Canons in American Poetry (Univ. of Wisconsin Press, 1995).

151 Mason, email interview, 21 Dec. 2001.

152 Mason, email to author, 14 Dec. 2001.

153 Finch, email interview, 17 Dec. 2001.

154 Finch, email interview, 17 Dec. 2001.

155 Both the West Chester Poetry Conference in Pennsylvania and the Teaching Poetry Institute in California are (or were) closely associated with New Formalism.

156 The Movement writers' reluctance to admit they were a bona-fide movement in the first place undoubtedly contributed to their reluctance to promote themselves nearly as extensively as the New Formalists have done.

157 So far as I know, neither Finch nor Varnes has written about these matters. Gioia and others have said that New Formalism was not hostile to women, to members of diverse racial groups, or to "new" ideas. Finch and Varnes maintain that the group was hostile. Since these are largely matters of personal perception—on all sides—they can be neither verified nor disproven. Certain "fringe" websites, such as Edge City Review and Expansive Poetry and Music Online, do appear to reject "new" ideas such as postmodernism and feminist theory, as do certain journals, such as Hellas and, to a lesser degree, The Formalist.

158 In an untitled 1990 review of Expansive Poetry, David Mason laments the absence of women from this major New Formalist publication (733).

159 Varnes, "Feminist Formalist," page 164. Varnes criticizes Alicia Ostriker, for instance, for equating formal poetry with anti-feminism and free-verse poetry with feminism. Nevertheless, in her discussion of Missing Measures, Varnes decries Steele's almost total neglect of women poets. Although "one book can't do everything," Varnes questions whether such an omission, which is not even explained in the book, confirms suspicions that New Formalism is politically conservative. Varnes also acknowledges that, ordinarily, Gioia "admires, encourages, even promotes the work of women writers," but she points out, rightly, that, in his essay "Notes on the New Formalism," he falls short. About this particular essay, she says, "When looking for formalist poets to praise, Gioia lists men; when looking for targets, women" ("Feminist Formalist," 162).

160 Hix presents several reasons that the New Formalists should heed postmodernism. For one thing, postmodernism, with its emphasis on relativity and "synchronic relationships" rather than strictly historical or chronological relationships, may provide New Formalists with "a fruitful way of thinking about what makes new formalism new" (148, 149). New Formalism's populist interests may also be supported by postmodernism's insistence on "'detotaliz[ing]' who society authorizes to tell what stories" (150). Furthermore, says Hix, New Formalists are closing themselves off to numerous formal possibilities by "construing form so narrowly": "A postmodernist would be wrong to think traditional forms have lost their power, but a new formalist would err in believing that only traditional forms are formal" (150, 151). And, finally, New Formalism would be wise "not [to] burn its bridges to the university," since academia is a prime location for the "thoughtful, intelligent citizens" the New Formalists hope to reach (152). In "New Formalism at a Crossroads," Hix also presents several suggestions for "maintaining an expansive posture in new formalism" (52).

161 An Exaltation of Forms, co-edited by Finch and Varnes, features poetic meters and forms from the "traditional" to the "popular." It also includes meters and forms from many parts of the world.

162 Addonizio quoted in "The Bards of the 'Burbs," page 75.

163 Mason, email to author, 16 Feb. 2001.

164 On page 34 of an article called "Is Wyatt to Petrarch as Ezra Pound to Arnaut Daniel?" Helen Dennis quotes Claude Lévi-Strauss's remark that "similarity does not denote influence." Post hoc ergo propter hoc, which translates "after which hence by which," is a familiar logical fallacy involving the assumption that because something happened after something else, the first event must have caused the second event.

165 Richard J. Gray, email to author, 16 May 2003.

166 Peacock, email to author, 21 April 2003.

167 Hacker, email to author, 17 April 2003.

168 Gwynn, email to author, 13 March 2003.

169 Nelson, Facebook message to author, 6 Sept. 2009.

170 All of the statements from Marilyn Nelson in these paragraphs (except those made directly to the author) are from her essay "Owning the Masters," which appears in After New Formalism: Poets on Form, Narrative, and Tradition, pages 8–17.

171 Pollitt, "Playground," Ecstatic Occasions, Expedient Forms, pages 178–179.

172 Maura Stanton, email interview, 29 Jan. 2007. Stanton was only loosely affiliated with the New Formalists, but her poems have been published in journals associated with them. She was also on the faculty of the West Chester Poetry Conference, which was created by Michael Peich and Gioia. The poems by Larkin that she saw in 1980 were distributed at a workshop by poet Stephen Dobyns.

173 Thiel, email to author, 23 Oct. 2004. Thiel says that some poems by Larkin and Gunn "gave [her] permission to write humorous poems, or at least with a lighter twist." The teacher at Brown University who introduced Thiel to the poetry of Larkin and Gunn was Michael Harper. According to Thiel, some of the epigrams in her collections Echolocations and Resistance Fantasies "don't speak directly to Gunn's poems" but "might have a similar energy and ironic turn (also Larkinesque)." Thiel explains that, in the lines "And Larkin, there's another to beware / between the sheets, for all I like his form," she is, "of course, using 'sheets' as both bedsheets and paper, and 'form' as both body and poetic form." Thiel also notes that various anthologists have compared her poem "The Minefield" to Larkin's "This Be the Verse." Thiel's, a narrative about the multi-generational impact of her father's

youthful wartime experiences, is serious and meditative, while Larkin's is raucous, vulgar, and humorously bitter. Thematic similarities can be purely coincidental, but in light of Thiel's longtime affection for Larkin's poetry, it may be more than coincidence that her poem, like his, deals with "the effect of one generation's trials on the next."

174 Thiel, email to author, 23 Oct. 2004.

175 All of Peacock's statements in this paragraph are from an email to the author, 21 April 2003.

176 Steele, All the Fun's in How You Say a Thing, page 217.

177 Richard J. Gray, note to author, March 2005. Also, my thanks to Professor Leon Burnett of the University of Essex for suggesting this line from Yeats's "Sailing to Byzantium."

178 I am borrowing the terms "discursive" and "essayistic" from a review of Steele's poetry, written by Kevin Walzer.

179 Hamburger, The Truth of Poetry, page 225.

180 Wezsteon, email interview, 12 March 2005.

181 As noted above, critics have also pointed out the similarities between Thiel's poem "The Minefield" and "This Be the Verse."

182 After reading a draft of these paragraphs, Peacock commented that the points I had made about connections between her poetry and Larkin's, which struck her as valid, had never been discussed before. She confirmed that "Home is So Sad" was indeed one of her favorite poems when she wrote "Our Room" and that it is still one of her favorites (email to author, 23 April 2005).

183 Steele's poems often contain "thesis statements" like those seen in Movement poetry, as seen in a sampling from three of Steele's earliest books: Uncertainties and Rest (1979); The Prudent Heart (1983); and Sapphics Against Anger (1986). "So much for dreaming," says the speaker of "With a Copy of Ronald Firbank" (Uncertainties and Rest, 3); "These days one sees a Kansas in retreat," says the speaker of "Over the Rainbow" (Uncertainties, 28); "There's nothing to the west but cold hills, / And the landmarks never change," says the fittingly laconic cowboy in "Cowboy" (Uncertainties, 29); "This is a child's forest," says the speaker of "This Is" (Uncertainties, 30); "Culture. It's an ingredient used in making / Pineapple yogurt, Gothic cathedrals," says

the speaker in the opening section of "Three Notes Toward Definition" (Uncertainties, 31). "Old letters are reproaches, mute petitions / Unlosable in some desk drawer / Or attic box," says the speaker of "Old Letters" (The Prudent Heart, 15). "The neighborhood, part Japanese and part / Chicano, wears its poverty like art . . . ," says the speaker of "Near Olympic" (Prudent, 21). "All life conspires to define us," says the speaker in "Last Tango," who also says, "In some less fallen world, an ease / Might grace our necessary fictions" (Sapphics Against Anger, 38); "The nominalist in me invents / A life devoid of precedents," says the philosophical speaker of "Chanson Philosophique" (Sapphics, 44); "Voluptuous in plenty, summer is / Neglectful of the earnest ones who've sought her," says the speaker of "Summer" (Sapphics, 51); "The prudent heart is like these plains, / Where quietness has grown immense . . . ," says the speaker of "Toward Calgary" (Sapphics, 65). (Several of the poems in Sapphics Against Anger first appeared in The Prudent Heart.)

184 Morrison, The Movement, pages 118–119.

185 Lentricchia quoted in Honicker, page 97.

186 This list comes from Thomas Cable, "Connoisseurs of Sound," page 59. Poets including Robert Graves, A. E. Housman, Edna St. Vincent Millay, Robert Fitzgerald, X. J. Kennedy, Howard Nemerov, James Merrill, Louis Simpson, J. V. Cunningham, Mona Van Duyn, and Weldon Kees are also cited as "masters" of the New Formalists.

187 Robert McPhillips has argued that the New Formalists are new because their language and cultural references tend to be more casual than those used by, say, 1950s Academic poets. New Formalists also tend to take a more relaxed approach to meter, rhyme, and form. But many New Formalist poems, especially those written by the "Wintersian" poets, can be packed with language, metaphors, and literary allusions just as esoteric as those of Hollander, Hecht, Wilbur, or Davie.

188 Solway, "Illuminating Ardor," page xiv.

189 All of the statements by Tillinghast are from his review, "Bookshelf: The Pleasures of Disciplined Verse," page A10.

190 Schoerke, "A Controversy Reignited," in New Expansive Poetry, page 84.

191 Lehman, "The Not-So-New Formalism," page 141.

192 Swiss, "Six Poets," page 303.

193 Conte, Unending Design, page 272.

194 Haines, "Rebels Not Yet Angels," page ii.

195 Hatch, "Rebels Without a Case," page 31.

196 Gioia, "Connect the Prose and the Passion," page 20.

197 Gioia, "Connect," page 20.

198 Gwynn, Introduction, New Expansive Poetry, page 11.

199 Mason, email interview, 19 December 2001.

200 All of the statements from Allen in this paragraph are from "Overcoming the Tic of Techniques," which is available online at https://www2.southeastern.edu/Academics/Faculty/jbedell/exp.html.

201 Phillips, "Assessing the New Formalism (So-Called)," page 150.

202 Link, "New Formalism," page 82.

203 All of the statements by Robert McPhillips in this paragraph are from his article "What's New About the New Formalism," which appears in New Expansive Poetry: Essays on the New Narrative and the New Formalism, pages 195–208.

204 In an entry on New Formalism in The Oxford Companion to Twentieth-Century Poetry in English, Robert McPhillips describes what he sees as the "distinct differences" between the "new formalism" and the "academic formalism that emerged out of the New Criticism in the 1950s": "While the [academic formalists] eschewed emotion in favour of irony, used elevated poetic diction and inverted syntax, and frequently looked to European culture for its subject, the New Formalists, by contrast, are more direct in their depiction of emotion, more colloquial in their diction, and more at ease with American popular culture as a source for formal poems (381)." As noted elsewhere, McPhillips's observations apply to many, but certainly not all, New Formalist poems.

205 Annie Finch says, "The single teacher who influenced my interest in formal poetry was Penelope Laurans (Robert Fitzgerald's widow, who teaches at Yale)," while "[John] Hollander influenced my criticism much more than my poetry" (email interview, 30 June 2004).

206 R. S. Gwynn says Lewis Turco, with whom he worked at a Bread Loaf Writers Conference, also contributed to his interest in formal poetry.

207 J. V. Cunningham is often described as a former student of Yvor Winters, but Timothy Steele emphasizes that he was not: "Contrary to what has been reported, Cunningham was never Winters's student. They were friends and colleagues" (Poems of J. V. Cunningham, xvii).

208 Wilbur, "For Better or For Worse," Mississippi Review, page 157.

209 Gioia refers to Davie as his "unofficial mentor" in an interview conducted by Gloria G. Brame and published online ("Paradigms Lost: Part Two").

210 New Formalists who argue for a strict adherence to meter, rhyme, and form are often called "Wintersians," a label that is not necessarily intended to be positive. In an online interview, appearing on the Cortland Review website, Timothy Steele, who is among this group, says that he has "no quarrel at all with a pluralism of poetic styles." At the same time, he also says that the "metrical tradition is the trunk of the great tree of poetry." In other words, he is saying that without this "trunk," poetry will die. Steele writes almost exclusively formal poetry himself, and in Missing Measures, he comes awfully close to saying that formal poetry is more legitimate than free verse. I suspect that, as a teacher of poetry, he is open-minded, but such a thing would be hard to determine. For future appraisals of the New Formalists, Steele's approach as a critic would be worth looking into, for it would help to show whether he is equitable in his treatment of both free verse and formal poetry. It would also be worth looking into the criticism of the others who are called "Wintersians."

211 Gioia, "Personal Tour," page 728.

212 Gioia goes on to say of Davie, "What other British critic could have made such a convincing case for the necessity of importing talents as diverse as Yvor Winters, George Oppen, Edward Dorn, Samuel Menashe, and Edgar Bowers—all poets not terribly well known even in America? Likewise, who else could have made such a suavely compelling plea for Americans to read Betjeman, Larkin, Tomlinson, Bunting, and Sisson?" ("Personal Tour," 727).

213 Bezner, "An Interview with Dana Gioia," page 40.

214 Gioia, "Donald Davie" (essay), Sequoia, page 16.

215 Gioia, "Donald Davie" (essay), pages 16 and 17.

216 Gioia, "Donald Davie" (essay), Sequoia, page 17. The ten poems listed by Gioia are "The Garden Party" (1955), "Remembering the 'Thirties" (1955), "Woodpigeons at Raheny" (1955), "Time Passing, Beloved" (1957), "The Mushroom Gatherers" (1957), "Via Portello" (1957), "Low Lands" (1964), "Pieta" (1969), "Tunstall Forest" (1969) and "Christmas Syllabics for a Wife" (1968–69). The poems published in the 1950s date from the Movement.

217 Gioia, "Donald Davie" (essay), Sequoia, page 17.

218 Gioia, "Donald Davie" (essay), Sequoia, page 18.

219 Davie, Thomas Hardy and British Poetry, page 3. As seen in H. T. Kirby-Smith's article discussed earlier, Hardy is also cited as an inspiration for the New Formalists.

220 Davie, Thomas Hardy, page 36.

221 Davie, Thomas Hardy, page 39.

222 Davie, Thomas Hardy, page 39.

223 Davie, Thomas Hardy, page 40.

224 Davie, "Remembering the Thirties," Collected Poems, pages 28–29.

225 Bezner, "An Interview with Dana Gioia," page 40.

226 Jarman, email interview, 28 May 2001. In a 1994 discussion of Ezra Pound's "Hugh Selwyn Mauberly," Jarman also briefly but respectfully mentions Davie, saying that the "stanzas are meant to last, to be, as Donald Davie has observed, carved in time, as an antidote to what the times demanded" ("Br'er Rabbit and Br'er Possum," 58).

227 Jarman, "A Shared Humanity," page 90.

228 Jarman, "A Shared Humanity," pages 100 and 101.

229 Jarman, "A Shared Humanity," page 93.

230 Jarman, email interview, 28 May 2001.

231 All of the statements in this paragraph by Jarman and McDowell are from "The Reaper's Non-Negotiable Demands," published in The Reaper Essays, pages 34–44.

232 One item in Jarman and McDowell's list of "non-negotiable demands" in The Reaper Essays is that poets must "Spring open the Jail of the Self" (43). Both groups have been inconsistent in their approach to autobiographical topics, however, suggesting that they have seen this demand as at least somewhat negotiable. These two groups are not, of course, the only ones who have either argued or implied that poets should write about subjects other than themselves, just as they are not the only groups to violate one of their own policies. Both groups might attempt to argue, however—with varying degrees of accuracy—that the autobiographical nature of their poems is countered by the "universality" of their themes.

233 All of Chambers' comments in this paragraph are from A Few Friends: Poems for Thom Gunn's 60th Birthday, page 5. Appearing in the poetry collection in honor of Gunn's 60th birthday along with Timothy Steele and Dick Davis are Edgar Bowers, Charles Gullans, August Kleinzahler, Raymond Oliver, John Peck, Jim Powell, Alan Stephens, Michael Vince, Robert Wells, and Clive Wilmer. Rather surprisingly, they are all males. The poets are formalists and free-verse poets, a fitting combination given Gunn's own writing practices and critical tastes.

234 All of Steele's statements in this paragraph are from page 44 in A Few Friends, page 44. (The poetry collection is listed under Edgar Bowers on the Works Cited page.)

235 All of Davis's statements in this paragraph are from page 13 in A Few Friends (which is listed under Edgar Bowers on the Works Cited page). After saying that he thinks of Thom Gunn as "the best living British poet," Davis then enumerates the qualities he admires in Gunn's poetry, including his "ability to use language persuasively," his "clarity," his "lack of pretension and fuss," and his "exactness," all of which combine to make Gunn a "great craftsman" (13). Although Davis does not mention Gunn's affiliation with the Movement, all of the traits he lists were valued by that group. Davis, too, appreciates those qualities. For him, though, the "intelligent sympathy with his subject matter that pervades everything [Gunn] writes" is even more important. Ending his tribute, Davis points out Gunn's potential as an inspiration for poets: "There is a kind of humility in Gunn's verse—both towards what he writes about and towards the craft of poetry—which has become very rare and which therefore seems all the more valuable and worth trying

to learn from." Strictly speaking, Davis does not say that Gunn has been an influence on his own poetry, but his tribute suggests the likelihood.

236 The nineteen poems by Gunn that appear in Selected Poems by Thom Gunn and Ted Hughes are "The Wound," "The Beach Head," "Tamer and Hawk," "For a Birthday," "Incident on a Journey," all from 1954; "On the Move," "The Unsettled Motorcyclist's Vision of His Death," "In Praise of Cities," "During an Absence," "The Corridor," "Vox Humana," all from 1957; "In Santa Maria del Popolo," "The Annihilation of Nothing," "Innocence," "The Byrnies," "Claus von Stauffenberg," "Considering the Snail," "'Blackie, the Electric Rembrandt'," and "My Sad Captains," all from 1961.

237 Steele, A Few Friends, page 44. (This collection is listed under Edgar Bowers on the Works Cited page.)

238 All of Lake's statements in this paragraph and the next are from his article "Old Adam in the New World Garden," pages 9–10.

239 I would use "abandon" where Lake uses "abandonment."

240 Hudgins made all of these statements in an email interview that I conducted with him on 28 April 2005.

241 Hudgins goes on to say that his initial reading of Gunn was not entirely fair: "But these were the impressions—hardly, thoughts—of an angry guy in his mid-twenties reading in the library with a chip on his shoulder, looking for a reason to reject the famous and successful. I haven't read Gunn closely since then, I'm sorry to say, except for The Man With Night Sweats" (email interview, 28 April 2005).

242 Allen made all of these statements in email interviews that I conducted with him, one on 26 March 2002 and the other on 6 Jan. 2004.

243 In an entry for The Oxford Companion to Twentieth-Century Poetry in English (1994), R. S. Gwynn points out that the 1957 edition of New Poets of England and America "introduced Philip Larkin, Kingsley Amis, Thom Gunn, and others to many American readers" (383). The 1957 edition contains the following poems by Movement writers: "Masters," "Against Romanticism," "A Bookshop Idyll," and "Departure" (Amis); "At Knaresborough," "The Evangelist," "The Garden Party," "Remembering the 'Thirties," and "Homage to William Cowper" (Davie); "A Mirror for Poets," "The Wound," "Incident on a Journey," "Tamer and Hawk," "Merlin in the Cave: He Speculates

Without a Book," "The Corridor," "Before the Carnival," and "The Nature of an Action" (Gunn); "Journey Through the Night," "The Light," "Elegy for an Estrangement," and "Warning to a Guest" (Holloway); "Delay," "Winter Love," "Weathercock," "Identity," "The Climbers," "The Idler," "A Way of Looking," "Not in the Guide-Books," "Beyond Possession," "Communication," "Mirrors," "Escape and Return," "Answers," and "In the Night" (Jennings); "Deception," "Church Going," "Toads," "Poetry of Departures," "At Grass," "Next, Please," and "Places, Loved Ones" (Larkin). Charles Causley, who is occasionally counted as a Movement writer (or at least mentioned as a poet who shares some ideas with the group), appears here as well. The anthology also features American writers often cited as influences on the New Formalists: Edgar Bowers, Charles Gullans, Donald Hall, Anthony Hecht, John Hollander, Donald Justice, Howard Nemerov, Louis Simpson, William Jay Smith, and Richard Wilbur.

244 While the 1957 edition of New Poets of England and America does not differentiate among British and American poets, the 1962 edition separates them according to nationality, suggesting that the trans-Atlantic divisions that came to typify British and American poetry of the 1960s and later were already beginning. The 1962 edition contains the following poems by Movement writers: "Autobiographical Fragment," "Sight Unseen," "Terrible Beauty," "A Tribute to the Founder," "Science Fiction," "On a Portrait of Mme. Rimsky-Korsakov," and "After Goliath" (Amis); "A Winter Talent," "Gardens No Emblems," "Hearing Russian Spoken," "The Wind at Penistone," "Time Passing, Beloved," "The Mushroom Gatherers," "Heigh-Ho on a Winter Afternoon," and "For an Age of Plastics, Plymouth" (Davie); "On the Move," "The Unsettled Motorcyclist's Vision of His Death," "Vox Humana," "In Santa Maria del Popolo," "The Annihilation of Nothing," "Innocence," "Considering the Snail," "Loot," "The Byrnies," and "My Sad Captains" (Gunn); "Old Man," "The Child and the Shadow," "Disguises," "The Parting," "Ghosts," "The Storm," "Teresa of Avila" (a prose poem, surprisingly enough), "The Room," "A World of Light," and "Harvest and Consecration" (Jennings); "Mr. Bleaney," "An Arundel Tomb," and "The Whitsun Weddings" (Larkin); "The New Sun," "Au Jardin des Plantes," "Anniversary," "Apology for Understatement," and "Poem Without a Main Verb" (Wain).

245 In one of the email interviews that I conducted with him (6 Jan. 2004), Dick Allen spoke at length about the poetic environment of his college

and graduate school days: "The split came with the Beats, [with] Donald Allen's anthology [The New American Poetry 1945–1960], and with the proliferation of volumes of modern and contemporary American poetry and classes in which ONLY modern and contemporary American poetry was studied. For many of us, the Beats and the increased influence of William Carlos Williams' poetry made most of British poetry seem stodgy and unimportant and uninteresting and many of us ceased to pay much attention to it. However, for those of my generation, the pattern and influences had been set . . . ." The "pattern and influences" mentioned by Allen included the view of Yeats as "the greatest poet in the English language recently" and Eliot as "a close second."

246 Additional articles by Dick Allen, including "Poetry Village," "Shifts," "The Donner Party," "To the Wall," "What Rough Beast: SF-Oriented Poetry," and "After the Avant-Garde," demonstrate the extent to which his ideas echo those of the Movement.

247 Gwynn made the statements in this paragraph in an email interview that I conducted with him (13 March 2003). Gwynn says, further, that the primary influences on his work have been "the Metaphysicals, Hardy, Housman, Browning, Wilbur, Hecht, Simpson, Kennedy, and lots of others, mostly formalists."

248 Gioia, "Personal Tour," page 724.

249 Gioia, "Personal Tour," pages 727–728.

250 Gioia, "Personal Tour," pages 727–728.

251 Gioia, "A Map of The Shires," pages 103 and 111.

252 All of Gioia's statements in this paragraph are from his review, "A Personal Tour," pages 724–729. In a 2001 review of The Secret of Poetry, David Kirby says surprisingly similar things about Jarman: "To him, the secret of good criticism is a sense of history and of context, of knowing where poems come from and how poets read each other" (84).

253 Gioia notes the argument of some critics who say that American poets write primarily with themselves, rather than readers, in mind. He does not dispute the critics' allegation. Instead, he describes Davie's claim that English poets consider the writing of poetry to be "a public and social activity," which, in Davie's view, sometimes comes uncomfortably close to pandering: "the sad fact is that English readers of contemporary

poetry—few as they are, and perhaps just because they are so few—have got used to being cajoled and coaxed, at all events sedulously attended to, by their poets" (Davie qtd. in Gioia, "Personal Tour," 726).

254 Unless otherwise noted, all of these comments are from a personal interview conducted on 20 Dec. 2001.

255 In "The Achievement of Weldon Kees" (1979), Gioia hints at similarities between Kees and Larkin: "Kees then is a poet of a very narrow scope, but this is hardly a damning criticism. Herbert, Hopkins, Houseman [sic], Larkin, not to mention continental writers like Trakl or Leopardi are all poets who could, in some sense, be accused of having narrow interests. It is not the breadth of a poet's response to life that assures fame with posterity, but rather the depth and intensity of that vision" (32). In Gioia's view, then, Larkin does not deserve to be "damn[ed]" for his "narrow scope" or his pessimism any more than Kees does, for both poets responded to life with a "depth and intensity of . . . vision." Similarly, in a 1981 review, Gioia compares Larkin and Donald Justice, saying that, "Like his English contemporary, Philip Larkin, Justice is content to excel within very definite, self-imposed limits" ("Three Poets in Mid-Career," 674). In this article, Gioia reviews poetry by Justice, Hecht, and Frederick Morgan.

256 McPhillips, "Dana Gioia Interviewed by Robert McPhillips," page 16.

257 McPhillips, "Dana Gioia Interviewed by Robert McPhillips," page 24.

258 McPhillips, "The Gods of Winter," page 114.

259 Flamm, "Yearning Disabled," page 45. Flamm almost admires Gioia's poem "The Room Upstairs," but he says that it ends up being "too much Frost's, from its conception down to its cadences."

260 All of Swarbrick's comments in this paragraph are from his review, "No Shocks Left from the Rude Poet," page 13.

261 Scott, "This Be the Prose," page 16.

262 In "This Be the Prose," A. O. Scott is reviewing Gioia's prose collection Disappearing Ink: Poetry at the End of Print Culture. Scott praises the first essay for its "inclusiveness" and for its accomplishments in "map[ping] out a wide and rich terrain" in contemporary poetry, from rap to cowboy poetry to "spoken-word performances" (16). He says, "Gioia deserves praise for taking up questions that lie outside the grazed-over pastures where tenure seekers ruminate and belch."

However, the review is almost entirely negative. Scott condemns Gioia for "taking genuinely interesting and urgent questions and making them seem, by the time he is finished considering them, much less so." He even says that the collection—written in "undergraduate prose"—"is pretty much useless either as cultural analysis or as literary criticism." I have not read this entire collection by Gioia, but I have read many of the essays that later made their way into it, such as the discussions of Weldon Kees, Elizabeth Bishop, and Longfellow. Scott claims that Gioia's "impeccable manners, his air of quiet sympathy and his well-worn phrases of comfort and conciliation" make him seem less like a "passionate defender of a beleaguered art in a troubled time" and "more like an undertaker." Comments like these remind me of the ad hominem attacks launched against—and by—the Movement writers.

263 All of Gioia's statements in this paragraph are from "Poetry Chronicle," Hudson Review 33.4, pages 611–627.

264 All of Gioia's statements in this paragraph are from his essay, "The Barrier of a Common Language: New British Poetry in the 1980s," which appears in his 2003 essay collection Barrier of a Common Language: An American Looks at British Poetry but was first published in 1984.

265 Gioia, "Still Sad Music," page 1.

266 Mason, email to author, 16 Feb. 2001. In a 1990 review of Expansive Poetry, Mason describes his regret that many of the essays in the collection are polemical and one-sided but says that "We really do live in a world where form is often lumped with tradition and dismissed as fascistic, where technique is confused with politics. We need to rediscover the promise of 'formal' poetry—not just old forms from the handbooks, but newly invented forms—and this promise is complex" (page 731). In one interview, Timothy Steele says that his situation as a young poet who wished to write formal poetry when few others seemed to share his interest "wasn't all that crushing," but in an article published in Brandeis Review in 1992, he says that "writing in meter and rhyme did make me feel at times like a living fossil" (Walzer, "Interview"; "Forms of Poetry," page 30). The obstacles Steele encountered (which were similar to those encountered by Mason) perhaps help explain his own attraction to Gunn, which dates back to 1969: "Occasionally, when I submitted material, editors questioned my interest in technique. And once a well-meaning fellow did advise me that meter and rhyme

were simply passé and that, though it looked like I had some talent, I'd never get anywhere if I stuck to writing in form" (Walzer, "Interview").

267 Mason, email to author, 21 Dec. 2001.

268 All of Gunn's comments in this paragraph are from "An Anglo-American Poet: Interview with Jim Powell," which appears in Shelf Life: Essays, Memoirs, and an Interview, pages 218–230.

269 Gunn, "Fever in the Morning: Jim Powell," page 121.

270 In some cases, criticisms of the New Formalists are undoubtedly justified. In other cases, they are not. For instance, Gioia mentioned in a letter to me (January 2001), that "some anti-formalists have dismissed [his] sonnets," even though at that time he had "never published a sonnet."

271 Baer, "An Interview with Timothy Steele," pages 39–40.

272 Gioia quoted in Link, "Dana Gioia," page 209.

273 Gioia, "Notes on the New Formalism," Expansive Poetry, page 174. (This essay also appears in Can Poetry Matter?) Davie was perhaps an influence on Gioia's concept of "pseudo-formal verse." In a 1972 essay, Davie says that "some of the sloppiest verse one encounters has been perpetrated by people who thought they were writing free verse when in fact they were writing, for instance, loose pentameters. And in general there is no excuse for not knowing what you are doing" ("Some Notes," 200). As for Gioia's belief that poets should feel free to write both free verse and formal verse, former students have said that Davie encouraged a similar approach, as embodied by his combination of Modernist "Poundian" attitudes and traditional "Wintersian" attitudes.

274 Gioia, "Notes on the New Formalism," Expansive Poetry, page 174.

275 Bartlett, "Thom Gunn: 'For a Sign of Other Than Love'," page 91.

276 Finch, email to author, 17 Dec. 2001.

277 Allen, email interview, 26 March 2002.

278 Mason, email to author, 21 Dec. 2001. Mason describes Larkin as his favorite Movement poet: "Surely Larkin is my favorite, though I think the Thwaite edition of his work contains far too many weak poems. Larkin's very substantial achievement, I think, is to leave behind a very strong sense of personality in his poems, a stance that is unlike

anyone else's. He's like Eliot and Auden in this respect, and damn few others. It's as if he found the perfect medium to convey his very specific, sometimes unattractive persona. Not very many poets ever accomplish a voice in quite that way" (email interview, 27 May 2001). Mason says that his favorite poem by Gunn is "'The Hug, which opens THE MAN WITH NIGHT SWEATS. It's a love poem that could be read by people of any sexual persuasion, and it has a quiet realism in its images of a long-term relationship" (email interview, 27 May 2001). Mason says further that he "love[s] Thom Gunn for his unwillingness to be pegged. He must seem too American to some Brits, too British to some Americans. I like his affection for Williams and the Bay Area poets like Duncan, but I especially love his unwillingness to give up such pleasures as meter and rhyme, to join the sanctimonious anti-formal Puritans of the modern era." The importance of his connections with Gunn and Larkin notwithstanding, Mason also describes many additional influences, beginning with those in his family who first awoke his interest in narrative poetry.

279 Gioia, personal interview, 20 Dec. 2001.

280 The "blurb" from Thom Gunn appears on the back cover of Lake's book Another Kind of Travel. Here is the blurb in its entirety: "The poems that I like best in this clean and cunning book are 'An Apparition' and 'South of the City.' In them Paul Lake attempts to grasp the ungraspable, thus putting a strain on the imagination that makes for the irregular movement of the explorer's warily placed perceptions."

281 All of Gunn's statements in this brief paragraph are from "Playing Politics with Poetry," pages 4 and 5 (published in 1981). In a review first published in 1976, Gunn also praised In the Distance, an early collection by Dick Davis, an English poet who lives in the United States and who is often associated with the New Formalists: "This book does not force itself on your attention. When I first read it, I thought: Well, that's nice. But I read it again, and then again, as things from it returned to my mind and I went back to confirm them. I began to realize that these poems will probably still be with me in ten years' time, and there are not many recent books of poetry I can say that about" ("Immersions," 138). About the same book, Gunn says, "It is a first book, but a very mature one. The style is firm, totally without pretension, but all art. The majority of poems are metrical: at a time when most American poets consider metre obsolete and most English

poets who use it do so as if it were obsolete, it is wonderful to find a poet (English) whose poetry lives through its metre. His handling of it is masterful, and you are never aware of effort. And the language is exact but relentless, like the perceptions. On the basis of this book, I would say that Davis is one of the best poets around" (141).

282 Gunn's praise of Steele's Sapphics Against Anger (1986) appears on the back cover of the book.

283 Gunn, letter to the author, 27 June 2001.

284 Gunn, personal interview, 27 Dec. 2001.

285 Steele, email interview, 25 May 2004. Steele explained that he spoke with Gunn at the request of Jan Schreiber, then the editor-in-chief of Boston publisher David Godine, who wanted to publish a chapbook written by Gunn. Steele says that he met with Gunn and that "the chapbook project did go forward."

286 In an online interview conducted by Cynthia Haven in 2000, Steele describes an experience that he had in the late 1970s involving his first book, Uncertainties and Rest, which was eventually published by Louisiana State University Press. An anonymous referee who had read Steele's manuscript queried, "Does the press want on its list at this time a collection that is characteristically witty, formal, and sophisticated?" On being told of the referee's question, Steele cheerfully embraced the oversimplified dichotomy implied by it and asked whether the press would "rather publish poetry that is dull, haphazard, and primitive." This very sort of dichotomy is, of course, one major reason those who write formal verse and those who write free verse have engaged in heated arguments over the years. Haven's interview with Steele appears online, on the Cortland Review website. Coincidentally, in a 1981 review of poetry by Kingsley Amis, Ted Hughes, and others, Gioia states that, for Amis, "intelligence, wit, form, and verbal ingenuity are the essentials of poetry" (616). Though any resemblance between Gioia's description of Amis and the anonymous referee's description of Steele undoubtedly is coincidental, it is striking nonetheless.

287 Steele, email interview, 25 May 2004. "Vermont Spring" appears on page 51 in The Color Wheel.

288 Gioia, email to author, 20 May 2004.

289 To "audit" a class means to sit in on the class without receiving academic credit for it. The information about Gioia's education and the makeup of Davie's Poetry-Writing Seminar appears in "Michael Dana Gioia: A Chronology," written by April Lindner (pages ix–xiii in Dana Gioia: A Descriptive Bibliography).

290 Brame, "Paradigms Lost: Part Two"; McPhillips interview, page 23.

291 In a 1972 essay, Davie says that he still believes what he said in his 1953 poem "Creon's Mouse," which is notorious for its thoroughly Movement-like suggestion that "loss of nerve" is a virtue rather than a failing: "This poem was seriously meant, and much of it I still subscribe to. A loss of nerve is what has saved us time and again in the years since 1953 . . . . On the other side of the balance, an alarming recovery of nerve, 'too much daring', was what took Britain into the Suez crisis and America into Vietnam ("Lucky Jim," 88)." See also Harvey Oxenhorn's "Donald Davie and the American Poetry Workshop," along with the 1977 interview of Davie conducted by Dana Gioia.

292 Gray, note to author, Oct. 2003.

293 All of Gioia's statements in this paragraph are from a personal interview that I conducted on 20 Dec. 2001.

294 In a note to me (date not specified), Richard J. Gray suggests that, in fact, "the degree of Davie's interest in poetic structure . . . sets him apart from most advocates of free verse. Free-verse poets and their adherents might well resent any implication that they are uninterested in poetic structure, but it is surely safe to say that formal poets tend to be more interested in structure than free-verse poets tend to be.

295 All of Gery's comments in this paragraph are from an email to the author, 19 May 2005.

296 All of Lake's comments in this paragraph are from an email to the author, 24 May 2004.

297 The interview of Davie conducted by Paul Lake and James Powell appears in a 1981 issue of Occident. James Powell is not typically counted among the New Formalists; indeed, he has made it clear that he does not share their beliefs. It may be telling that Gunn's 1989 review of Powell opens with a vehement dismissal of not only the New Formalists but also the Language poets. Also, when Powell interviewed

Gunn in 1989, both criticized the New Formalists for "drawing on" a tradition that was "far too narrow" ("An Anglo-American Poet," 227).

298 In his reply to my enquiries about the connections between the Movement and New Formalism (24 May 2004), Paul Lake had this to say: "I think your fundamental insight that the Movement and New Formalism have an interesting relationship is on the money. What drew Donald Davie to Stanford was the legacy of Yvor Winters, an advocate of formalism in verse. So it was quite natural for people like me and Vikram Seth and John Gery to be selected by Stanford when we applied there." In a 1998 article, "Disorderly Order: Free Verse, Chaos, and the Tradition," Lake quotes Davie several times to support his own arguments.

299 All of Oxenhorn's comments in these two paragraphs are from his article, "Donald Davie and the American Poetry Workshop," which appears in Donald Davie and the Responsibilities of Literature, pages 64–73.

300 Gunn, "On a Drying Hill: Yvor Winters," page 202.

301 Davie, "Talking with Millicent Dillon," pages 45 and 46.

302 Unless otherwise indicated, all of Jarman's statements in this paragraph are from an email interview with the author, 13 July 2001. Jarman is generally associated with the New Narrative strand of Expansive Poetry. His book-length poem, Iris (1992), for instance, is not only about poet Robinson Jeffers and the importance of his poetry to a young woman late in the twentieth century, it is written in the long free-verse lines of Jeffers. Jarman does, however, write formal poetry, as in his Unholy Sonnets.

303 Jarman, email interview, 28 May 2001.

304 Murphy, "A Conversation with Mark Jarman," page 65.

305 McDowell, email interview, 18 February 2002.

306 Leslie Monsour is generally described as a second-generation New Formalist, although, as noted earlier, the generational lines are quite blurry. Monsour's comments about Larkin, Gunn, and others appear in an online interview, conducted by Alex Pepple, for Able Muse. Although Monsour says she has been "disappointed" by Gunn "a few times lately," she places both Gunn and Larkin amidst a distinguished group of her "poetic influences," including Frost, Jeffers, Bishop,

Dickinson, Auden, Wilbur, Keats, and "the three Wills: Shakespeare, Blake, and Wordsworth." Monsour names an eclectic group of poets whom she admires, many of them formalists: Homer, Ovid, Horace, A. A. Milne, Edward Lear, Robert Louis Stevenson, Timothy Steele, Wendy Cope, Dick Davis, X. J. Kennedy, Timothy Murphy, Dana Gioia, Charles Martin, Anthony Hecht, Mary Jo Salter, Brad Leithauser, Amy Clampitt, Gwendolyn Brooks, Mark Strand, William Logan, Billy Collins, Rhina Espaillat, John Ridland, Kate Light, Kevin Durkin, Dolores Hayden, "even Robert Service."

307 Molly Peacock made these remarks about Gunn and Larkin in an email interview (21 April 2003).

308 Annie Finch made these remarks about Larkin and Davie in an email interview (30 June 2004).

309 Katha Pollitt made this remark in an email interview (23 Sept. 2005). Pollitt does not call herself a New Formalist, but her poetry has appeared in journals or anthologies associated with the group.

310 Pollitt, "Philip Larkin," Grand Street 9.3 (Spring 1990), pages 253, 256, 260. In this review, Katha Pollitt offers an emphatic defense of the very poems that are grumpy, bleak, or Philistinic: ". . . the poems Larkin wrote in his curmudgeon vein are extraordinarily spirited productions, instantly memorizable, and often very funny . . . . 'They fuck you up, your mum and dad', 'Books are a load of crap', 'Life is first boredom, then fear' (amended by Amis as 'life is first boredom, then more boredom')—they may not be 'A thing of beauty is a joy forever', but are they not as confidently asserted, and as true?" (252). Although she dislikes the "muddled" arrangement of The Collected Poems, edited by Anthony Thwaite, she appreciates what it reveals about Larkin: "the main . . . message of the Collected Poems is that Larkin was more productive than we knew, and somewhat more—well, not hopeful exactly, but open to the possibility of hope" (253). Pollitt also says that, of contemporary poets, only Larkin is "regularly described as 'loved'" and that "His commitment to communicating is surely one of the reasons for his immense popularity . . . " (257). "One needn't be a Philistine," she says, "to plunge with happy relief into poetry that needs no footnotes or prose scenarios and professorial champions." Larkin's popularity, she says, also stems from his bleakly accurate descriptions: "The world we find in Larkin . . . is unmistakably the world we live in: car parks and glass-and-steel towers and tract housing, pointless jobs

and domestic routine, greed and glitz, small pretty cherished things that make us sad because, like the old lady's sheet-music covers in 'Love Songs in Age', they hint at a happiness that eludes us" (259). Larkin, she says, "transcends the darkness" of this world by "crystallizing it in verse so sharp and exact and surprising that, once read, it is never forgotten" (260).

311 Mason, email interview, 16 Feb. 2001.

312 Mason, email interview, 16 Feb. 2001.

313 David Mason described his admiration for both Larkin and Gunn in an email interview (27 May 2001).

314 Rachel Wetzsteon may be described as a second-generation or possibly third-generation New Formalist, though the generational lines are quite blurry. Wetzsteon described her affection for Larkin and Gunn in an email interview (12 March 2005) and an email message (1 April 2005).

315 Kirsch made this comment in an article called "In Memory, and Admiration, of Rachel Wetzsteon." The New Republic. 30 Dec. 2009. http://www.tnr.com/article/books-and-arts/rachel-wetzsteon. Accessed 24 Feb. 2010.

316 Chapman made this comment in an article called "The Life and Death of Rachel Wetzsteon." Easy Street: A Magazine of Words and Culture. 25 May 2015. http://www.easystreetmag.com/life-and-death-of-rachel-wetzsteon/. (Although the semicolon in Chapman's sentence should be a colon, I have chosen not to interrupt the sentence by writing "sic" next to the error.)

317 Seth quoted in "Poetic License," page 66. When Vikram Seth went to Stanford University to work a PhD in economics, he met Timothy Steele, and the two arranged to meet weekly to discuss poetry. In those sessions, Steele introduced Seth to his own poetry, as well as poetry by Frost and Larkin.

318 Seth quoted in "Poetic License," page 66.

319 Steele's remarks about the poets in the "older generation" who gave hope to younger poets appear on page 28 of an interview conducted by William Baer and published in The Formalist.

320 Allen, email to author, 1 September 2017.

321 Unless indicated otherwise, all of Allen's statements in this paragraph are from his review, "The Gift to Be Simple," which appears in Poetry 124.2 (May 1974), pages 103–116.

322 In his 1974 review of a collection by poet Mary Baron (mentioned in an endnote for Chapter One), Timothy Steele uses "Movement" criteria throughout. Speaking of Baron's poetry, Steele says, "There is in her best poems that fusion of feeling and control characteristic of all fine poetry" ("Keeping Angels in Line," 193). Steele also praises the "great tact and skill" in Baron's poetry, as well as her focus on "customary human concerns" (191). So far as I know, the Movement-like quality of "tact" is seldom pointed out in poetry reviews.

323 All of Shaw's statements in this paragraph are from his review, "Philip Larkin: A Stateside View," which appears in Poetry Nation 6 (1976), pages 100–109.

324 Leithauser, "Confinement of Free Verse," page 4. Leithauser's list also includes Robert Frost, John Crowe Ransom, W. H. Auden, Louise Bogan, Patrick Kavanagh, Robert Lowell, Elizabeth Bishop, James Merrill, Malcolm Lowry, and Seamus Heaney.

325 Rachel Hadas's description of Elizabeth Bishop and Philip Larkin as "diverse, skilled, and original" appears on page 256 of her article "On Bonnefoy." She prefers Bonnefoy's "vatic voice" to the "unformulated but strong aesthetic of the poem as either anecdote or photograph," which, she says, governs the poetry of Bishop, Larkin, and "a swarm of lesser writers." Bonnefoy is "working," she points out, "in a tradition of prophecy." Although Hadas does not mention the Movement writers, it is clear that Bonnefoy is quite different from them, for they shunned the "tradition of prophecy."

326 Andrew Hudgins's remarks about Larkin appear in a 1990 "Poetry Chronicle," published in Hudson Review (page 681).

327 Wyatt Prunty, another poet often associated with the New Formalists, was familiar with Davie's poetry as early as 1979, but I have not included his remarks in the body of this chapter because they are neutral, neither positive nor negative. In a 1979 review, in response to a comment made by Davie that "British and American poets have trouble hearing each other," Prunty points out that Davie himself is "read on both sides" of the Atlantic ("Reciprocals," 640). He says further that Davie, an English poet named Peter Dale, and an American poet named Timothy

Steele "can hear each other perfectly well" because they are all "writing formal poetry derived from a tradition which persists on both sides of the Atlantic." Prunty was responding to comments made by Davie in 1978 or 1979 at a meeting of the Modern Language Association in Atlanta, Georgia.

328 Gioia, "Still, Sad Music," page 1. Gioia also uses a well-known Larkin line—"What will survive of us is love"—as the title for a 1994 review of an autobiography by Philip Levine, The Bread of Time: Toward an Autobiography, first published in The New York Times Book Review, 20 Feb. 1994.

329 Gioia's comments in this sentence and the next are from an email to the author, 10 Feb. 2018.

330 Gioia, "Poetry and the Fine Presses," page 491. In his 1993 article "The Still, Sad Music of Philip Larkin," Dana Gioia states that Larkin secured his stellar literary reputation "By a rare combination of imaginative and critical genius," resulting in "mature collections" in which every poem is "genuinely interesting," with "at least two dozen of them rank[ing] among the best English language poems of the century." Though acknowledging the unappealing sides of Larkin's character, Gioia believes that Larkin "was a quietly visionary poet" who "found a way of making the unhappiest truths darkly beautiful" (1, 9).

331 Brame, "An Interview with Poet and Critic Dana Gioia. Paradigms Lost: Part Two."

332 Gioia, email to author, 20 May 2004.

333 Peschiera, "America and the Culture of Poetry," page 92. In addition to Davie and Yvor Winters, Gioia also names Hugh Kenner, Northrop Frye, Georg Lukacs, and Leslie Fiedler.

334 Bezner, "Interview with Dana Gioia," page 40.

335 In this sentence and the next, I am quoting from Gioia's written responses to questions that I sent to him by post in May of 2001 (exact date not specified). In a letter that he sent to me in January 2001, Gioia says that the Movement "was the most important impulse of its time because it brought Larkin to prominence."

336 Steele, "Symposium," page 103.

337 The passage from which I have excerpted Steele's praise of Larkin's "Whitsun Weddings" and "Church Going" appears on page 217: "More specifically, extended stanzas seem particularly to suit a kind of middle-length poem—a poem of, say, fifty to one hundred lines—well represented by such works as Keat's "Ode to a Nightingale" and "Ode on a Grecian Urn," Yeats's "Prayer for My Daughter," Winters's "California Oaks," and Larkin's "Whitsun Weddings" and "Church Going." Though these poems differ in many respects from one another, they all combine lyrical grace with a thematic and argumentative richness that we customarily encounter only in much longer poems or in such prose forms as the essay, short story, or novel." It is intriguing to see that Steele values two characteristics that were also important to the Movement: "lyrical grace" and "argumentative richness." Of course, most poets espouse "lyrical grace." In contrast, the number of poets who espouse "argumentative richness" in poetry is probably quite limited. Steele has so often made positive remarks about Larkin and Gunn that it would be repetitive to include them all in the body of this chapter. In addition to the remarks that I have included, others can be found in a symposium featured in a 1989 issue of Crosscurrents dedicated to "Expansive Poetry" and edited by Dick Allen; in Steele's own book Missing Measures (1990); in an interview conducted by Kevin Durkin in 2000; and in a 2002 interview conducted by William Baer. Steele also makes positive remarks about Larkin and Gunn on the following pages of All the Fun's in How You Say a Thing: 87, 217, 218, 225, 258, 314. In this same book, Steele recommends criticism written by Winters, Gunn, and Davie. See, for instance, pages 293, 299, and 304.

338 Martin, "Just a Smack at Larkin," Hudson Review, pages 400–401.

339 Martin, email to author, 16 May 2005.

340 Mason, email to author, 30 Aug. 2017. Unfortunately, when "Larking for Larkin" was published in Sewanee Review, the word "toad" was changed to "load," thus obscuring the reference to the poem by Larkin that inspired Mason's own poem.

341 Timothy Steele's remarks about the poets in the "older generation" who "gave . . . great hope" to younger poets appear on page 28 of an interview conducted by William Baer and published in The Formalist.

Before that, on pages 26–27, he says, "... Of the contemporaries, I'm particularly indebted to Richard Wilbur, Philip Larkin, X. J. Kennedy, Louise Bogan, Anthony Hecht, Thom Gunn, Janet Lewis, and Edgar Bowers....

342 So many reviews suggest thematic and formal parallels between the two groups that there simply is insufficient room to mention or discuss them in the body of this chapter. The Movement writers might have thought, for instance, that William Oxley's description of Gioia's poetry—that its "authority derives from humility, perhaps a troubled humility, but humility all the same"—would fit their own (101). John N. Miller says that the balance of "Sociability and privacy, candor and reserve, expression and reticence create a civilized dialectic in several of Steele's poems" (60). On the other hand, the Movement writers were also criticized for the very same tendency for which Robert McPhillips criticizes Steele: being "particularly even-tempered on all occasions" (314). According to John Press, writing in 1962, "it is absurd to pretend that in our affluent society a poet can find nothing to arouse his compassion or his savage indignation" (11). Along these same lines, Paul Breslin quotes Dick Allen's claim that "New Formalist poems are typically 'more passionate and involved than intellectualized and distanced'" (143). In response, Breslin says, "The New Formalism may be less mannered than the old, but the words 'involved and passionate' do not spring to one's head" (145). In an article about the poetry featured in New Lines, Ian Hamilton dismissively says of Gunn, "One doubts that Gunn had learned anything, at this stage, from any modern poet" (73). Decades later, McPhillips criticizes Steele for almost exactly the same reason: "He writes as if the Modernist movement had never occurred" ("Reading," 314). Ironically, Larkin (as well as Conquest and Amis) would probably have seen such a remark as high praise. In a 1959 review of John Betjeman, for instance, Larkin "attributed much of [Betjeman's] popularity to his 'rejection of modernism'," approvingly noting that "For him there has been no symbolism, no objective correlative, no T. S. Eliot or Ezra Pound" (qtd. in Morrison, 134). In contrast, Davie soon developed the opposite view, as suggested by his indictment of the "silent conspiracy which now unites all the English poets from Robert Graves down to Philip Larkin, and all the critics, editors and publishers too, the conspiracy to pretend that Eliot and Pound never happened" ("See, and Believe," 193). Kevin Walzer rightly insists that Steele "is well aware that the modernist movement

occurred," though his assessment of it has not endeared him to most of his peers, for in his book Missing Measures (and in other contexts), he alleges that the adherents of Modernism have done grave damage to poetry.

343 Turco, "Year in Poetry," Dictionary of Literary Biography Yearbook: 1986, page 179.

344 Felix Stefanile's comments appear on page 42 of his review "Poets of Emulation: Dana Gioia and Jay Parini" (published in a 1990 issue of Voices in Italian Americana). Stefanile is reviewing Gioia's Daily Horoscope and Parini's Town Life. Although Stefanile never mentions the Movement, I find it striking that so many of the characteristics he points out are also Movement characteristics. For instance, Stefanile says that Gioia and Parini write about such quotidian matters as "family, jobs, traffic, commerce," and "civic life." They write "the poem of responsibility, of summing up, of work and money, the poem of 'other people'" as opposed to "the mooning, private self-oriented lyric of so many free verse poets practicing at this time." In their poems about "work and money," they are not writing "biting satires laced with the humor of contempt," and, in fact, there is "not a political idea in sight." In both "little statements as well as large," their poetry is "accessible." Still, they are "vividly concrete poet[s], hard-minded and forthright," writing poems that present a "vivid portraiture of contemporary life and civilization." In Stefanile's view, Gioia and Parini are "tinkerers, in the homely yet grand sense of that word when good mechanics use it," approaching each poem with "love and passion and persistence" and creating an "artefact [that] becomes art."

345 Miller, "A Renewable Disguise," page 60.

346 Link, "Dana Gioia," page 213.

347 McClatchy, "Summaries and Evidence," page 642.

348 Press's comments appear in Rule and Energy, on page 48 and page 9.

349 John Miller's comments in this section are from his review "A Renewable Disguise," Chowder Review (1980), pages 60–62.

350 Kinzie's comments in this section are from her review "The Overdefinition of the Now," American Poetry Review (1982), pages 16 and 17.

351 Brownjohn, "A View," page 247.

352 Brownjohn, "Jennings," page 254.

353 Chappell, "Once Upon a Time," page 370.

354 Russell, "Dana Gioia and the New Formalism," page 16.

355 Flamm, "Yearning Disabled," page 45.

356 Press, Rule and Energy, page 11.

357 Corcoran, English Poetry Since 1940, page 98. In his description of Davie's poetry, Corcoran follows the typical pattern of implying that English poetry is "constrained" and "corseted" by its supposed "decorums." His metaphor is suggestive (in more than one sense of the term). Evidently, in his view, English poetry is a Victorian maiden (or matron) restricted by rigid undergarments and prudish morals, while American poetry is a twentieth-century woman: liberated, passionate, perhaps even a bit licentious, hampered by no such corsets or constraints.

358 Gioia, "Poetry Chronicle," Ontario Review, page 102.

359 All of McClatchy's statements in this paragraph and the next are from his review, "Mortal Listeners," which appears in Poetry 149.1 (October 1986), pages 31–47.

360 Press, Rule and Energy, page 49.

361 Both of these comments are from Michael Hamburger, The Truth of Poetry, pages 220 and 231.

362 Poems by Larkin that focus on failure and limitation appear in his Collected Poems: "Next, Please" (52), "Success Story" (88), "Dockery and Son" (152), "The Building" (191), and "Poetry of Departures" (85). Additional poems with much the same theme are easy to find. In the poem "Coming" (33), childhood is "a forgotten boredom." "I Remember, I Remember" (81) focuses entirely on what the speaker's childhood lacked. According to "Talking in Bed" (129), love invariably diminishes to the point that "It becomes still more difficult to find / Words at once true and kind, / Or not untrue and not unkind." The opening stanza of "Continuing to Live" (94) reduces life to futile "habit": "Continuing to live—that is, to repeat / A habit formed to get necessaries—/ Is nearly always losing, or going without. / It varies."

363 Gioia's description of his first encounter with a poem by Larkin appears in an online interview called "Paradigms Lost: Part Two."

364 Davie's "Hawkshead and Dachau in a Christmas Glass" appears on page 32 of his Collected Poems.

365 The phrase "another world . . . / behind the ordinary" appears in Gioia's poem "Daily Horoscope," which is divided into numbered sections. (From his 1986 collection, also titled Daily Horoscope.) This phrase appears in the section called "The Stars Now Rearrange Themselves . . . ." For similar ideas, see also "Do Not Expect . . . ," "Flying Over Clouds," "The End," and "The Journey, the Arrival, and the Dream."

366 Press's comments in this paragraph are from Rule and Energy, pages 46–47.

367 Hamburger, The Truth of Poetry, page 225.

368 Gray, note to author, March 2005; emphasis added.

369 All of Walzer's comments in this paragraph are from "The Poetry of Timothy Steele," pages 16–30.

370 Morrison, The Movement, page 170.

371 Morrison, The Movement, page 159.

372 Morrison, The Movement, page 148.

373 In "Davie, Larkin, and the State of England," Bernard Bergonzi deals with this criticism of Movement poetry. Davie accused Larkin, for instance, of being "interested exclusively in humanity and not in nature as something other and self-subsistent" (qtd. in Bergonzi, 352). Bergonzi defends Larkin, arguing that Davie is misreading him, but one may question whether poets without such an interest are somehow inadequate in the first place. Surely not. Actually, although the Romantic poets are often seen as the ultimate literary "nature lovers," they tended to focus on nature not so much as an entity in itself but as it connected to humans—or symbolized them. Indeed, this pattern may be typical for most "nature poetry." We humans are, after all, egocentric and anthropocentric creatures and unavoidably see things through our own eyes. The Movement writers were also reacting against clichéd images of nature and what they feared were anti-human tendencies in some nature poetry. Regardless, survey of Movement poetry shows that nature is a frequent topic, even if it is typically inhabited or shaped by humans. In my discussion of Davie's poem "Low Lands" and Gioia's poem "California Hills in August," I touch on some of these ideas.

374 The phrases "enervate dullness" and "bookish smell" appear on pages 61 and 62 of John Lucas's review of Rebel Angels. The paragraph about the "ersatz ratiocination" in Movement poetry appears on page 62. The terms "hesitations" and "qualifications" appear on page 102 of Morrison's The Movement. The two Movement-like lines quoted by Lucas—"Odd, how his genius courts expectancy," and "Yet time yields shape and history"—appear in "The Wartburg, 1521–1522," and "Joseph," both by Timothy Steele (Rebel Angels, pages 210–211 and 219–220). The Larkinesque phrase "bodied forth" appears in "Old Bachelor Brother," by Brad Leithauser (Rebel Angels, 158).

375 Morrison, The Movement, page 159.

376 Press, Rule and Energy, page 47.

377 Davie quoted in Morrison, The Movement, page 99.

378 Although Morrison ultimately defends "the cautious self-qualification" seen in many Movement poems, he acknowledges that it "might be seen as evidence of a fear of being committed to any opinion lest ridicule or discredit ensue" (The Movement, pages 100 and 102).

379 Several New Formalist poems that, in my view, feature the "hesitations," "qualifications," and "dithering binaries" so disliked by John Lucas and John Press appear on the following pages of Rebel Angels: Rafael Campo, "For J. W." (13); Dana Gioia, "Counting the Children" (39–45); Rachel Hadas, "The Red Hat" (101–113); Andrew Hudgins, "The Hereafter" (112); Mary Jo Salter, "What Do Women Want?" (202). The two poems by Gioia in Rebel Angels that feature variations on the phrase "I suppose" are "Lives of the Great Composers" (36–37) and "Guide to the Other Gallery" (46). Gioia's "Maze Without a Minotaur" (47) contains a Movement-like "turn" similar to those Lucas finds annoying: ". . . Yet who / could bear to see it all?" "My Confessional Sestina" (48–49) is filled with such phrases: "Let me confess"; "I don't think so"; "Let's be honest"; "Granted"; "Perhaps." I don't necessarily find such phrases troubling, especially if they seem intended to create a conversational tone in the poems.

380 As Blake Morrison points out, poets including Coleridge, Keats, Eliot, and Empson qualify or amend their thoughts and descriptions by using phrases such as "it seems" and "perhaps" (103). Elizabeth Bishop, one of the models for the New Formalists, often does this very same thing. In fact, Mary Jo Salter's poem, from its mid-sentence corrections to its

use of exclamation points, seems to have been inspired by Bishop. (It reminds me, for instance, of "The Filling Station.") Nevertheless, it is intriguing to find this "Movement" characteristic throughout New Formalist poetry. In an interview conducted by J. M. Spalding, Mark Jarman describes characteristics in poetry that "move" him emotionally (Cortland Review, 1999). As he does so, he sounds much like a Movement writer.

381 Rachel Wetzsteon made these remarks about Larkin and Gunn in an email interview (12 March 2005). She recalls that she first read these two poets in the early 1990s.

382 The Movement consisted of eight men and only one woman, all Caucasian, all from more or less the same social class, and all graduates of Oxford or Cambridge. While the narrowness of the constituency of the Movement is troubling, it is helpful to take into account how movements begin. Surely one must generally begin with people one knows. If a movement lasts long enough, and if its members are open to new people and new ideas, then the movement may evolve and broaden. Given the era in which it existed, not to mention the narrow ways in which it defined itself, the Movement itself would probably never have evolved or broadened in meaningful ways. In its early years, New Formalism was also criticized—and rightly so—for the narrowness of its constituency. To its credit, it almost immediately began to evolve and expand in terms of gender and race, as well as ideology. New Formalism has also extended to England, in the persons of Anne Stevenson and Michael Donaghy, both Americans living in England (until Donaghy's death in 2004). Gioia also has many ties with the U.K., including regular "appearances" on BBC Radio and his involvement as co-founder of Dark Horse, a Scottish literary journal. It is my understanding that there are also Canadians and Australians associated with New Formalism. Even so, New Formalism—if it continues to exist as a movement at all—may always be primarily an American phenomenon simply because the members of a movement generally need proximity to one another, something that is difficult to achieve on an international level.

383 Powell, "New Lines," page 382.

384 This description of Charles Martin appears on the Poetry Foundation website:

http://www.poetryfoundation.org/archive/poet.html?id=4408.

385 This description of David Mason appears on the Poetry Foundation website:

http://www.poetryfoundation.org/archive/poet.html?id=4430.

386 This description of Rachel Wetzsteon's poetry appears in a New York Times article about her death, "Rachel Wetzsteon, Poet of Keen Insights and Wit, Dies at 42." 31 Dec. 2009. http://www.nytimes.com/2010/01/01/books/01wetzsteon.html. An article called "Philip Larkin and Happiness," by Wetzsteon, was posthumously published on the Contemporary Poetry Review website: http://www.cprw.com/Misc/larkin1.htm.

387 Finch, email to author, 25 August 2000.

388 Gioia, personal interview, 20 December 2001.

389 Link, "Dana Gioia," page 217.

390 "The Oven Bird," by Robert Frost, appears on pages 119–120 of his Collected Poems. The following poems by Thom Gunn appear in his Collected Poems: "Lazarus Not Raised" (7–8); "The Unsettled Motorcyclist's Vision of His Death" (54–55); "In Santa Maria del Popolo" (93–94). "Success Story," by Philip Larkin, appears on page 88 of his Collected Poems. "The Burning Ladder" (3), by Dana Gioia, appears on page 3 of Daily Horoscope. "Failure," also by Gioia, appears on page 6 of Interrogations at Noon. The following poems by Donald Davie appear in his Collected Poems: "Creon's Mouse" (17), "Jacob's Ladder" (39).

391 Larkin's "Success Story" goes on to question whether this "explanation"—"To be ambitious is to fall in love / With a particular life you haven't got"—is adequate or even accurate, but the poem eventually makes it clear that those who have failed must tell themselves such things as they attempt to comfort themselves and rationalize their lack of ambition.

392 Phillips, "An Interview with Paris Review," page 74. (Phillips is interviewing Philip Larkin.)

393 In "An Interview with Paris Review," interviewer Robert Phillips mentions the belief of Peter Davison, another poet and critic, that Larkin's "favourite subjects [are] failure and weakness" (74). Larkin replies, "I think a poet should be judged by what he does with his subjects, not by what his subjects are. Otherwise you're getting near

the totalitarian attitude of wanting poems about steel production figures rather than 'Mais où sont les neiges d'antan?' Poetry isn't a kind of paint-spray you use to cover selected subjects with. A good poem about failure is a success." Incidentally, given his stated belief that "foreign languages [are] irrelevant" and that "A writer can have only one language, if language is going to mean anything to him" (69), it is ironic that—in the very same interview—he quotes a line of French poetry to support his point. Such a contradiction is, as noted elsewhere, characteristic of the Movement.

394 Davie himself points out that "Jacob's Ladder" is also, simply, the name given to the "spur of the mountain Kinderscout in the Derbyshire Peak" ("Notes," Collected Poems, 606).

395 Larkin, "Waiting for breakfast, while she brushed her hair," Collected Poems (20–21). Gioia, "View from the Second Story," Daily Horoscope (75).

396 Gioia, "Poetry Chronicle," page 615.

397 The "mothers loud and fat" and the "uncle shouting smut" appear in "The Whitsun Weddings" (114); the "boy puking his heart out in the Gents" appears in "Essential Beauty" (144); the "children with their shallow violent eyes" appear in "How" (176); the "crooks and tarts" appear in "Going, Going" (190); the "old fools" appear in a poem by the same name (196). Gioia praises the "visionary note" in Larkin in two articles: a 1981 review of Larkin and Amis and a 1993 review of Andrew Motion's biography of Larkin. Katha Pollitt, who is also loosely associated with the New Formalists, said that the poetry in Larkin's Collected Poems shows that he was "not hopeful, exactly, but open to the possibility of hope" (253).

398 McDowell, "New Schools and Late Discoveries," page 675.

399 Larkin, "Mr Bleaney," Collected Poems (102–103). Gioia, "The Room Upstairs," Daily Horoscope (81–85).

400 Martin, Philip Larkin, page 59.

401 In Gioia's poem, which fits the themes of "diminished things" and "the failure of nerve," the landlord's regrets become clear through the story he tells and through the advice he offers the potential tenant, who listens silently: "Never look for what / You truly want. It comes too easily, / And then you never value it enough—/ Until it's gone." The landlord

also states that he designed the house himself, "A modern house, . . . / The rooms squared off and cleared of memory," but it immediately becomes obvious that he did not successfully clear the house of memory, as indicated by the long, impassioned story he tells about the former tenant named David.

402 In at least some of his letters, Larkin appears to have been putting on a "persona" of sorts, perhaps to amuse the recipients of his letters. As Anthony Thwaite describes in the introduction to the Selected Letters, Larkin wears many "masks" in his letters, which are "an informal record of the lonely, gregarious, exuberant, desolate, close-fisted, generous, intolerant, compassionate, eloquent, foul-mouthed, harsh and humorous Philip Larkin" (xiv, xv).

403 Gioia, "Still, Sad Music," page 9.

404 Gray, note to author, March 2005.

405 Jonathan Raban describes "Mr Bleaney" as a "remarkably successful example of a poem which is very much like a political democracy of a peculiarly muddled and English kind" (Society, 32). He goes on to say that the poem is "multilingual," with "each idiom correspond[ing] exactly to a social tone, even if the idioms are defined in rather literary terms: the declassed 'narrator', the proletarian 'character', and the essentially aristocratic voice of 'poetry'."

406 In a 1942 letter to Kingsley Amis, Larkin describes a woman, evidently his own landlady, who could easily have been the model for the one in "Mr Bleaney": "Mrs G[. . .] is that unbearable character, an interesting and irritating person, insofar as a stupid, insensitive, lower middle class woman can be interesting. . . . She lets fall appalling tragedies—such as her mother dying of consumption—in the most casual of ways; the most amusing anecdotes—such as making a pair of camiknickers . . . out of 1/4 yard of silk and 3/4 yard of lace (or something like that)—in a most unamused tone" (Selected Letters, page 42).

407 Breslin, "Two Cheers for the New Formalism," page 145. Quoted in this same article, Robert McPhillips says that the New Formalists "accept their cultural tradition as firmly established" (also on page 145).

408 Davie, "In the Stopping Train," Collected Poems (337–344). Larkin, "The Whitsun Weddings," Collected Poems (114–116). Gioia, "In Cheever Country," Daily Horoscope (19–21). As noted in Chapter Two, Davie's poem was written long after the Movement disbanded,

but Larkin's was written while the Movement was active. Davie's poem, which is written in stanzas of various lengths and configurations, even looks drastically different from a Movement poem.

409 Jarman, "A Shared Humanity: 'In the Stopping Train' and 'The Whitsun Weddings'," page 9.

410 According to Bruce Martin, Larkin's poem "combines generous affection with objective insight" (Philip Larkin, page 60). The poem's speaker, says Martin, realizes that he has "intimately shared an experience with people toward whom he initially felt indifference." Furthermore, although he feels a "sense of separating," as suggested by the "arrow-shower" at the end of the poem, he also feels a "sense of an almost miraculous fertilization," as suggested by the very same image (60–61). The "arrow-shower" metaphor at the end of "The Whitsun Weddings" is also implicitly violent, but as this issue is not immediately relevant to my discussion of the connections between this poem and the one by Gioia, I have not pursued it.

411 Writing about "In the Stopping Train," Neil Corcoran describes the "poem's tropes of doppelgänger and of a self-punishing journey in a stopping train": "'In the Stopping Train' is a poem in which self-rebuke is enacted by the splitting of the self in two: the poem's subjective first person castigates its objective third in a way that conveys the potential duplicity of such emotion, where the capacity for self-disgust may actually be a sly self-regard" (English Poetry, page 100).

412 All of Jarman's comments in this section are from his article "A Shared Humanity," pages 89–101.

413 All of Walzer's comments in this section are from his article "Dana Gioia and Expansive Poetry," pages 24–40.

414 Peters, "Commuter Poetry," page 52.

415 Atkinson, "An Interesting American Poet," page 65.

416 In Chapter One, I describe Greg Kuzma's review, "Dana Gioia and the Poetry of Money," as one of the most blatant class-based attacks on a New Formalist. Although I, too, I question this poem's depiction of social classes and social inequity, I don't go as far as Kuzma does.

417 In a 1991 review of The Gods of Winter, Thomas D'Evelyn says that Gioia's "best poems confirm family responsibilities" (14). He also notes "Gioia's belief that our workaday worlds should penetrate our poetic

dreams." In his discussion of "Becoming a Redwood," D'Evelyn points out the strong undercurrent of nostalgia but says that "thought wins over nostalgia." All of these characteristics are reminiscent of Movement poetry (though the Movement writers emphasized responsibility in general rather than restricting the focus to responsibility towards one's family). As D'Evelyn compares Gioia's themes to those of Yeats, he touches on political aspects that also come up in discussions of Movement poetry: "Gioia's larger thematic ends . . . are traditional in the way W. B. Yeats's were traditional. This has nothing to do with right- or left-wing politics, everything to do with the continuity of the affections and the concern for quality of life; it is both 'hard-headed' and 'spiritual'."

418 The speaker in "The Whitsun Weddings" uses negative class-based stereotypes to describe the people standing on the platforms or boarding the trains, but Larkin's poem does not explore social class as an issue. While Gioia's poem describes the artifacts of exploitative wealth and middle-class suburbia, it does not probe their significance, nor does it say anything about the contrasts between the lives of the workers and the lives of the factory owners. Social class does not seem to be a concern at all in Davie's poem.

419 Jarman, "A Shared Humanity," page 90.

420 Jarman, "A Shared Humanity," page 89. The following is the full remark that Jarman makes about the apparent connection between "In the Stopping Trains" and "The Whitsun Weddings": "'In the Stopping Train' seems, in part, a response to 'The Whitsun Weddings' and not merely because both record journeys on stopping or local trains, but because the former presents a totally different role for the poet from that of the latter."

421 The term "meander" is frequently used in connection with slow, leisurely walking, but I am using it in its geographical sense, which describes the way that a river (or stream) twists, turns, and curves through the landscape. The way that a snake moves also resembles "meandering" used in this sense.

422 Gioia's "California Hills in August" appears in Daily Horoscope (4). Davie's "Low Lands" appears in his Collected Poems (141).

423 Gioia's essay about Davie appears in the "Donald Davie Issue" of Sequoia, which was published in 1977 or 1978. (The copyright date is listed as 1977, but the cover says Winter 1978.)

424 Gioia's "The Homecoming" appears on pages 39–52 in The Gods of Winter, a collection published in 1991. The poems by Larkin discussed or mentioned in this section appear in his Collected Poems: "Home is So Sad" (119) and "Poetry of Departures" (85–86). The two poems by Gunn mentioned or discussed in this section appear in his Collected Poems: "A Mirror for Poets" (24–25) and "Incident on a Journey" (33–34). Davie's "Homage to William Cowper" appears on page 8 of his Collected Poems. Davie says that this poem is a reaction to a poem by Cowper. Davie says, further, that "Cowper's poem, 'On the Death of Mrs. Throckmorton's Bullfinch', in its controlled hysteria, is surely one of the most frightening poems in English" ("Notes," Collected Poems, 605).

425 Both Larkin and Gioia may simply have used a standard expression to describe the sheet music and its location—it is music, after all, and it has to be stored somewhere—but since it is by no means a certainty that a household will have a piano or a collection of sheet music, Gioia's inclusion of these items may have been inspired by Larkin's inclusion of them.

426 Jarman, email interview, 28 May 2001. Although the similarity may be completely coincidental, it is striking to me that the title of Jarman's first book, North Sea (1978), which focuses largely on his youth in Scotland, echoes the title of Larkin's first book, The North Ship.

427 The child in "My Parents Have Come Home Laughing" is, in fact, oddly omniscient. He does not understand everything, but he knows a great deal about his parents' feelings and about the events at the evening's "feast," which he did not attend. My guess is that this inconsistent semi-omniscience may be a result of Jarman's relative inexperience as a poet when he wrote this poem.

428 As a young man, Jarman appeared to question the teachings of his father and grandfather, both Protestant ministers. In North Sea (1978), the few poems that deal with religious matters are skeptical. The dedication of 1981's The Rote Walker—"For my father and in memory of my grandfather"—makes it seem that Jarman was beginning to move away from this skeptical stance, but more than half of the poems in

this collection express doubts similar to those seen earlier, questioning prayer, miracles, Christianity, and God. In the few poems that deal with religious issues in The Black Riviera (1990), Jarman seems far less skeptical than in his earlier books. Two later collections, Questions for Ecclesiastes (1997) and Unholy Sonnets (2000), continue to express some skepticism but also affirm Jarman's faith. When Questions for Ecclesiastes won the 1998 Lenore Marshall Poetry Prize, Charles Simic commented, "Alongside the New Formalism, there seems to be a reappearance in poetry of faith, spirituality, religion and even a kind of New Yearning. Jarman finds himself smack in the middle of this" (29). He also quotes Jarman, who said that his aim in this collection was "somehow to crack open the silence of heaven and force a divine presence from a divine absence." Reviewer Dulcy Brainard says that, in Questions for Ecclesiastes, "Jarman posits—and challenges—a God remote from human experience" (62). In 2001, Jarman told me that, in his poetry, he suspects he comes across "as an anxious Christian with an affectionate regard for the natural world" (email interview, 13 July 2001).

429 Davie, "The Evangelist," Collected Poems (29–30). Larkin, "Faith Healing," Collected Poems (126). Jarman, "Comparisons of Wonder," The Rote Walker (39).

430 Martin, Philip Larkin, page 82.

431 Larkin said at the time that he based "Faith Healing" on a television documentary he had seen (Martin 82). But, of course, fiction writers and poets are not restricted to "the truth." If Larkin had wanted to present a less one-sided and unflattering view of the event and the people who were there, he could easily have described the women in less insulting terms, just as he could easily have included men among those who hoped to be cured by the preacher. He could also have depicted the preacher more sympathetically. All of the details he includes about the women suggest misogyny and snobbishness. The post-menopausal facial hair is the first, and most noticeable, detail. The women's "flowered frocks" also sound like dresses that are baggy and loose, intended to be worn around the house rather than in public. After they have been prayed over by the evangelist, some women "stay stiff, twitching and loud / With deep, hoarse tears." They are so hungry for kindness and attention that when they feel a "voice / At last calls them alone," they are overwhelmed with emotion, making "Their thick tongues blort,"

and "their eyes squeeze grief." Larkin may intend to be sympathetic, but his language fails him.

432 In the poem, the evangelist's supposed question is punctuated with a comma rather than a question mark. In my discussion, I have had to end it with a period to make it fit the syntax of my sentence. In either case, what is ostensibly a question comes across as an order or command.

433 Davie's "The Garden Party" appears on page 22–23 of his Collected Poems. The two poems by Gunn that are mentioned in this section appear in his Collected Poems: "Carnal Knowledge" (15–16) and "A Plan of Self-Subjection" (46–47). Larkin's poems appear in his Collected Poems: "Lines on a Young Lady's Photograph Album" (71–72), "I Remember, I Remember" (81–82), "Reference Back" (106). Jarman's "Greensleeves" appears on page 10 in The Rote Walker, which was published in 1981, and "Between Flights" appears on pages 15–16 in The Black Riviera, which was published in 1990.

434 Gray, note to author, March 2005.

435 Richard J. Gray also says of Jarman's poem "Greensleeves" that, if he had not known otherwise, he "would have guessed . . . that it came from an English (as in British) poem" (note to author, March 2005).

436 To be precise, some of Gunn's poems also feature doppelgängers or voyeurs who are the main characters. As mentioned in an earlier endnote, these poems include "The Secret Sharer" (Collected Poems, page 13), "Incident on a Journey" (33), "The Corridor" (85), "The Monster" (96), and "Behind the Mirror" (293).

437 Morrison, The Movement, pages 94–95.

438 Jarman, "The Home," The Black Riviera (36–41). All of the poems by Larkin that are discussed or mentioned in this section appear in his Collected Poems: "If, My Darling" (41), "Mr Bleaney" (102–103), "Reference Back" (106), "The Whitsun Weddings" (114–116), "Ambulances" (132–133), "The Large, Cool Store" (135), "The Building" (191–193), "Heads in the Women's Ward" (194), "The Old Fools" (196–197).

439 Larkin also moves between third-person pronouns and second-person pronouns in the first stanza: "Do they somehow suppose / It's more grown-up when your mouth hangs open and drools, / And you keep on pissing yourself, and can't remember / Who called this morning?" The

shift in the second stanza, however, seems clearly intended to address the reader, whereas the shift in the first stanza seems primarily to follow the colloquial pattern of using "you" in casual speech.

440 The terms "whippet" and "whip-thin" may share the same ancestry. The dictionaries I consulted say that the word "whippet" has unclear origins but that it may have arisen in the late 1400s as a command to "whip it," meaning to "move briskly."

441 Baer, "An Interview with Timothy Steele, page 28.

442 "Wedding Wind" is, in fact, the only Larkin poem I can think of that features tumultuous weather. This is also one of the few poems by Larkin that are obviously "persona" poems or dramatic monologues.

443 "Aubade" was not included in any of the poetry collections Larkin published in his lifetime (The North Ship, The Less Deceived, The Whitsun Weddings, or High Windows). It did, however, appear in the Times Literary Supplement in 1977. About this poem, Katha Pollitt says that it has been "famous ever since in samizdat" ("Philip Larkin," 254). According to the unabridged Random House Dictionary of the English Language, the term "samizdat" refers to "a clandestine publishing system within the Soviet Union, in which forbidden or unpublishable literature is reproduced and circulated privately." Pollitt's reference to the political and literary situation in the Soviet Union is perhaps intended as a wry clue to the situation in the United States in the second half of the twentieth century. The often negative responses to formal poetry, as described elsewhere in my discussion, may help explain the perception—melodramatic though it may have been—that a formal poem was "forbidden," able only to be "circulated privately" through a "clandestine publishing system."

444 Comments made by Dick Allen are pertinent to this discussion of the use of "I" and "we" in poetry. In one of the two email interviews that I conducted with Allen, he said that he admires poetry "which tells us who we are" (email interview, 26 March 2002). In this same interview, he went on to say that, for him, "the emphasis is upon the 'we' or the 'you', not the 'I'."

445 Harvey, "Illusions Not Illusions Any Longer," page 91. Steele's "Coming Now" appears in The Prudent Heart (19). Steele's "Hortulus" appears in The Color Wheel (48). These two poems by Steele appear in Sapphics Against Anger: "Old Letters," (9–10), "Sapphics Against Anger" (17–

18). The poems by Larkin discussed or mentioned in this section appear in his Collected Poems: "Coming" (33), "Going" (3), "Dockery and Son" (152–153), "Reference Back" (106), "Love Songs in Age" (113), "Deceptions" (32), "Talking in Bed" (129), "Born Yesterday" (84), "Success Story" (88), "Toads" (89–90), "Mr Bleaney" (102–103), and "Aubade" (208–209). The poems by Gunn discussed or mentioned in this section appear in his Collected Poems: "To Yvor Winters, 1955" (69–70), "Legal Reform" (77–78), "Tamer and Hawk" (29), "On the Move" (39–40), "Lerici" (23), The poems by Davie discussed or mentioned in this section appear in his Collected Poems: "The Garden Party" (22–23), "Hypochrondriac Logic" (16), "Jacob's Ladder" (39), "Creon's Mouse" (17). Jarman's "Ascension of the Red Madonna" appears in The Rote Walker (14). Gioia's "His Three Women" appears in Daily Horoscope (72–73).

446 Harvey, "Illusions Not Illusions Any Longer," page 95.

447 Harvey, "Illusions Not Illusions Any Longer," pages 95–96.

448 Harvey, "Illusions Not Illusions Any Longer," pages 96–97.

449 Steele uses a strikingly similar phrase in his poem "Autobiography": ". . . he [the autobiographer] and the reader are / Equally deceived, and his words define the / Deception" (page 35, Uncertainties and Rest, 1979). Gunn's own poem called "Autobiography" appears on pages 285–286 of his Collected Poems. Both poems deal with the necessity to be honest in autobiography, but otherwise they bear little resemblance to each other.

450 Gunn is particularly fond of wordplay and oxymoronic lines: "My circle's end is where I have begun" (the last line of "A Plan of Self-Subjection); "I am my own and not my own" (a line repeated several times within "Jesus and His Mother"); "This was the end and yet, another start" (the first line of "Merlin in the Cave: He Speculates without a Book"); "Resisting, by embracing, nothingness" (the last line of "In Santa Maria del Popolo"); "I was still separate on the shadow's ground / But, charged with growth, was being altered, / Composing uncomposed" (the ending of "Words"); "He escapes, he does not escape, he is the same, he is other" (a line midway through "Behind the Mirror," one of many "doppelgänger" poems by Gunn); "Mastered by mastering, / I so much belong to the wind / I become of it" (lines toward the end of "Small Plane in Kansas"); "What was the pain / he needed to kill / if

not the ultimate pain / of feeling no pain?" (the ending of "Painkillers"); "... the speed contains its own repose" (lines toward the end of "The Life of the Otter"); "Only an infinite finitude I see / In those peculiar lovely variations" (lines toward the end of "The Annihilation of Nothing").

451 Shaw, "Philip Larkin: A Stateside View," page 104.

452 Harvey, "Illusions Not Illusions," page 96.

453 In a 1990 review of Larkin, Katha Pollitt says, "'Born Yesterday' is almost a parody, with fairy-godfather Larkin able to wish for an infant girl's happiness only by presenting it in terms more suitable for household chores" (255). Pollitt's review is almost entirely positive except for remarks like this one, though even this one seems more amused than critical.

454 A number of Steele's poems touch on the subjects of failure and limitation, often in a pensive yet oddly upbeat way: "Sunday Afternoon," "For Ying Lew," and "Don Juan: A Winter Convalescence" appear in Uncertainties and Rest (1979); "In the King's Rooms," "Near Olympic," and "The Question of Identity" appear in The Prudent Heart (1983); "On the Eve of a Birthday" appears in On Harmony (1984); and "Last Tango" (a revision of "The Question of Identity") appears in Sapphics Against Anger (1986). An entire section of Uncertainties and Rest is titled "Sufficiencies."

455 In Steele's "Family Reunion," from 1979, the gathered family members are "Staid, / Together for the past, if nothing more," and they "share the same relaxing masquerade—/ A life that's always gentle, never strict . . . ." The Movement writers endorsed these qualities in their own poetry, though they would also likely have argued that life can be "strict" while also being "Staid" and "gentle." (It is interesting to note that the life described by Steele is a "relaxing masquerade," suggesting that it is not possible to have a life "that's always gentle, never strict.")

456 Steele, "Spring," The Color Wheel, page 51.

457 Steele, email interview, 25 May 2004.

458 "Vermont Spring," according to Donald Stanford, "rejects Eliot" ("American Formalism," 386). He also says that, in the poem, "Gunn is praised as a man who '[r]etains the vernal tang of mind of heart'."

459 Elizabeth Jennings's "Modern Poet," an early Movement "manifesto," implicitly argues for an "austerity" that creates its own kind of "beauty":

This is no moment now for the fine phrases,
The inflated sentences, words cunningly spun,
For the floreate image or the relaxing pun
Or the sentimental answer that most pleases.
We must write down an age of reckless hunger,
Of iron girders, hearts like plumb-lines hung,
And the poet's art is to speak and not to be sung....
(qtd. in Morrison, 21–22)

460 I interviewed Robert Conquest on 28 December 2001. In Chapter One, I also refer to his letter to The New Statesmen.

461 Chambers, A Few Friends, page 5.

462 Two of the poems by Steele appear in A Few Friends: Poems for Thom Gunn's 60th Birthday: "Decisions, Decisions" (46) and "Dependent Nature" (47). "Small Lives," also by Steele, appears on page 11 in Sapphics Against Anger. The poems by Gunn mentioned or discussed in this section appear in his Collected Poems: "On the Move" (39) and "Considering the Snail" (117).

463 Morrison, The Movement, page 275.

464 The "small bug, purposeful, unwary," that "Explores a page's printed prairie," in Steele's poem "Jaracanda" (Sapphics Against Anger, 47), also calls to mind the snail in Gunn's "Considering the Snail," which the speaker says is "drenched there / with purpose" and driven by "slow passion."

465 The two poems by Steele discussed or mentioned in this section appear in Sapphics Against Anger: "Near Olympic" (20–23) and "From a Rooftop" (3–4). Gunn, "In Praise of Cities," Collected Poems (59–60). Larkin, "An Arundel Tomb," Collected Poems (110–111).

466 Walzer, "The Poetry of Timothy Steele," page 20.

467 Steele, "Mockingbird," Sapphics Against Anger (12). This poem also appeared two years earlier in a 1984 chapbook called On Harmony. (The pages are unnumbered.) Gunn, "Patch Work," Collected Poems, 427–428.

468 I lean toward Gunn's view of mockingbirds rather than Steele's. True, these birds do "steal" their tunes from "real" songbirds (and from other sources). However, the tunes resulting from their "patch work" are often very impressive musically. Much like avant-garde musicians, they

are even known to incorporate such sounds as the meowing of cats, the barking of dogs, and the beeping alarm issued by some vehicles when they are in reverse gear. It follows, then, that I also lean toward Gunn's view of poets rather than Steele's.

469 Gunn, "Adventurous Song," Shelf Life, page 143.

470 Gunn, "Adventurous Song," Shelf Life, page 143.

471 In 1989, Gunn contributed a poem to a chapbook, edited by Steele, in honor of the sixtieth birthday of poet and critic Charles Gullans. Also, as noted elsewhere, Steele contributed three poems to a 1989 chapbook in honor of Gunn's sixtieth birthday. In 2001, both Gunn and Steele, along with other formalist poets, including Edgar Bowers, X. J. Kennedy, Gerry Cambridge, Mary Jo Salter, Dick Davis, and Robert Burns Shaw, appeared together in a poetry chapbook called Profile, Full Face: A Small Anthology of Poems, in memory of Edgar Bowers (who died in 2000).

472 This is a partial list of additional poems that merit further examination: Steele's "Sunday Afternoon" (Uncertainties and Rest, 4) and Gunn's "Wind in the Street" (Collected Poems, 6); Steele's "Last Night As You Slept" (Uncertainties and Rest, 49) and Gunn's "Touch" (Collected Poems, 168); Steele's "Mornings in a New Apartment" (Uncertainties and Rest, 80) and Gunn's "Thoughts on Unpacking" (79) and "Waking in a Newly Built House" (115); Steele's "But Home Is Here" (Sapphics Against Anger, 58) and Larkin's "Home Is So Sad" (Collected Poems, 119); Steele's "The Question of Identity" (The Prudent Heart, 29), Larkin's "Dockery & Son" (152), and Gunn's "Black Jackets" (108). Steele's epigram #8 (Uncertainties and Rest, 19) about a "rake" who "swears he'll settle down" and "take a wife"—the speaker asks "Whose?"—resembles a comic and lighthearted version of Gunn's two poems named "Modes of Pleasure" (101 and 102). "Reading Habits" (Uncertainties and Rest, 18) bears no resemblance to Larkin's "A Study of Reading Habits," but it may be significant that the title of Steele's poem echoes Larkin's. Steele's "Short Subjects" includes a numbered section called "Family Album" that echoes Larkin's "Lines on a Young Lady's Photograph Album." Steele has also written a number of poems that focus on the "diminished" nature of the world or the necessity to accept the world as it is. He typically advocates a peaceful and contented acceptance rather than a grudging resignation. In Uncertainties and Rest (1979), these include "Sunday Afternoon" (4); "Suburbs of the

Sea" (7); "Homecoming in Late March" (25); "Over the Rainbow" (28); "Three Notes Toward Definitions" (31); "Nightpiece for the Summer Solstice" (43); and "Baker Beach at Sunset" (46). I have not, thus far, spotted any additional poems by Steele that seem related to poems by Davie.

473 Steele, email to author, 30 June 2006.

474 There are a surprising number of American poems about mockingbirds, their imitative behavior, and their artistry or lack thereof. See, for instance, "The Mockingbird of Mockingbirds," by Denise Levertov, and "Letter to a Poet," by Robert Hass. The mockingbird also makes recurrent appearances in Walt Whitman's "Out of the Cradle, Endlessly Rocking." (Charles Bukowski also has a poem called "the mockingbird," but it focuses on the bird's tendency to harass cats, which turns out to be fatal in this poem, rather than its songs.) Steele points out that the mockingbird is "arrested in a state of perennial imitation. He isn't inspired: that's his pathos. None of his notes are original" (email to author, 30 June 2006). As a side note, I question assumptions that animals lack awareness, for such assumptions strike me as arrogant and anthropocentric.

475 These remarks by Pollitt are from page 260 of her 1990 article called "Philip Larkin," which appeared in Grand Street.

476 Gunn, "Adventurous Song," page 143.

477 Some might wonder what sorts of political and philosophical leanings might appear in those New Formalists who have been inspired by the Movement writers. Although such a question is understandable, I also find it slightly troubling. For one thing, writers are surely not required to hold any particular beliefs. For another, it is possible to appreciate a writer's work while acknowledging—and even quarreling with—the characteristics and ideas to which one objects. My own political and philosophical views are vastly different from those of Larkin, for instance, but I still appreciate many of his poems. Gunn's early poetry, with its swaggering and stereotyped masculinity and its almost nihilistic emphasis on violence, is also problematic, but I am able to enjoy much of it nevertheless. If one were to look at all the New Formalists who seem to have been inspired by the Movement, I suspect that one would find a wide variety of poetic and political stances, from

conservative to liberal. Those who claim Larkin as an inspiration may tend to be conservative, whereas those who claim Gunn may tend to be liberal, and those who claim Davie may be somewhere in the middle. But what of those who—like Allen, Jarman, Monsour, Steele, Thiel, and Wetzsteon—claim both Larkin and Gunn or those who—like Gioia—claim all three? Questions like these would be difficult, if not impossible, to answer, for similarities (and differences) in these areas may be mere coincidence. What can be established are the younger poets' attitudes towards the older poets. What can also be established is that many of them have written poetry responding to that of the older group.

478 This question, while interesting, can be answered with only a limited degree of certainty. Although I believe that poetry written by the New Formalists has often benefitted from their acquaintance with the Movement writers, I cannot necessarily pin down the ways in which it has benefitted, nor can I prove that the Movement writers are the source of particular aspects of the poetry. If the younger writers are able to use form felicitously, for instance, they could have learned their skills from any number of poets and sources that they have studied and emulated. The "restraint" that often characterizes New Formalist poetry—whether it is a good thing or a bad thing—could also have come from any number of sources. Likewise, the themes with which they deal could have been inspired by any number of poets. However, the textual evidence clearly suggests that the themes, the situations, the images, and even the language of a number of New Formalist poems have been inspired by poetry written by Davie, Gunn, or Larkin.

479 Molly Peacock, an American, has lived in Canada for many years. Anne Stevenson, also an American, has lived in England for decades. Stevenson was the keynote speaker for the 2005 West Chester Poetry Conference. Michael Donaghy is another American who lived in England for many years, until his death in 2004. As mentioned earlier, he was one of the "New Gen" poets who were apparently quite the literary phenomenon in England in the 1980s. I have also read that some who identify themselves with the New Formalist group live in Australia. Marilyn Hacker, who dislikes being grouped with the New Formalists, lived in France for many years. Pinning down the identity of people is tricky, of course, for they may see themselves in one way, while others may see them as something else entirely. Marilyn Hacker illustrates this point, for she is often called a New Formalist despite her

objections. Rita Dove, who is African American, does not necessarily like to be associated with the group, but she is featured in at least two New Formalist anthologies: A Formal Feeling Comes and Poetry After Modernism. Other African American poets who are often associated with New Formalism are Allison Joseph, Marilyn Nelson, Carolyn Beard Whitlow, and Elizabeth Alexander. Gioia, Rafael Campo, and Julia Alvarez are of Hispanic descent. Seth is of Indian descent. So far as I know, most other New Formalists are Caucasian and Anglo-European.

480 Keith Tuma points out that, for Larkin, the "common reader is not student nor literate man aware of the conventions of English verse so much as he is a caricatured lower middle-class individual suspicious of being duped and intent on speaking back to an academic elite" (Fishing, 74). Tuma also points out that Larkin's criticism is based on a "consumerist logic holding that the audience, whatever audience, knows what it wants and is prepared to accept it" (75). Both of these observations strike me as true. But I think that Larkin also has in mind the kind of person who may not be educated but who is intelligent and concerned about issues such as fear, death, grief, loneliness, frustration, the ridiculousness and the meaning in ordinary lives, and so on. My attitude toward the importance of appealing to "ordinary" readers has undoubtedly been molded by a number of factors: my own working-class background, my status as a first-generation college student, my years of experience as a teacher of introductory college writing classes (which are filled with many students who have backgrounds much like my own), and my reading of numerous articles and books about social class and the complexities of its interactions with education, academia, culture, and literature. I should also note that I am aware of the complexities and problems with some of the terms I am using, such as "traditional" and "accessible" and "ordinary," as well as "culture" and "literature." I use them here without delving into those complexities simply because it would be inappropriate and unwieldy to engage in such explorations within the confines of my discussion.

481 Davie quoted in Bradley, The Movement: British Poets of the 1950s, page 105.

482 Regan, "The Movement," A Companion to Twentieth-Century Poetry, pages 213–214.

483 Again, Frank Lentricchia is the source of the idea that Ezra Pound wanted artists to "make contemporary what is old" (quoted in Honicker, 97).

484 Davie, "Talking with Millicent Dillon," Trying to Explain, page 46.

485 In a letter written to me shortly before he died, Enright characterized the Movement as "a loose association at its peak" (30 May 2001). Gunn characterizes the Movement as a "lot of categorizing foolishness" in "My Life Up to Now" (174). The description of the Movement as "a false situation" is from Wain's Living in the Present (qtd. in Morrison, 238). The description of the Movement as "dead" is from a 1962 letter from Larkin to Conquest (Selected Letters, 340).

BIOGRAPHICAL NOTE

Theresa Malphrus Welford, who grew up in a small, working-class town near Savannah, Georgia, received a PhD in English Literature from the University of Essex in 2006. A two-time nominee for the Pushcart Prize, Theresa has published poetry, creative nonfiction, book chapters, and scholarly articles, as well as two edited collections of poetry: *The Paradelle* and *The Cento* (both published by Red Hen Press). She is currently working on two textbooks and a number of picture-book manuscripts. Theresa and her husband, Mark Welford, happily share their home in Statesboro, Georgia, with countless rescued animals (cats and dogs).